St Ann's, The Final Chapter

Peter Richardson

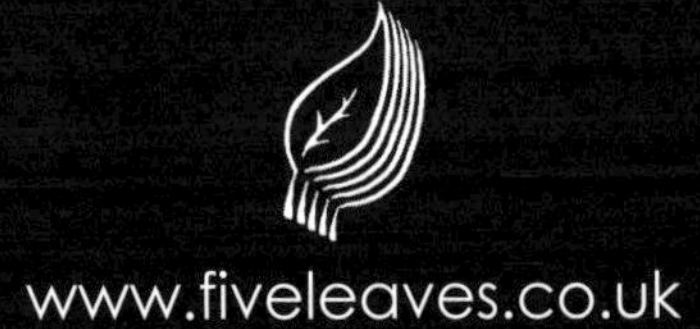

www.fiveleaves.co.uk

St Ann's, The Final Chapter

Peter Richardson

Published in 2021 by Five Leaves Publications

14a Long Row, Nottingham NG1 2DH

www.fiveleaves.co.uk

www.fiveleavesbookshop.co.uk

peterrichardsonphoto@me.com

ISBN (paperback) 978-1-910170-85-4

ISBN (hardback) 978-1-910170-86-1

Printed in Great Britain

Contents

"'There must be somebody, like the kids playing in the street who would be in their 60s now, who might recognise themselves or their parents or grandparents."

Introduction

By the 1890s St Ann's, an area of Nottingham, had 10,000 houses packed into it. Two thirds of them had no hot water and three quarters had no bath, toilets being outside in a yard. They were mostly terraced houses with no garden. Factories, workshops and other industrial buildings were built alongside the houses so that workers did not have far to travel. By the end of the 19th century the whole area was virtually filled with high-density housing to form a self-contained suburb with churches, chapels, schools, shops, banks, pubs and even a railway station on the Nottingham Suburban line.

In the1950s Nottingham City Council began a programme of slum clearance, and St Ann's turn came in 1967 with the first clearance order. In previous redevelopments the policy was to demolish unfit houses but leave the more expensive pubs and industrial buildings. A much more radical approach was adopted in St Ann's, and vast areas were razed to the ground. Although the main thoroughfares were retained, many of the old grid-plan streets disappeared.

Critics argued that some of the older houses could have been retained and improved. Many residents, especially those who had lived in St Ann's all their lives, regretted the loss of the neighbourliness which had existed in the closely-packed streets. Others welcomed the move from cramped houses without modern amenities to new ones with central heating, gardens, bathrooms and space for refrigerators and washing machines.

During this clearance, which took place in the late 1960s and early 1970s, many residents had to continue living and working amongst the rubble until new houses were built to replace theirs. These photographs portray those people and how life was towards the end of the demolition and clearance. For continuity, and to create context, one or two of the photographs or subjects of the first book, *St Ann's, The End of an Era*, are repeated.

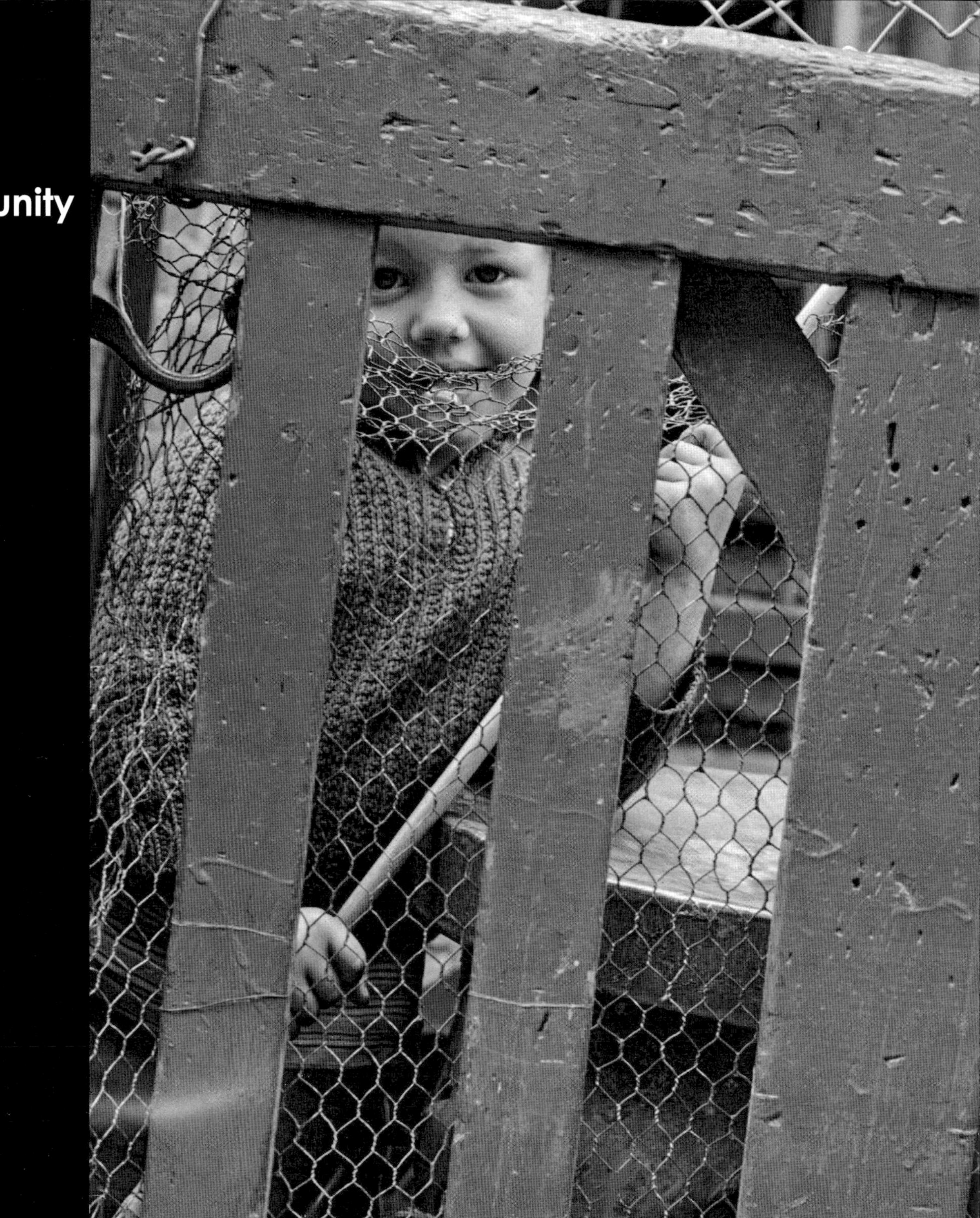
the Community

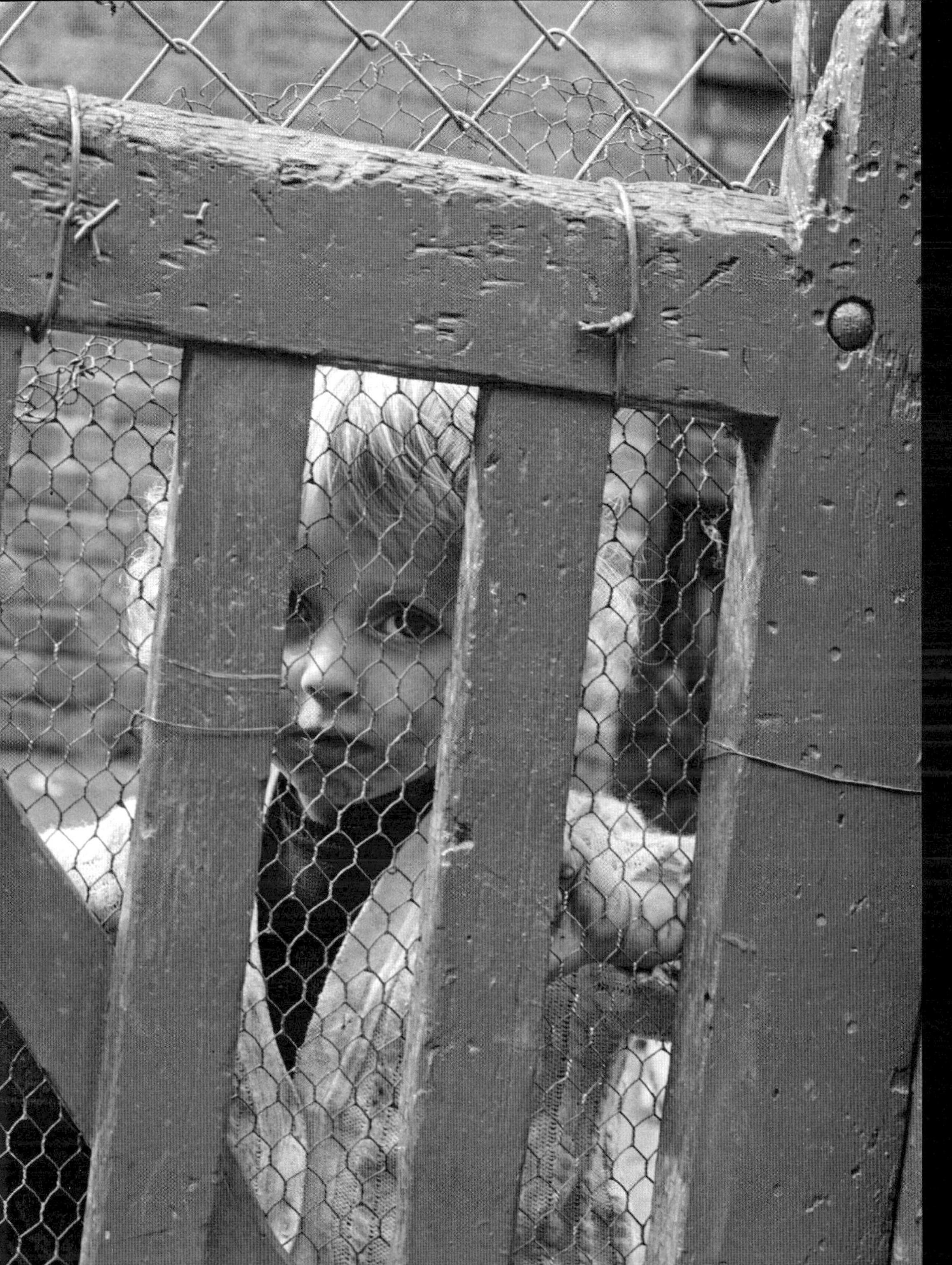

"It was a communal back yard. It served the whole of the terrace, and we did have a coal house, and a toilet outside, which froze every winter."

"The back yards were swilled down, with the water from the dolly tubs after a day's washing. Toilets were whitewashed, and newspaper squares hung neatly on a string and nail."

Jean Taylor

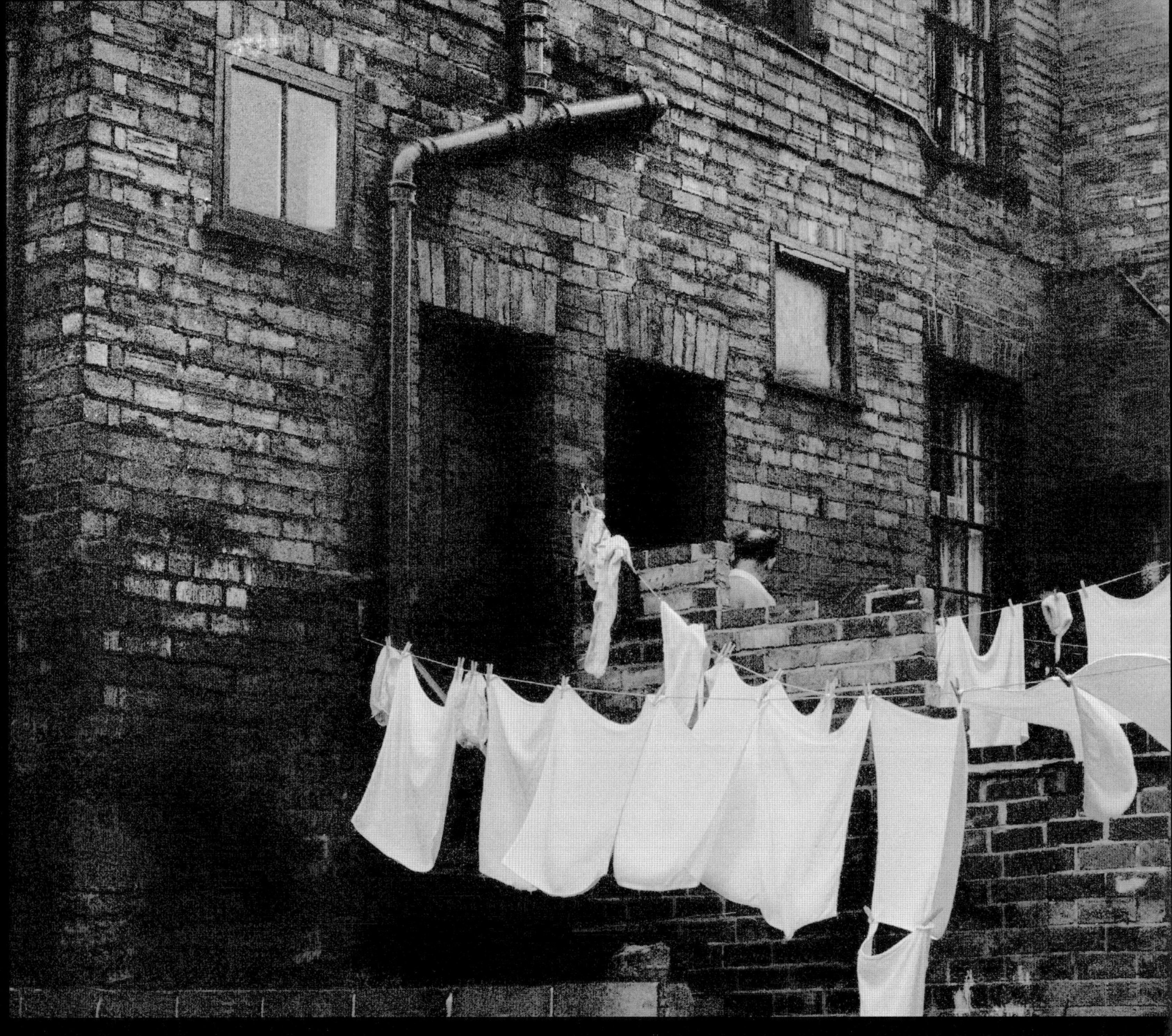

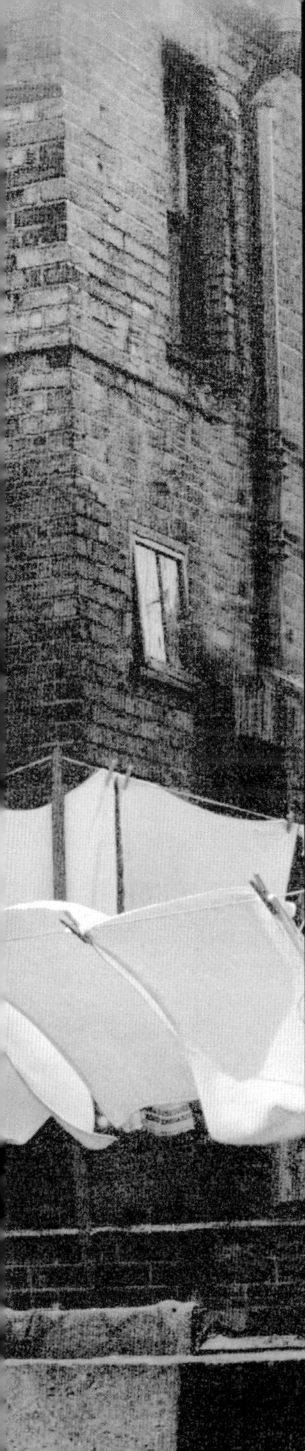

The Monday wash still went ahead despite the dust and dirt created by the demolition going on around

"No bathrooms, and in our backyards we had wash mangle, dolly tub, ash bin and grate."

"The constant rumble of factories, thick smoke and smog. Chips eaten out of newspaper. Credit on the slate."

Audrey Jackson

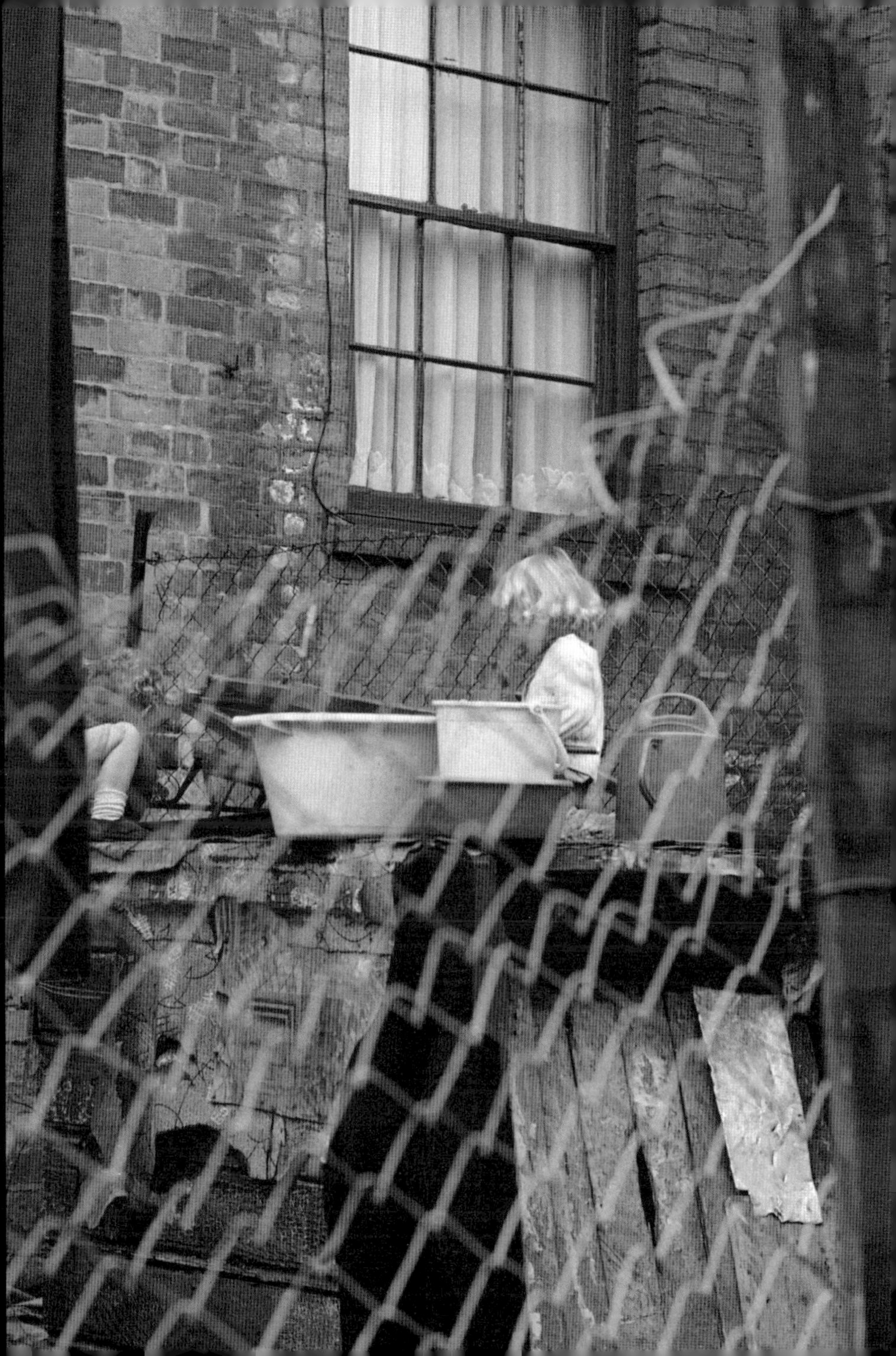

Messing with dad's motorbike and sidecar

These were very popular as most people couldn't afford a car.

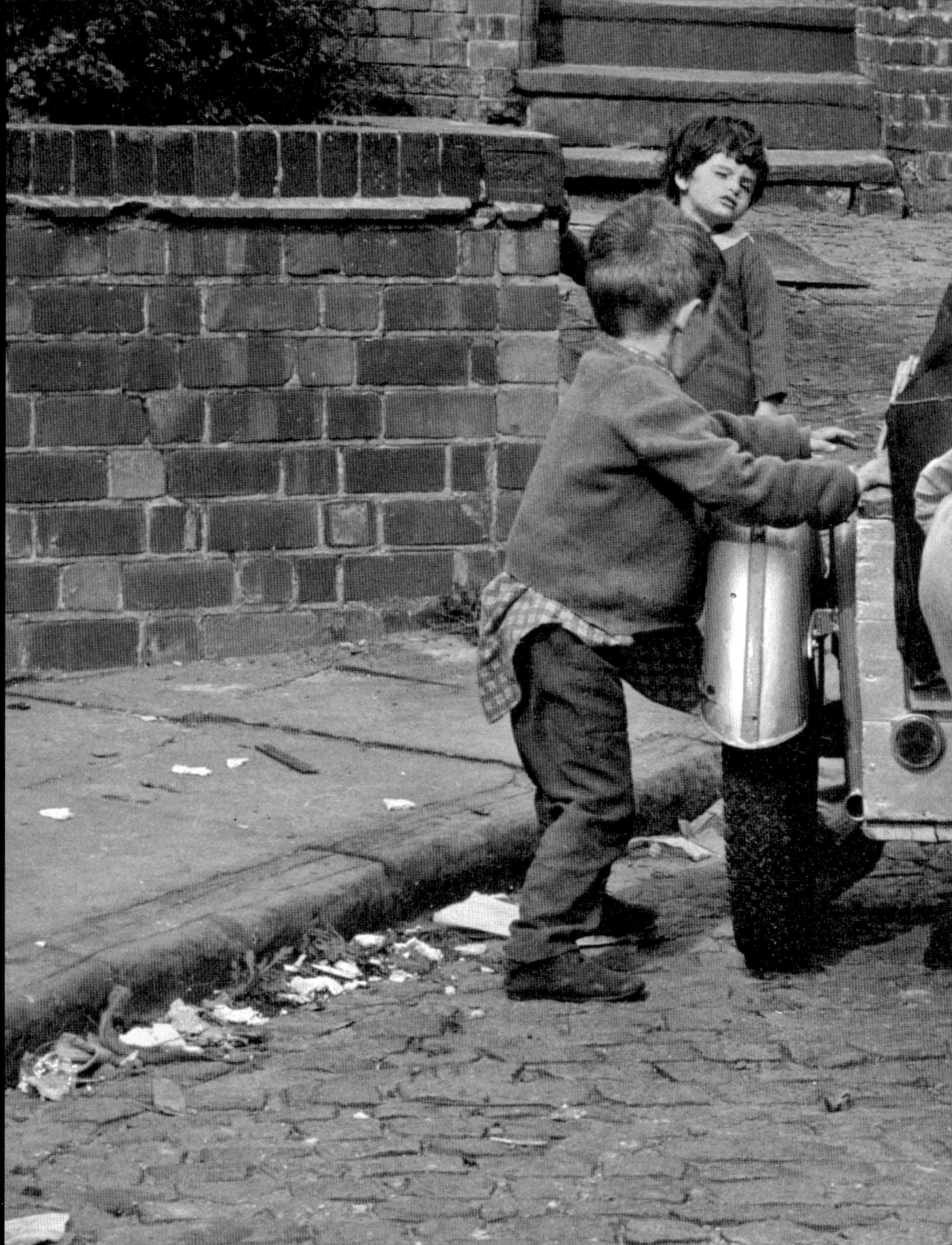

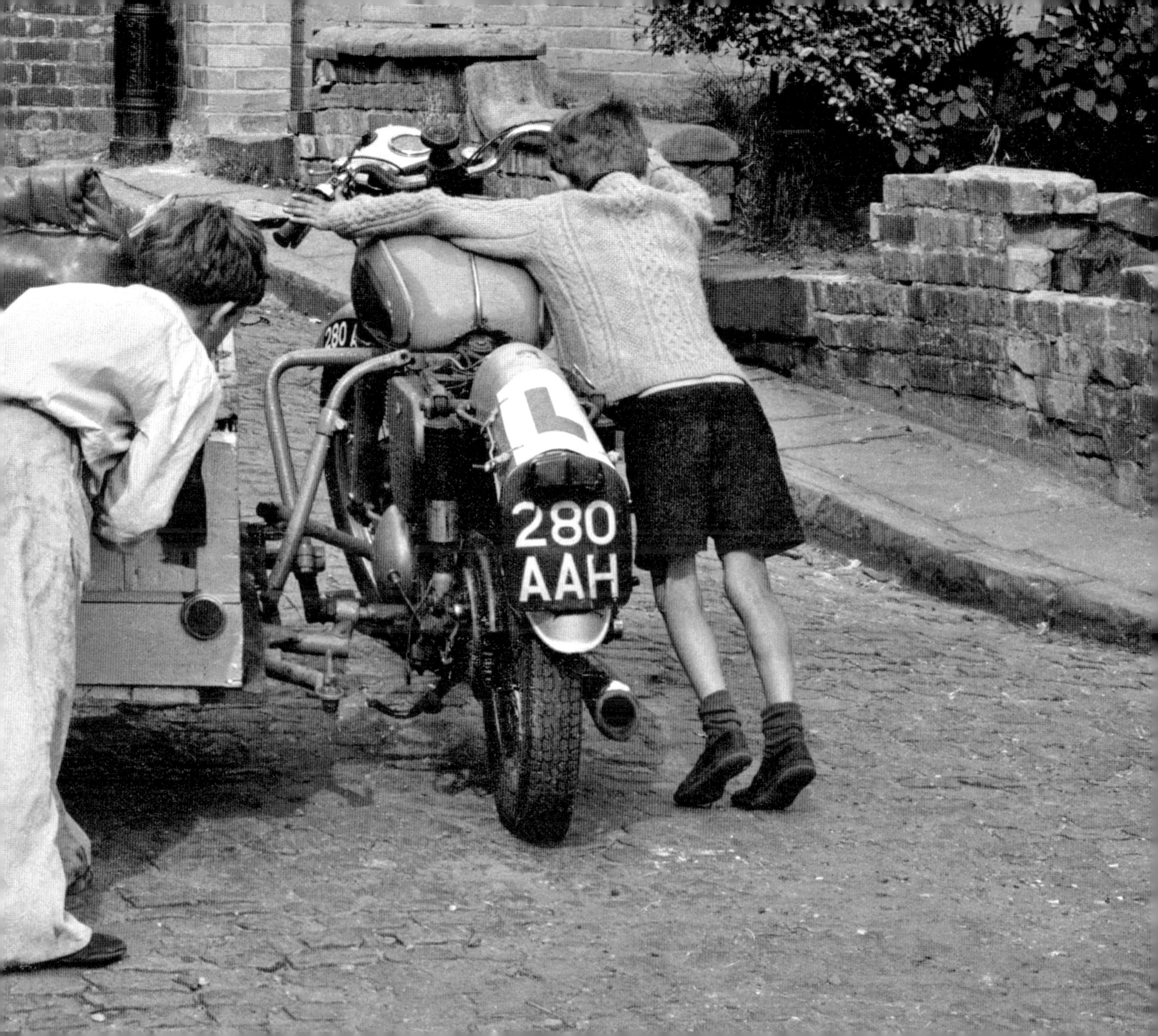

280 AAH

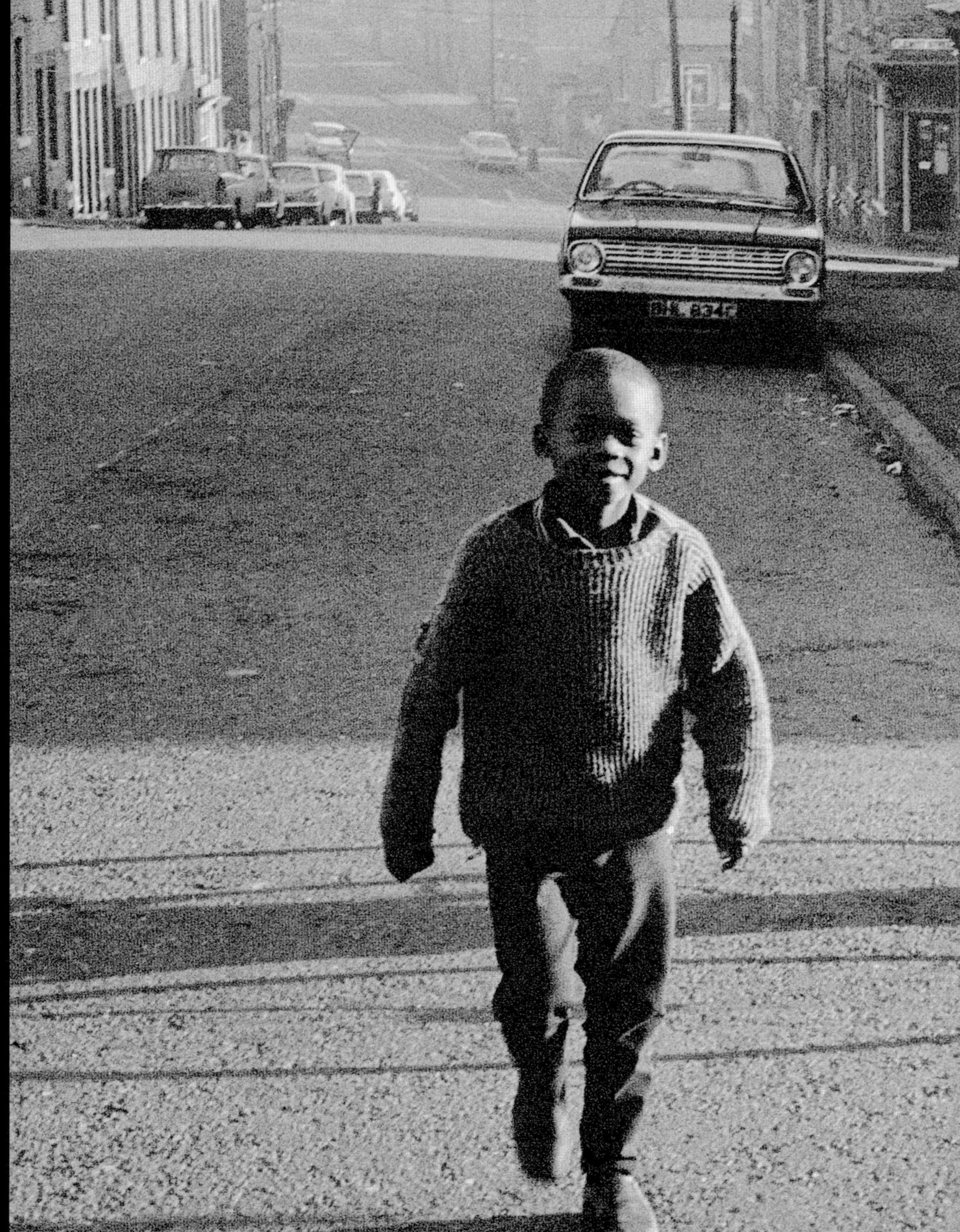

Junction of Pym Street and Sanderson Street

Boys returning from an errand to the shops to fetch a light bulb. The corner shop behind them is at the top of Flewitt Street. It is the one depicted on the front cover.

"Had all the little shops, mainly on Alfred Street, butchers, fishmongers, sweetshops, didn't go often in the sweet shop but when we did it was great, used to always have Kali so I could dip my finger in it and my fingers would go different colours, me tongue used to go different colours but always had Kali, sugar! Lots of sugar."

Anne Binns

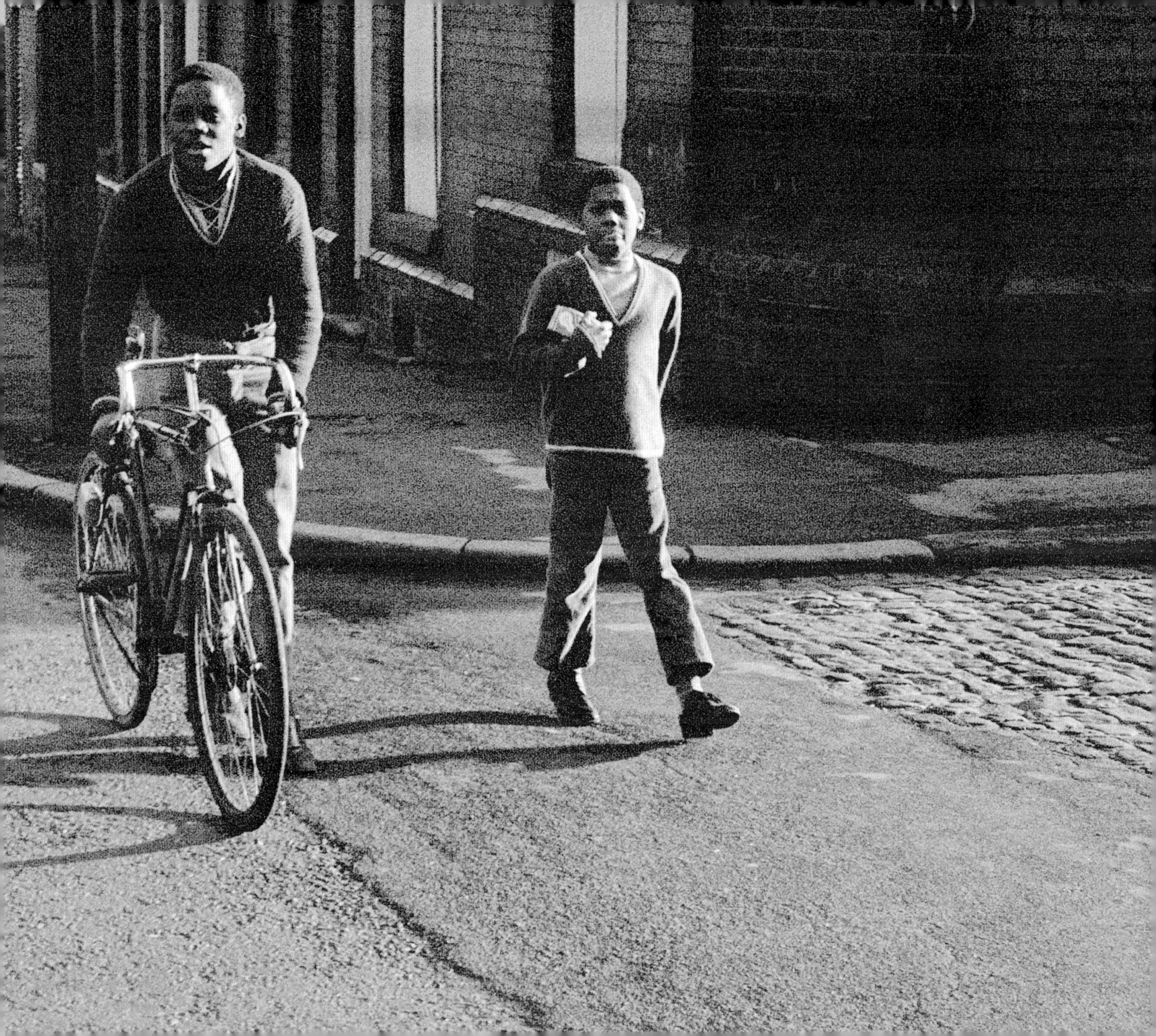

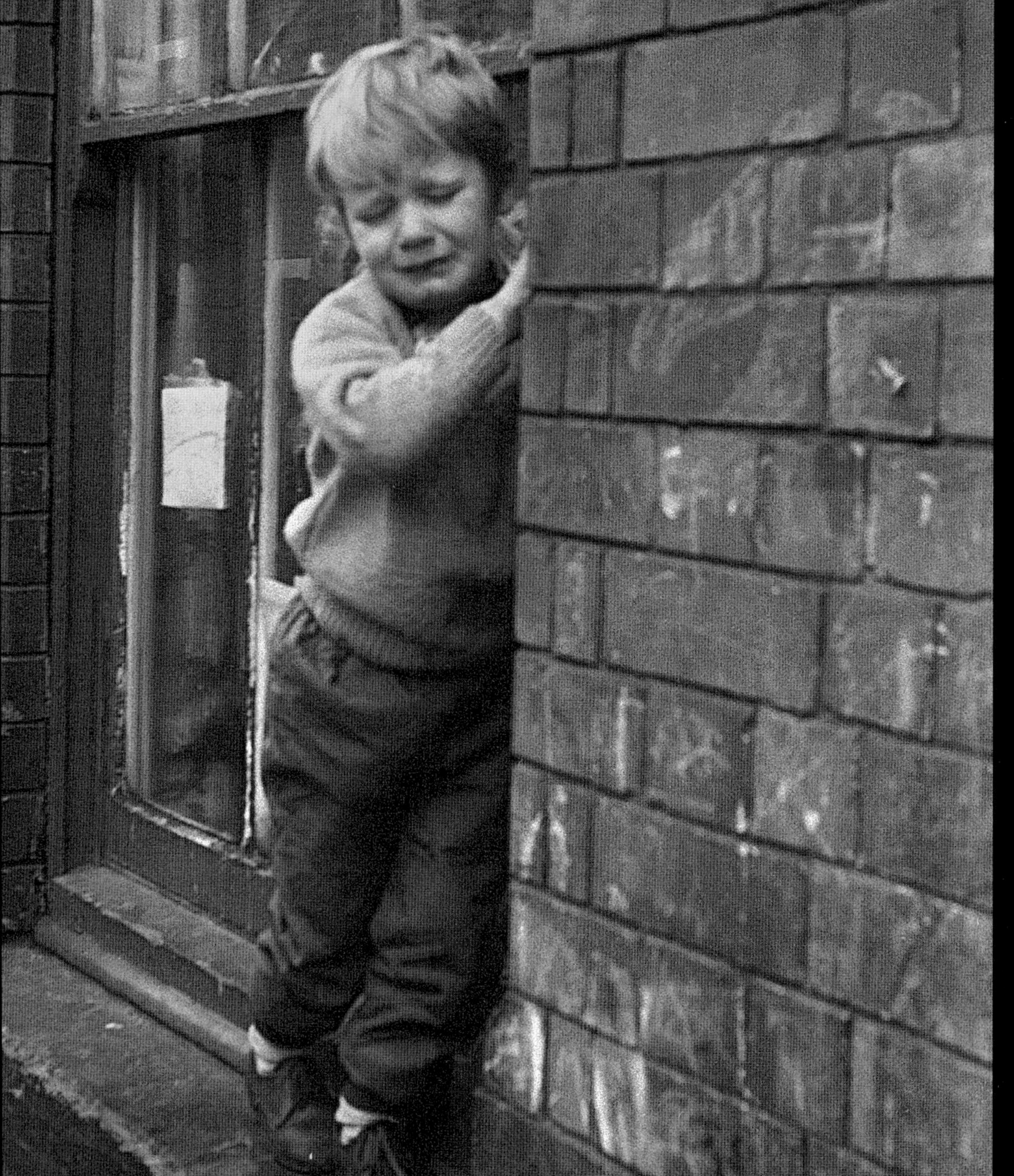

Crying boy standing on a windowsill outside his house

"Houses unfit for human habitation, so the council said. What about the people? St Ann's was a community like no other. You could always rely on your neighbours. If your mum went out to work (most did) a neighbour would always keep an eye on you till Mum came home from work."

Susan Dawn

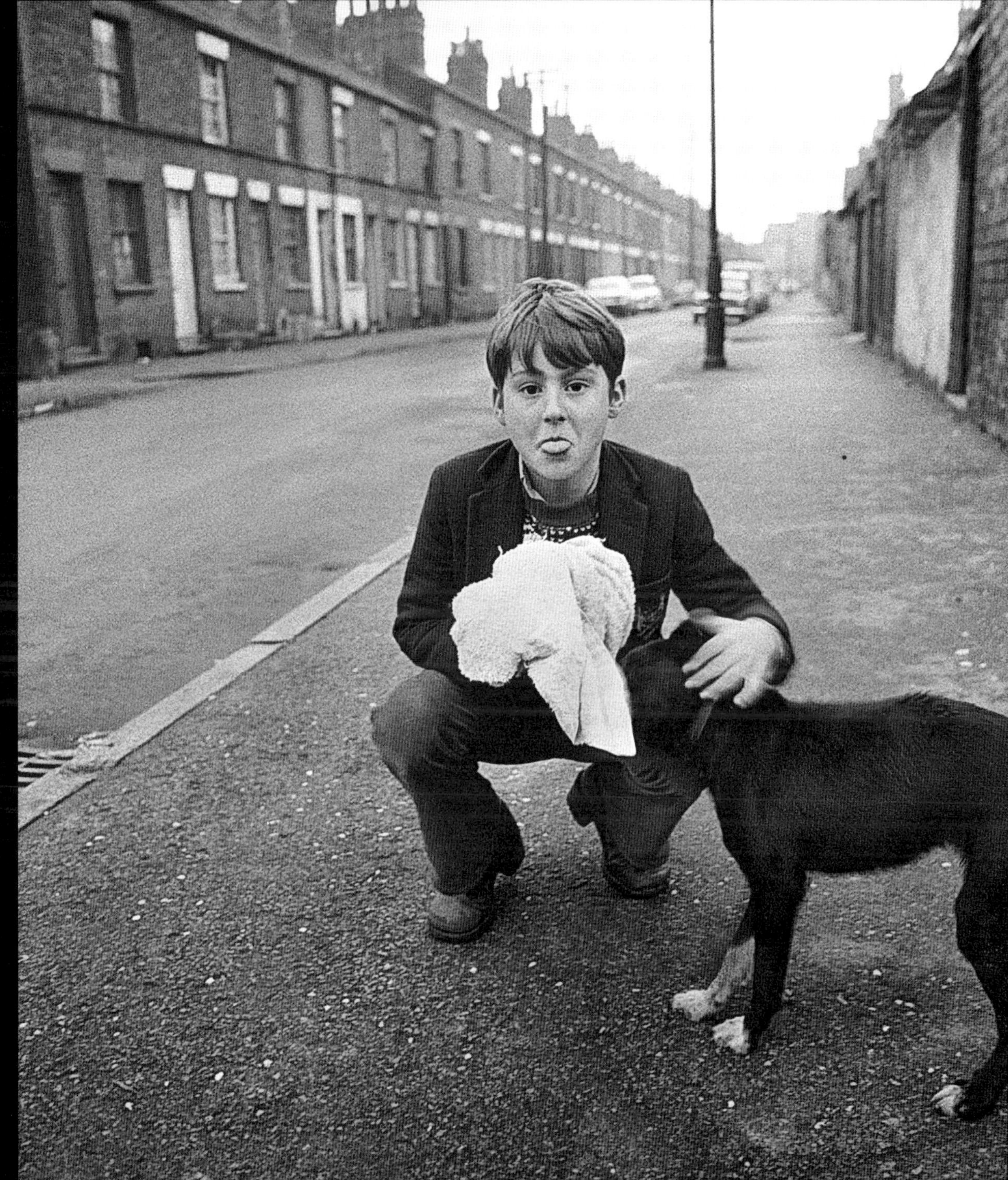

Boy with his pet dog cheekily putting his tongue out at me

A towel in his hand suggests he's on his way back from the Victoria Baths.

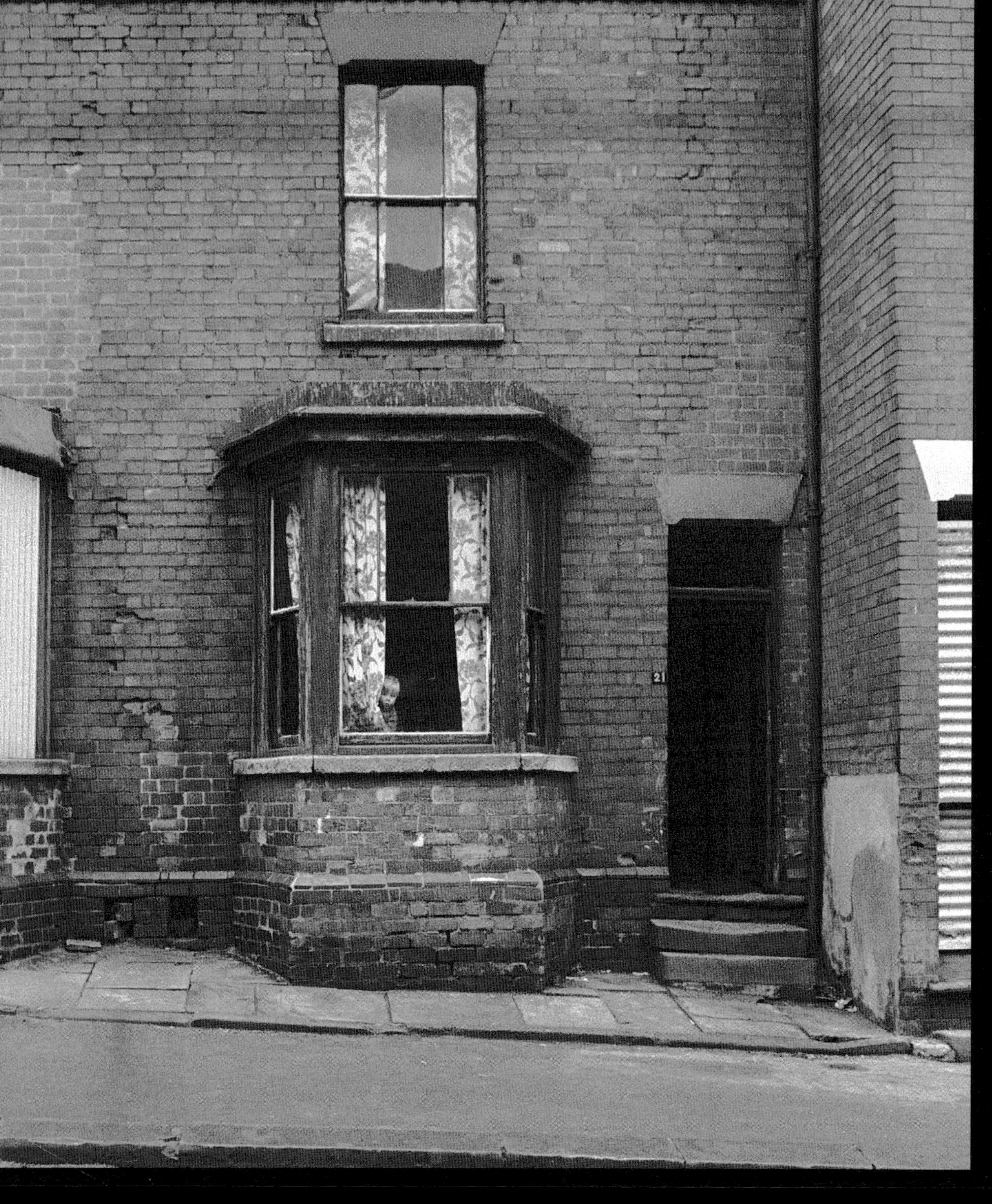

Young child peeking from behind the curtains of the front room window

During the clearance many families found themselves isolated on streets of empty houses.

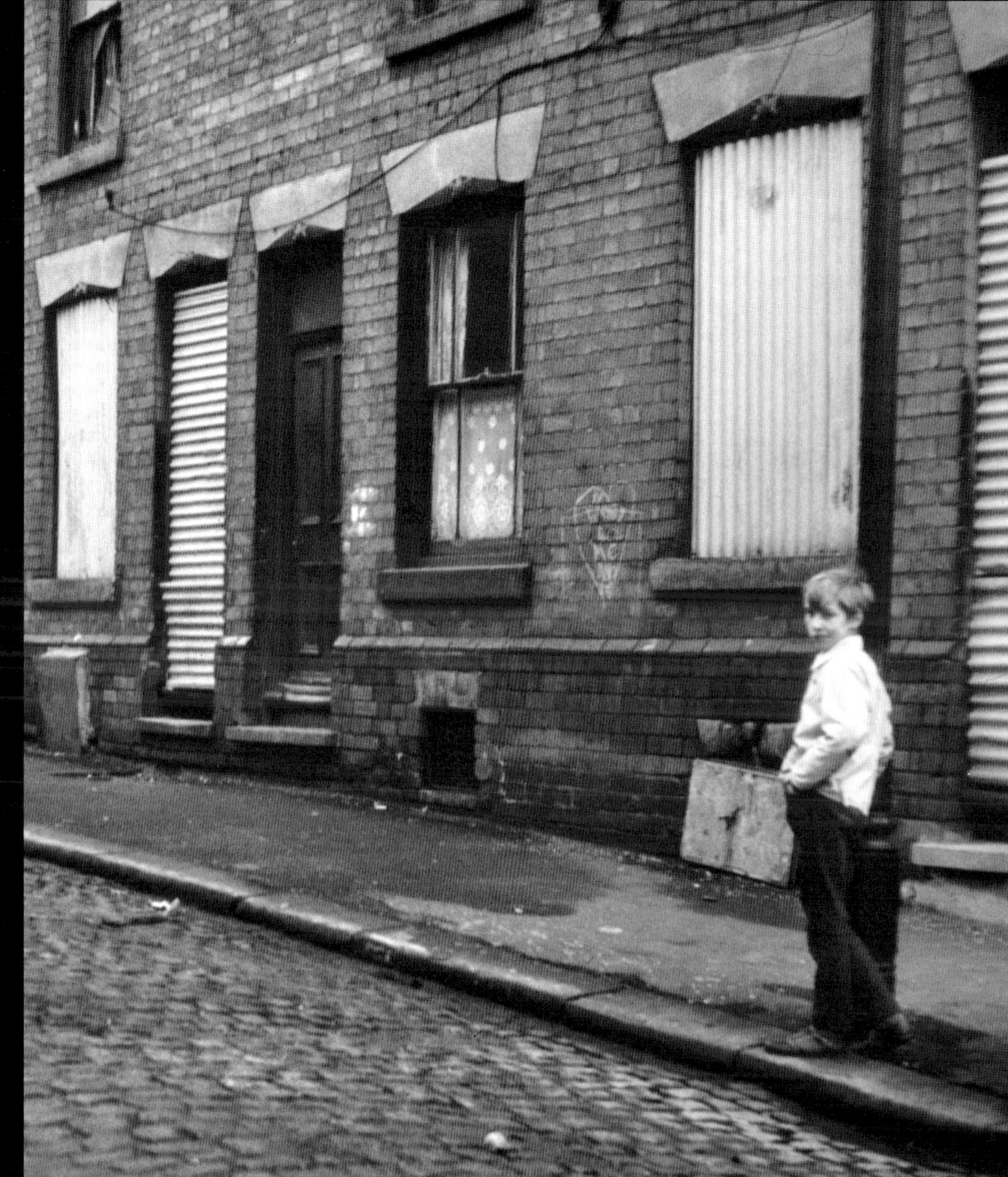

Boy leaning on a lamppost outside his house

Many children lost all their friends as houses were boarded up or demolished and families dispersed to different areas of the city.

"We all played on the streets in those days. There was dozens, literally dozens of kids playing on the street at night as soon as they came home from school. They'd be out there till 7 or 8 o'clock at night."

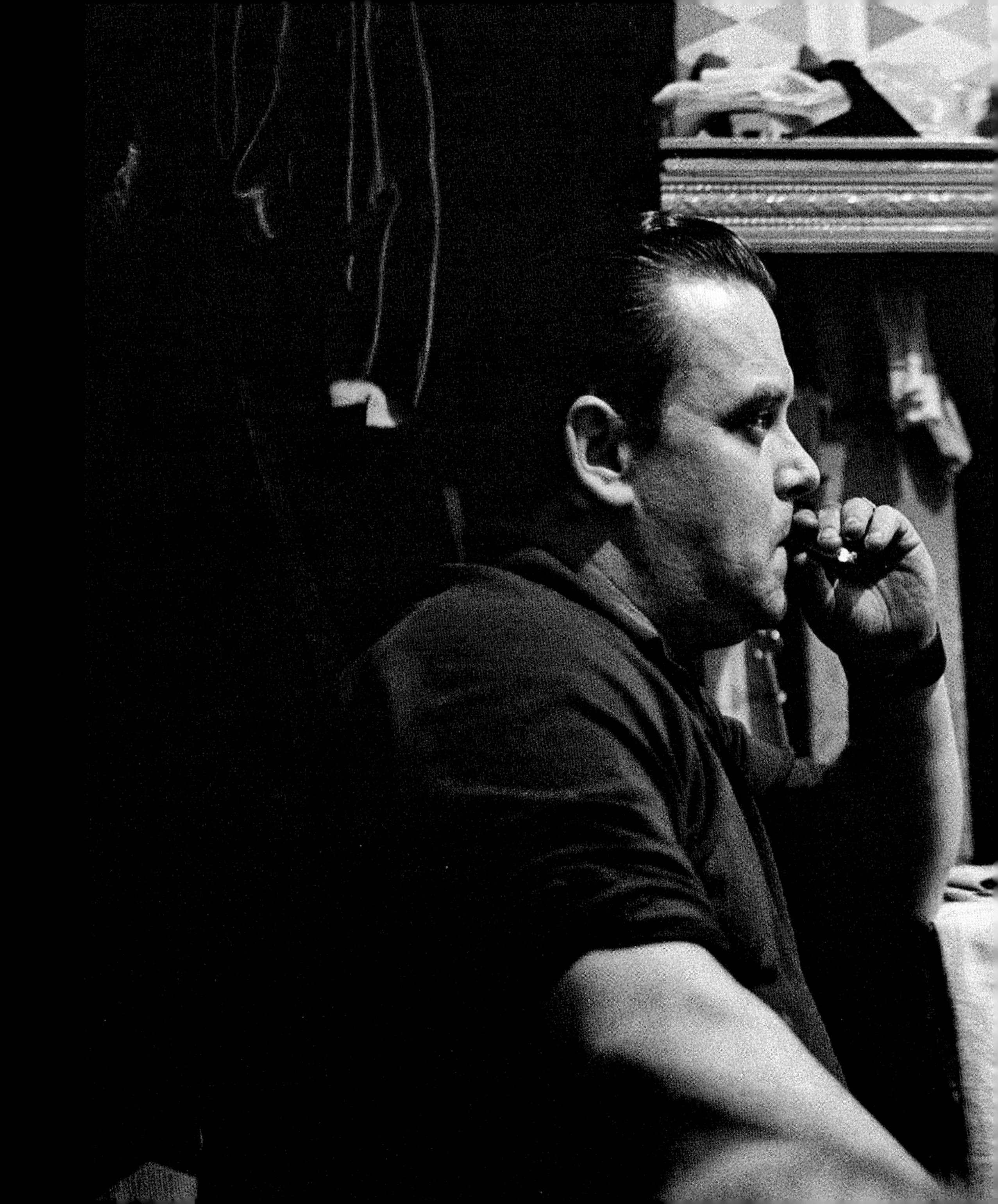

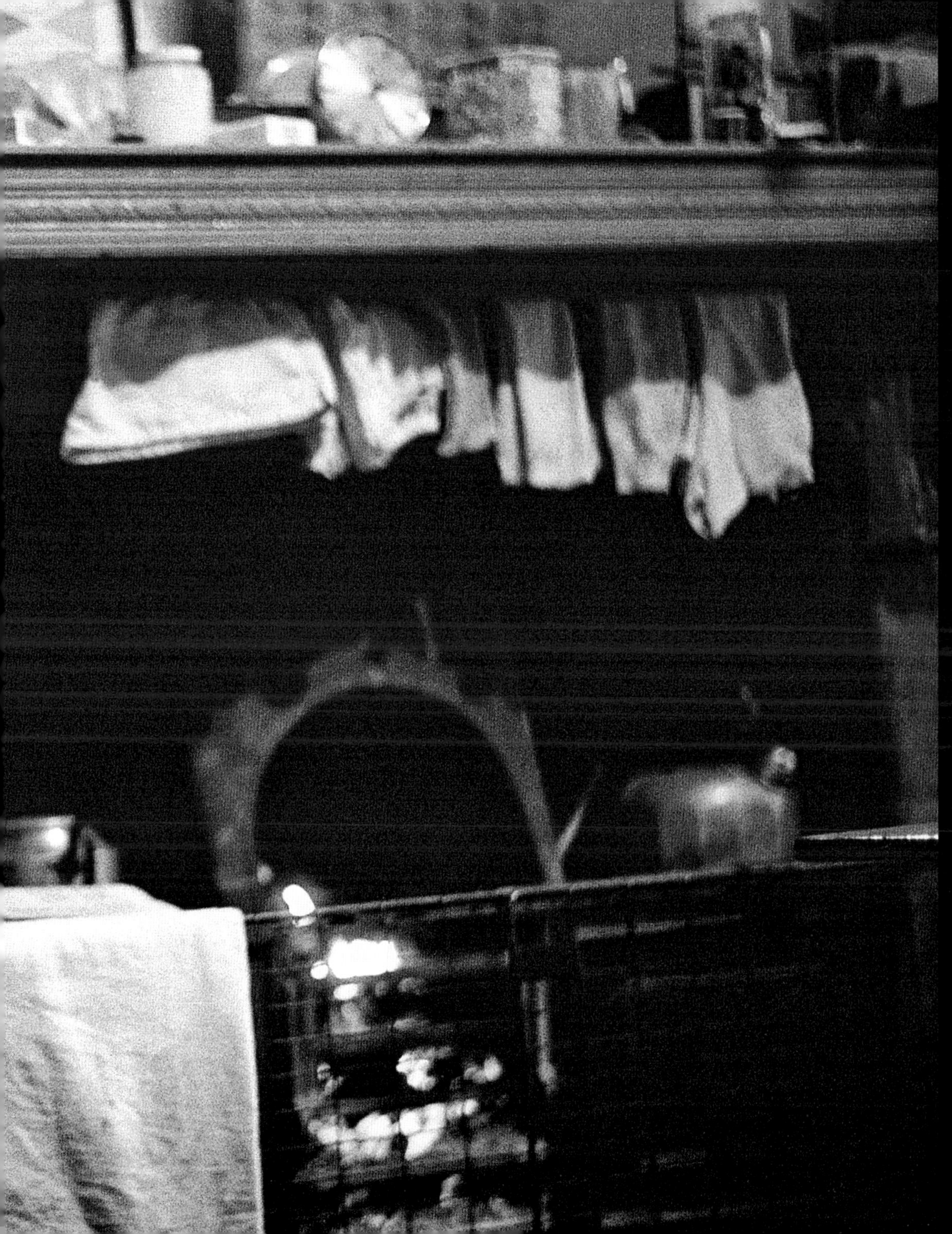

Traditional cast iron cooking range

This possibly provided the only source of heat in the house. On wet days washing was often hung on lines across the room.

"Looking at it now, it's grim but we never gave it a second thought then. We were poor, but so was everyone else around us."

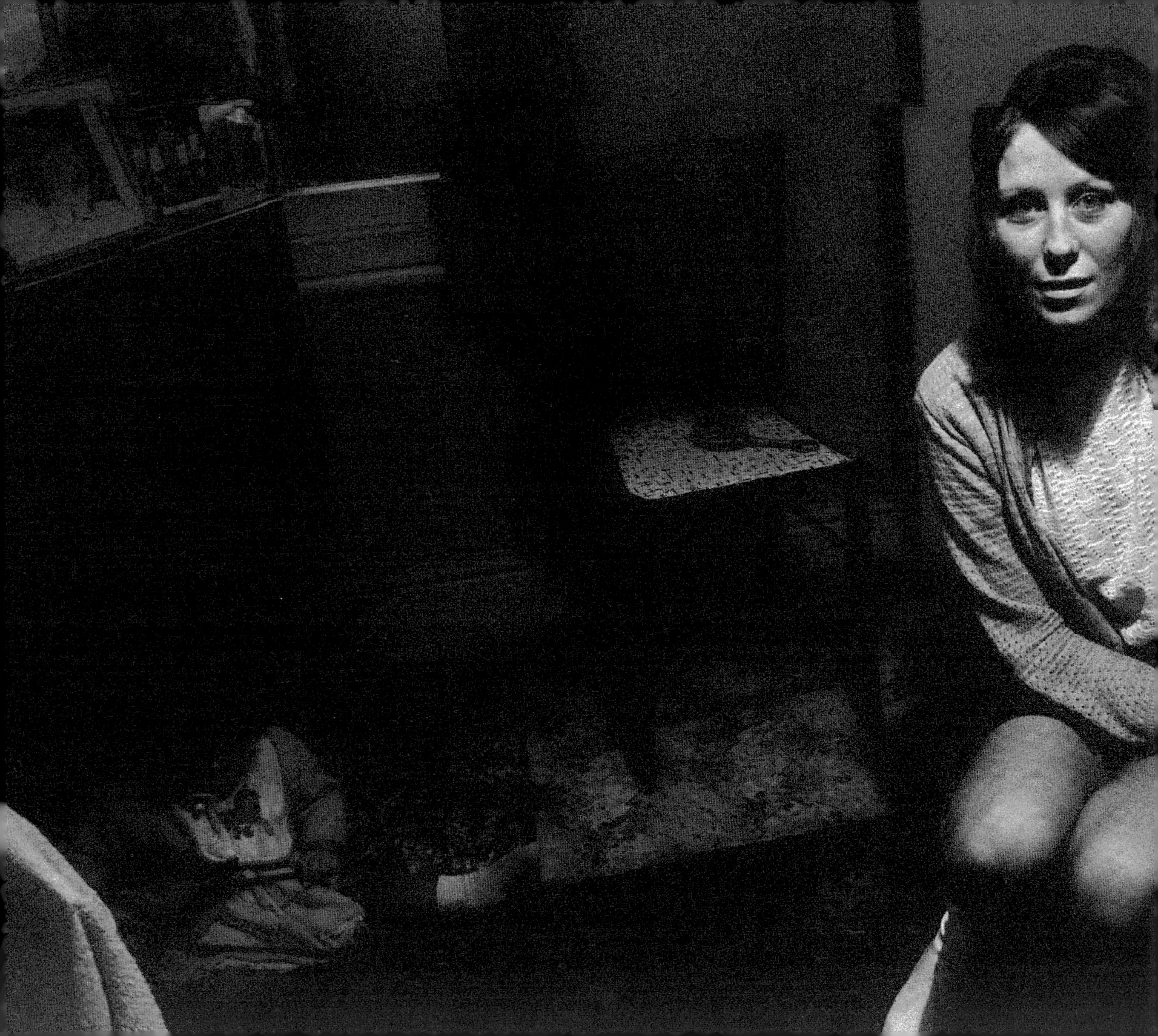

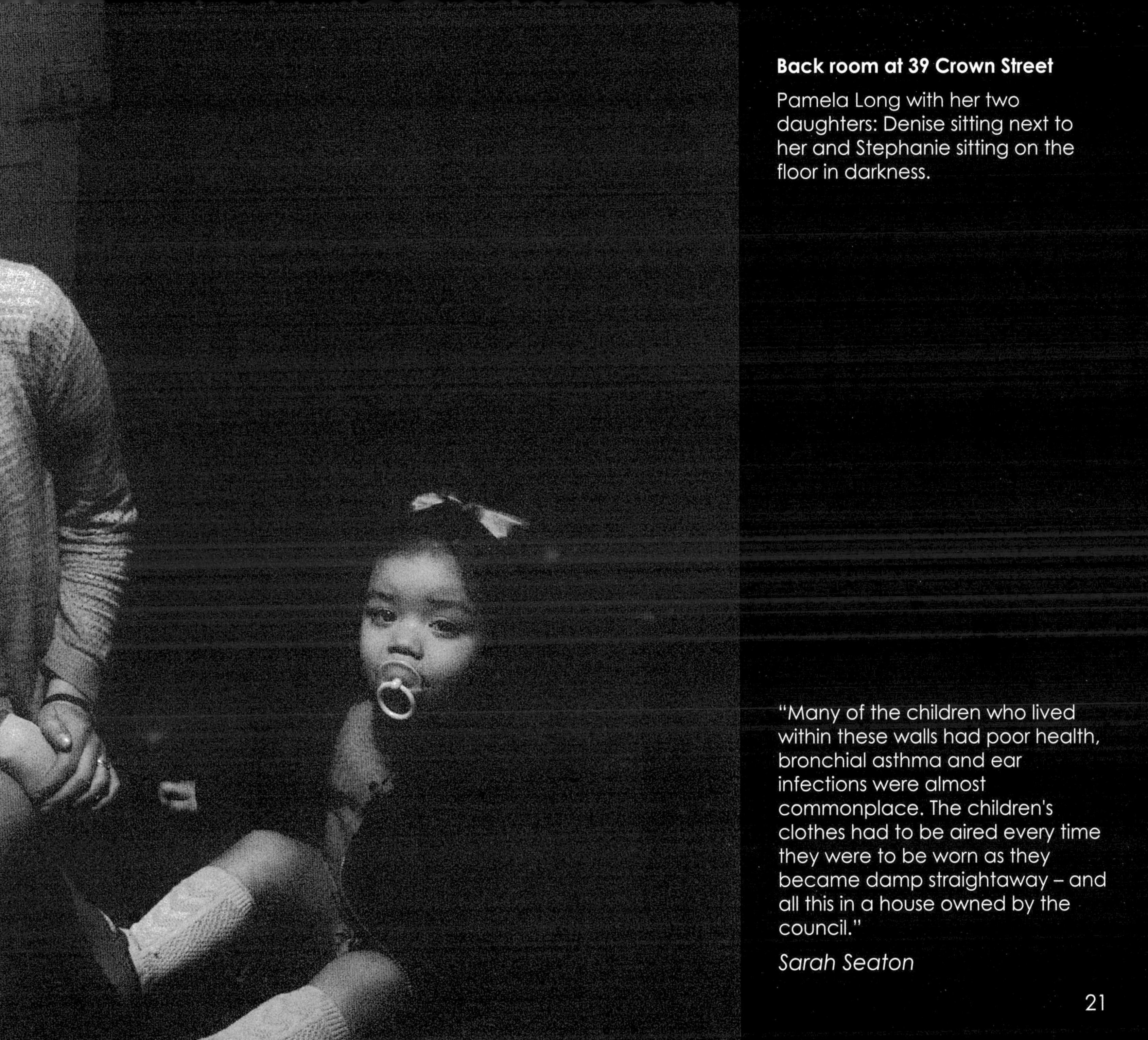

Back room at 39 Crown Street

Pamela Long with her two daughters: Denise sitting next to her and Stephanie sitting on the floor in darkness.

"Many of the children who lived within these walls had poor health, bronchial asthma and ear infections were almost commonplace. The children's clothes had to be aired every time they were to be worn as they became damp straightaway – and all this in a house owned by the council."

Sarah Seaton

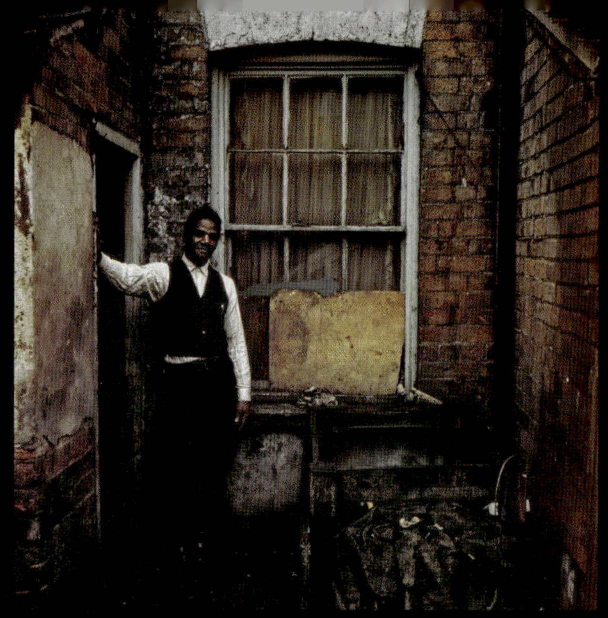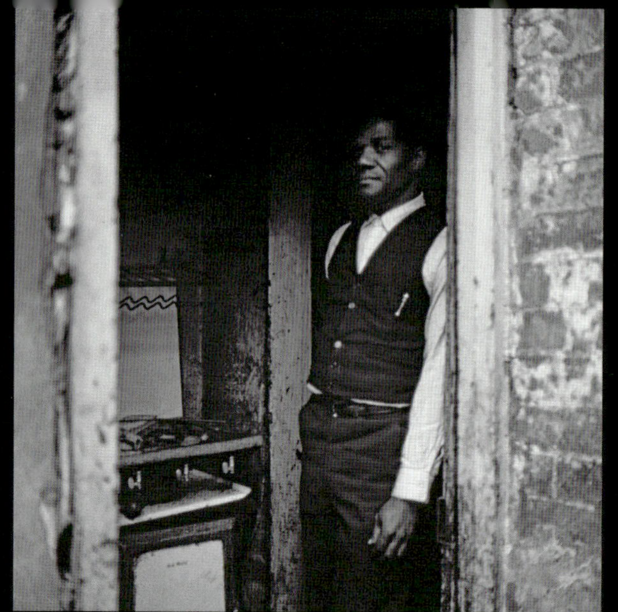

I visited many residents on a regular basis and captured stages of their lives and how they lived. Often when I returned I found that they had been rehoused and their old homes were boarded up or even demolished.

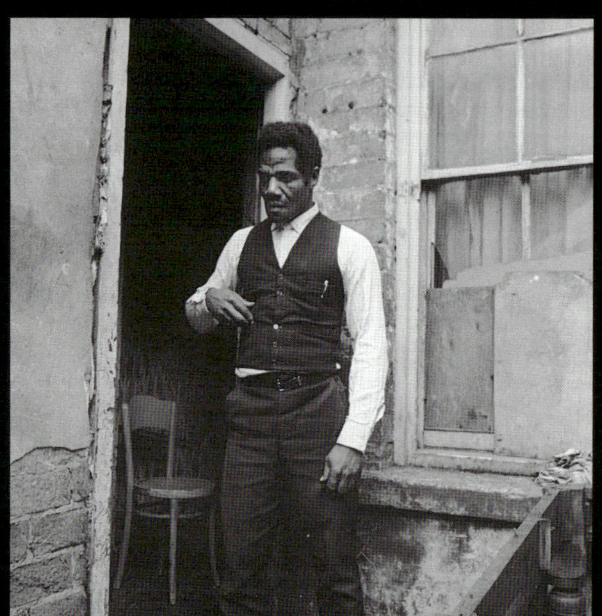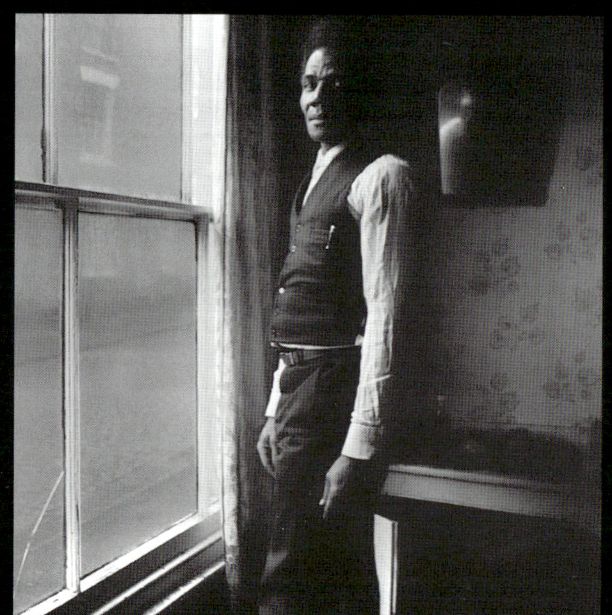

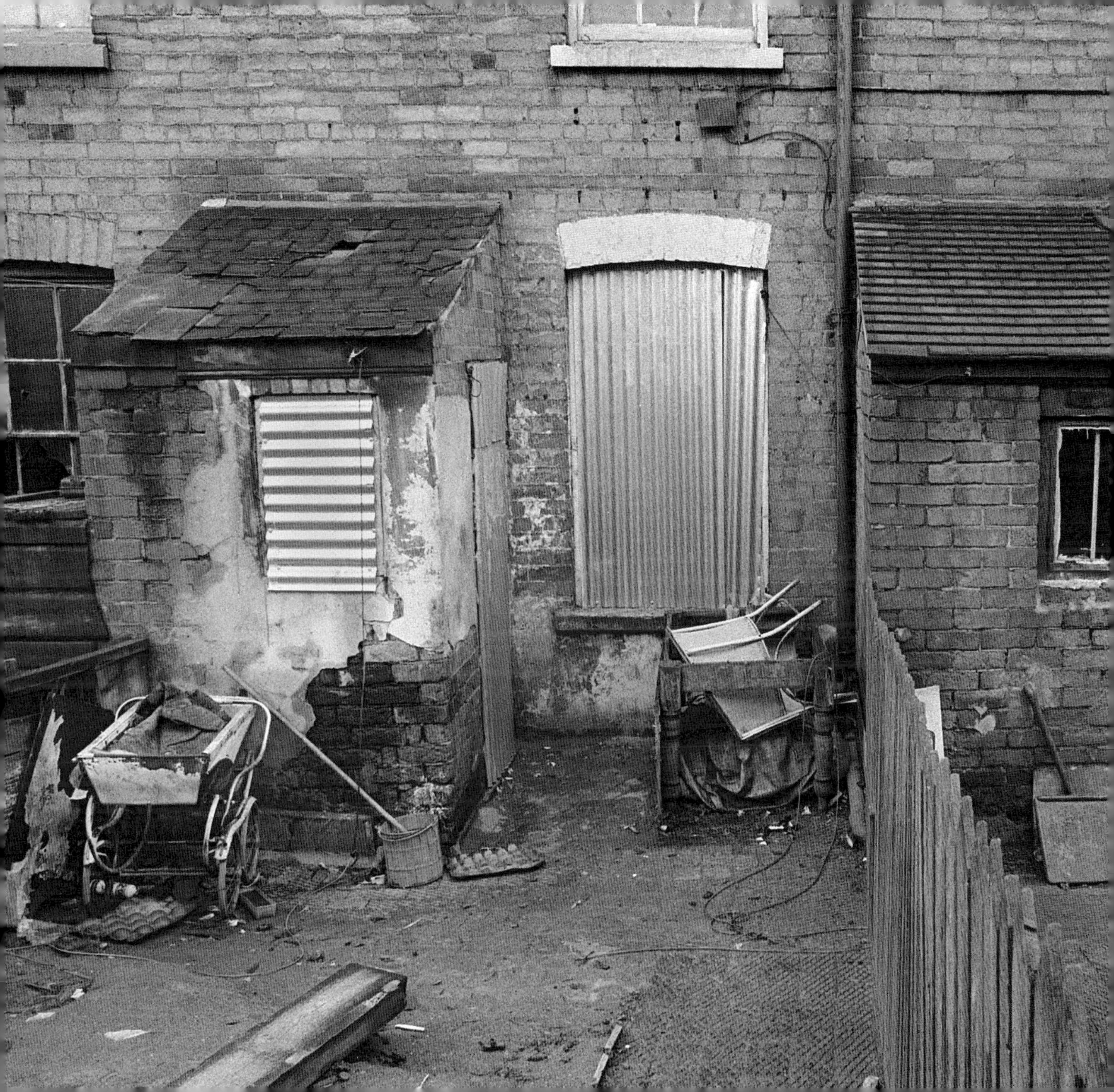

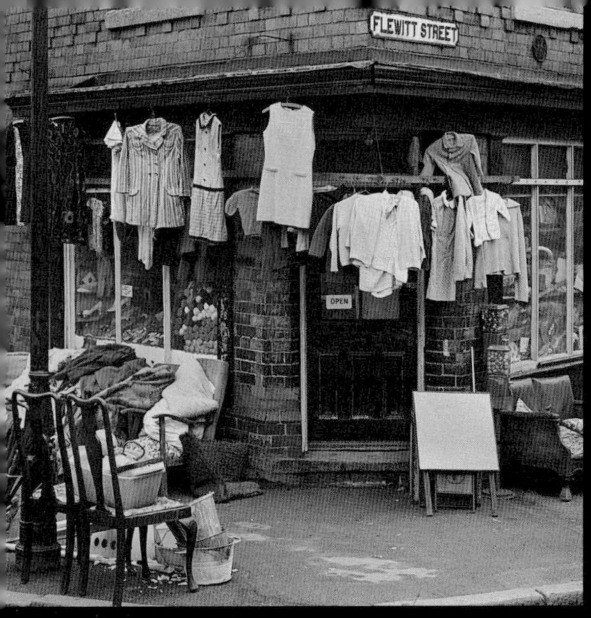

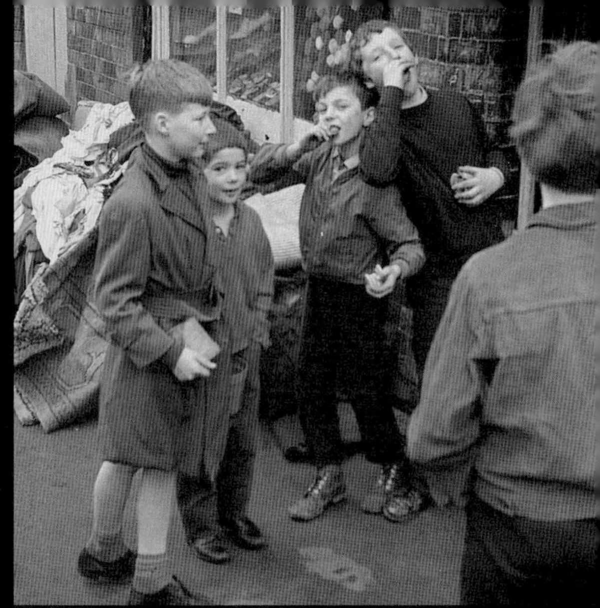

This shop at the top of Flewitt Street features in many photographs from the first book and was a large part of many residents' lives. Its sad end portrays that of many shops and homes in the final stages of the demolition of St Ann's.

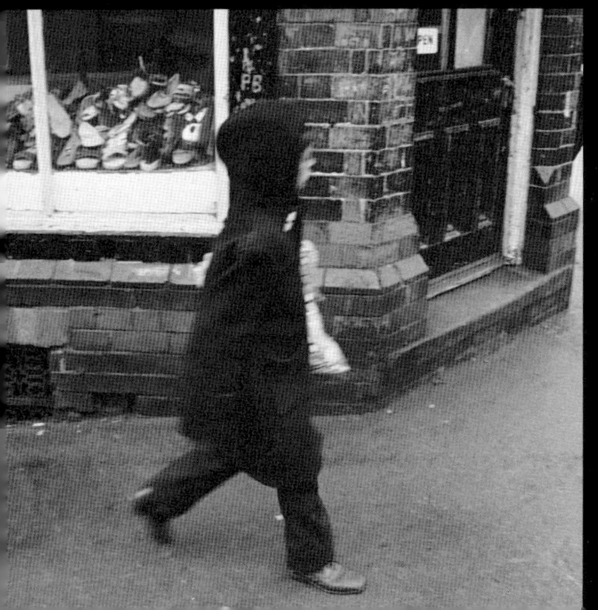

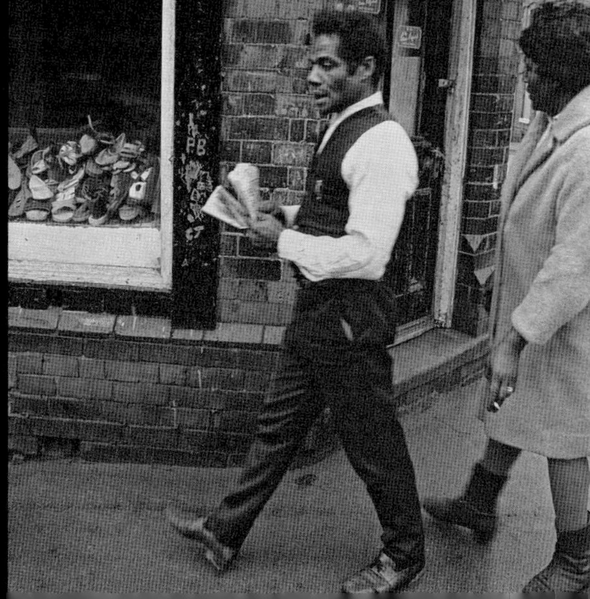

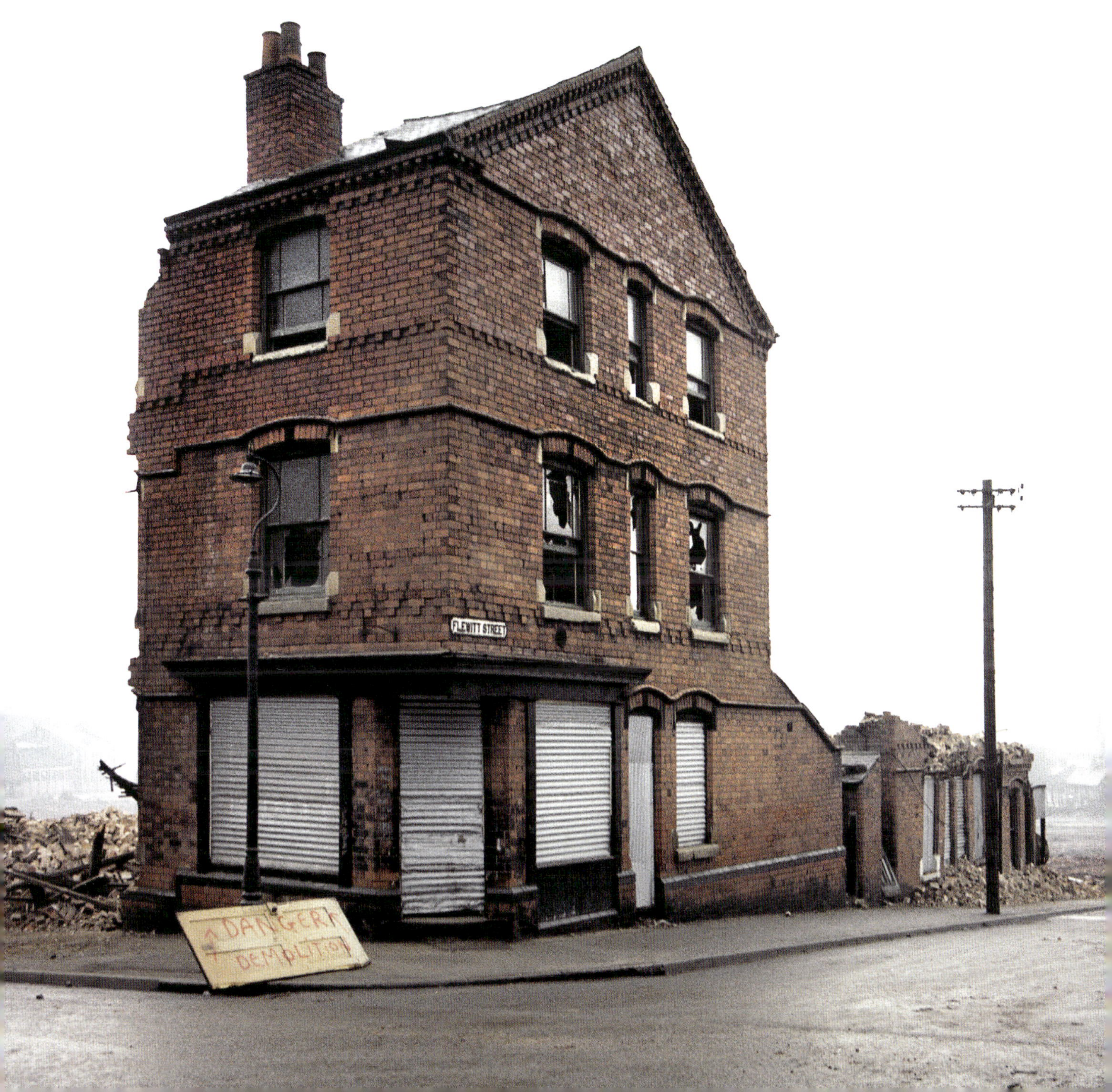
FLEWITT STREET
↑ DANGER ↑
↑ DEMOLITION

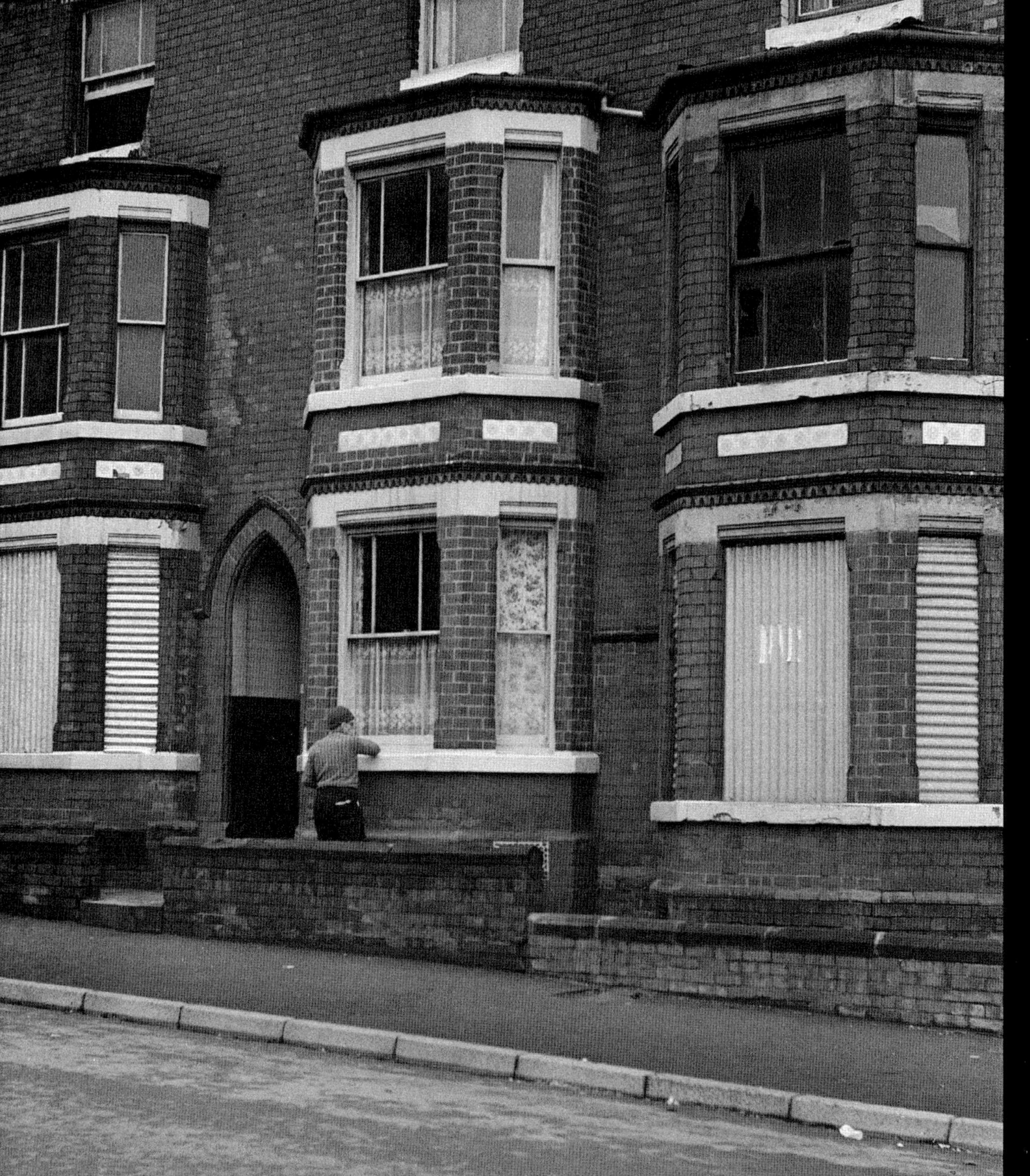

Despite the dirt and mess of demolition people still took a pride in their houses

"It was a regular Saturday morning job for me and my sister to share the chores of scrubbing the front/back doorstep, and the outside toilet step and floor. Then as we had brass door knobs and house number on the front door, out came the Brasso. We learnt at a very early age how to do the cleaning."

Lesley Dudley

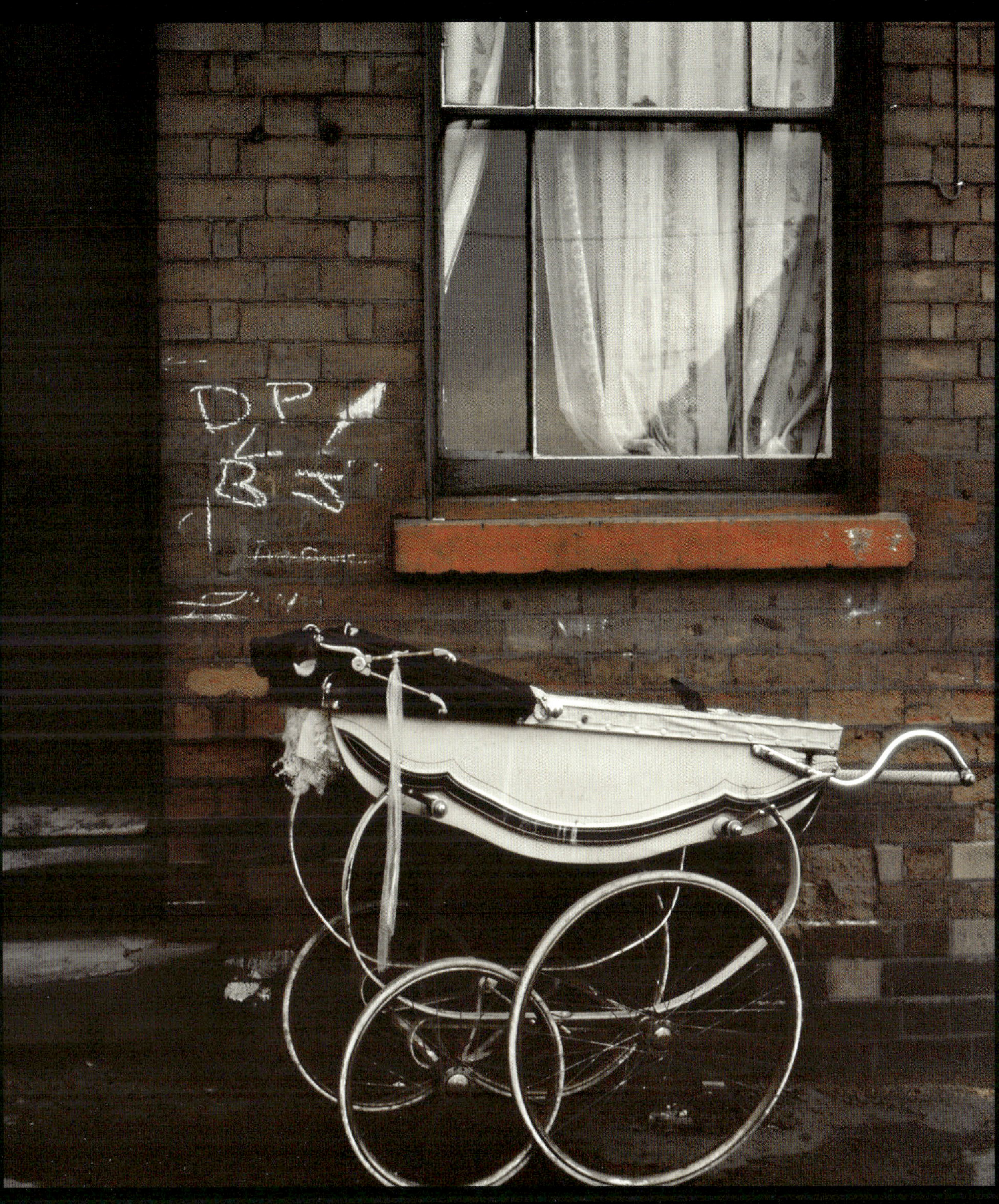

"That's why the pram was
used a lot in those days.
You never got rid of your
prams 'cause you carted
your lace work round
and that."

Off to Bath Street
    Washhouse – when
    the wet days come.
With washing piled high
    in a pram – through
    the rain we often ran.
There was sinks, dryers,
    ironers, a hard day's
    work for all.
You had a ticket at your
    turn the attendant
    would call.
'Oh I was only watching'
    – sat with all parked
    prams.

Jean Taylor

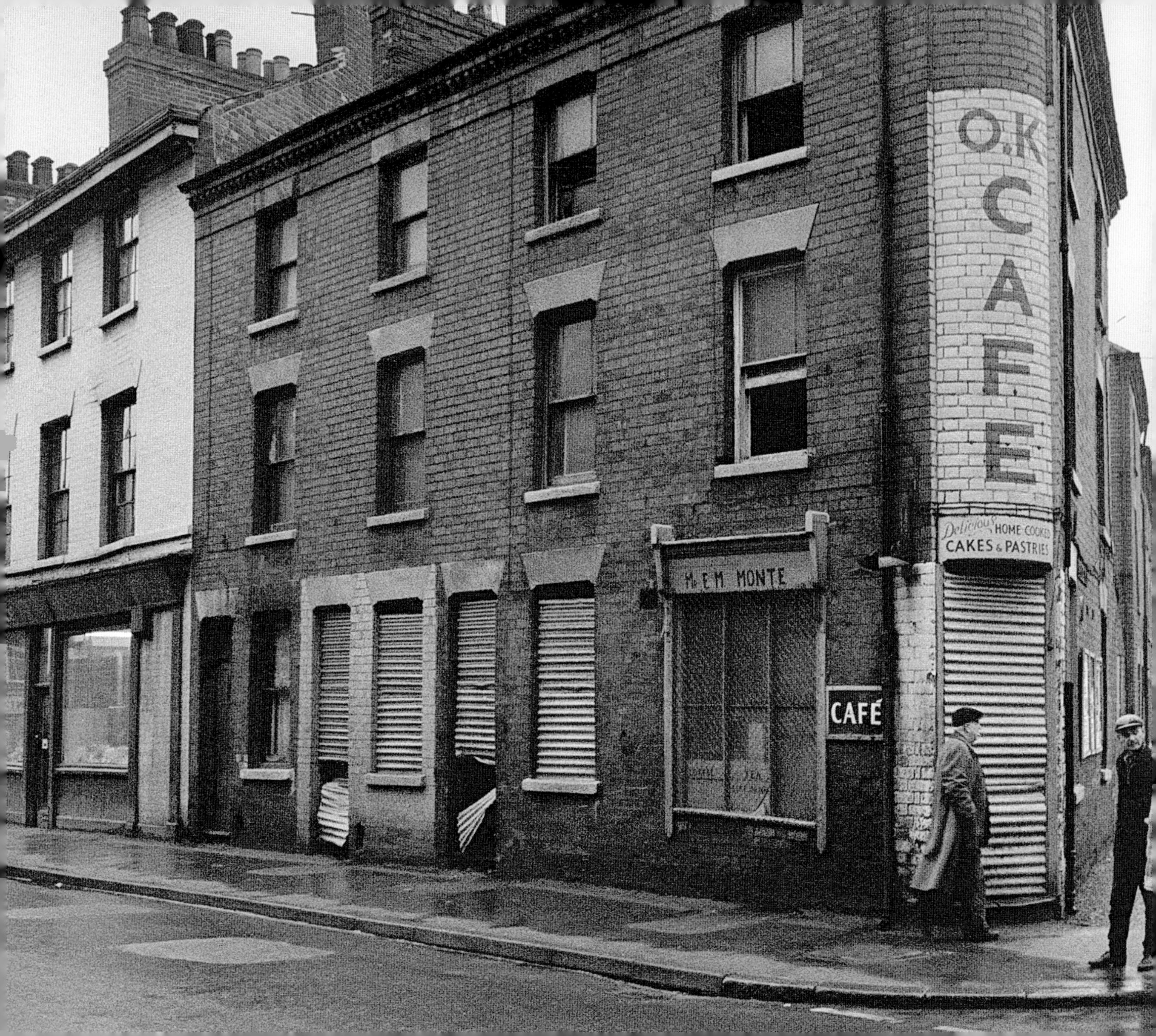

O.K. CAFE
Delicious HOME COOKED CAKES & PASTRIES
M. E. M. MONTE
CAFÉ

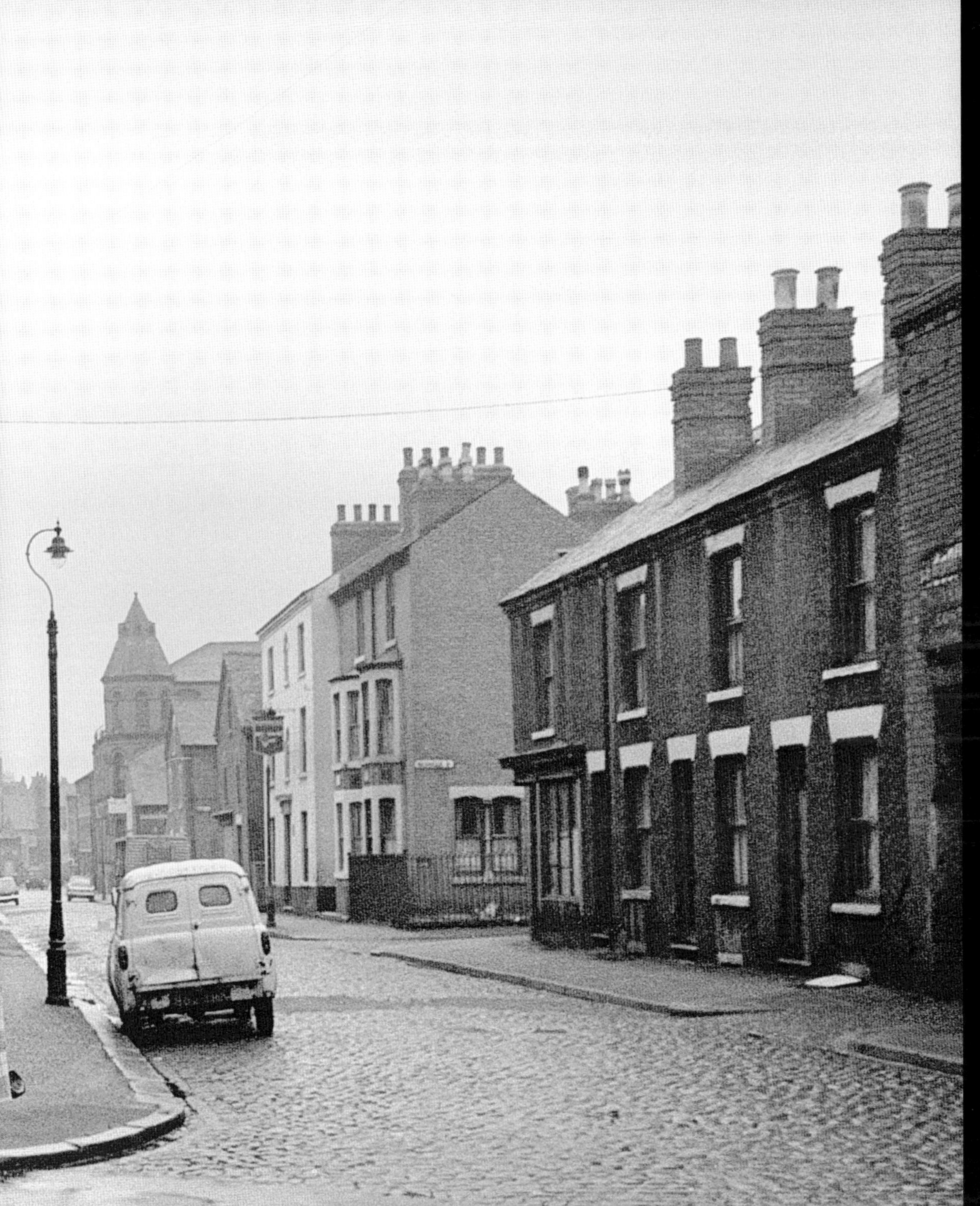

Alfred Street South at the junction with Hawkridge Street

To the left of the picture is Peas Hill Post Office and the Devonshire Arms public house is just visible down Hawkridge Street, along with the plumber's yard (on the far right of the picture) depicted on page 65 after it had been shuttered up.

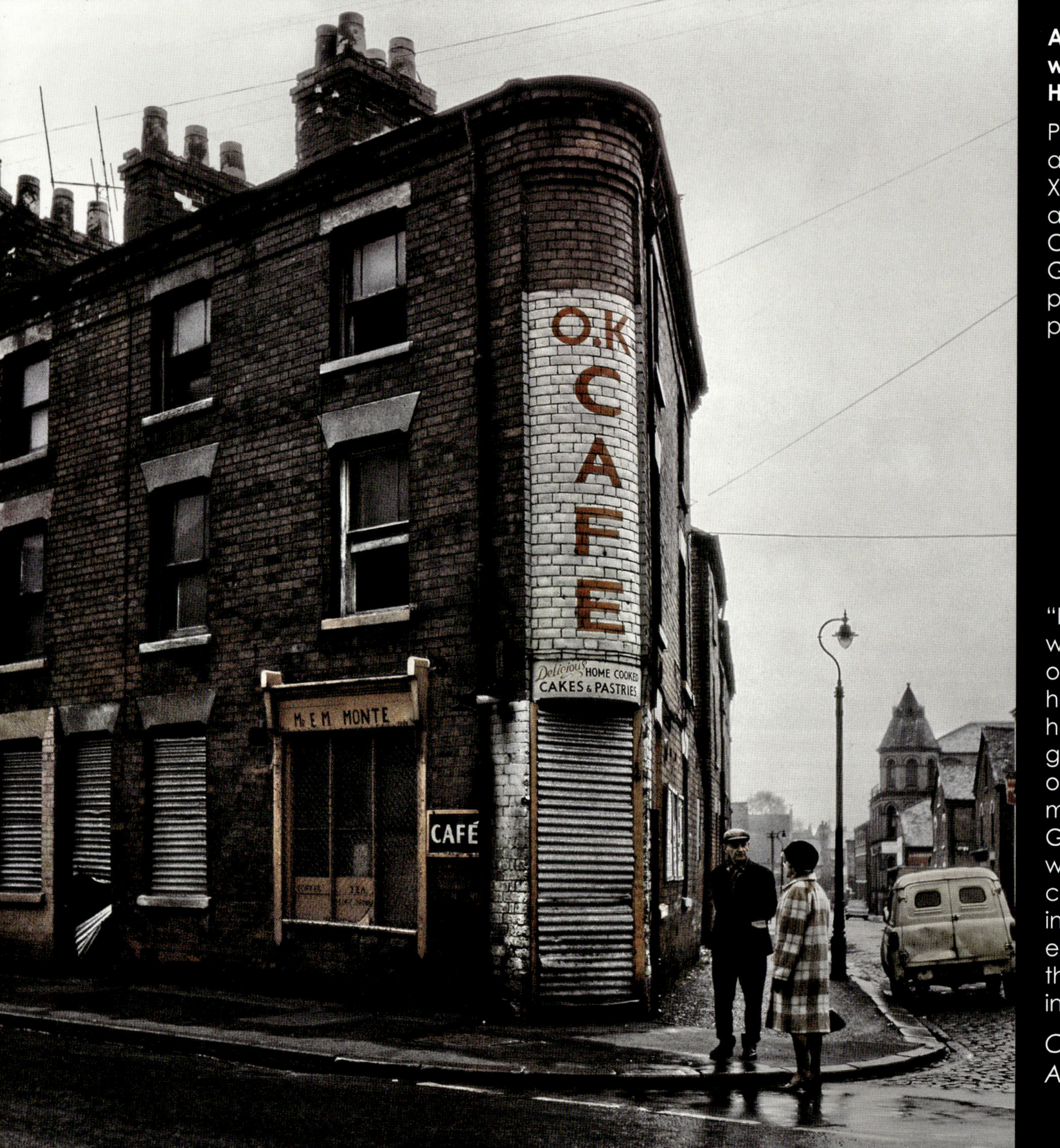

Alfred Street South with the junction of Hawkridge Street

Posters on the wall advertising for chest X-Rays, Horse Racing and miners' jobs at Calverton and Gedling Collieries paying £18 and £19 per week.

"I remember in 1970 when the miners went on strike and we only had electricity four hours a day. I used to go down the Wessie off licence and buy my dad his Stones Ginger Wine. While I was there I would get change to put money in the gas and electric meters. Boy, they were some interesting times."

Clarence George – Antonio Shim

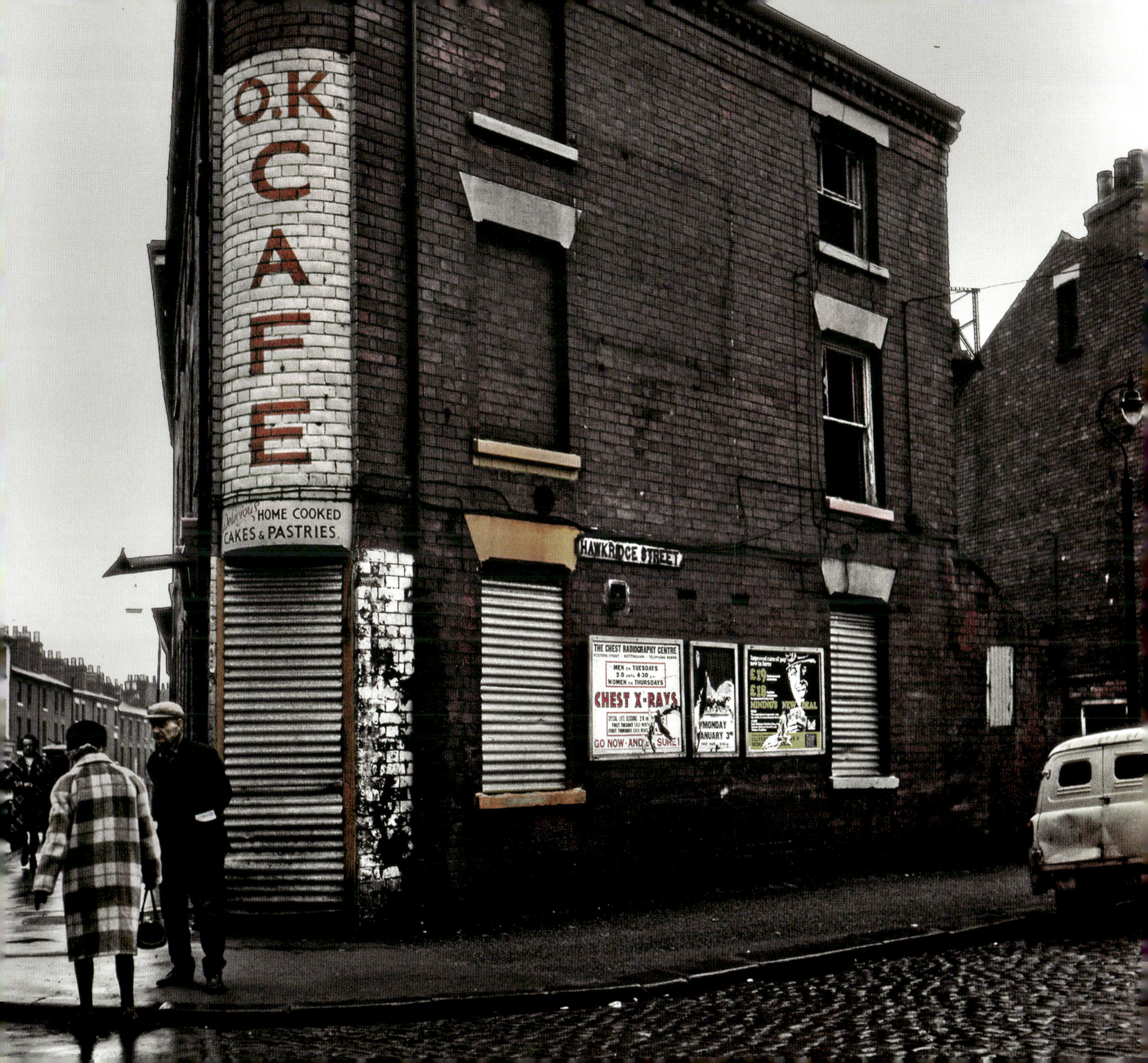
O.K
CAFE
Delicious HOME COOKED
CAKES & PASTRIES.
HAWKRIDGE STREET
THE CHEST RADIOGRAPHY CENTRE
MEN on TUESDAYS
2.0 until 4.30 p.m.
WOMEN on THURSDAYS
CHEST X-RAYS
GO NOW AND BE SURE!
£19
£18

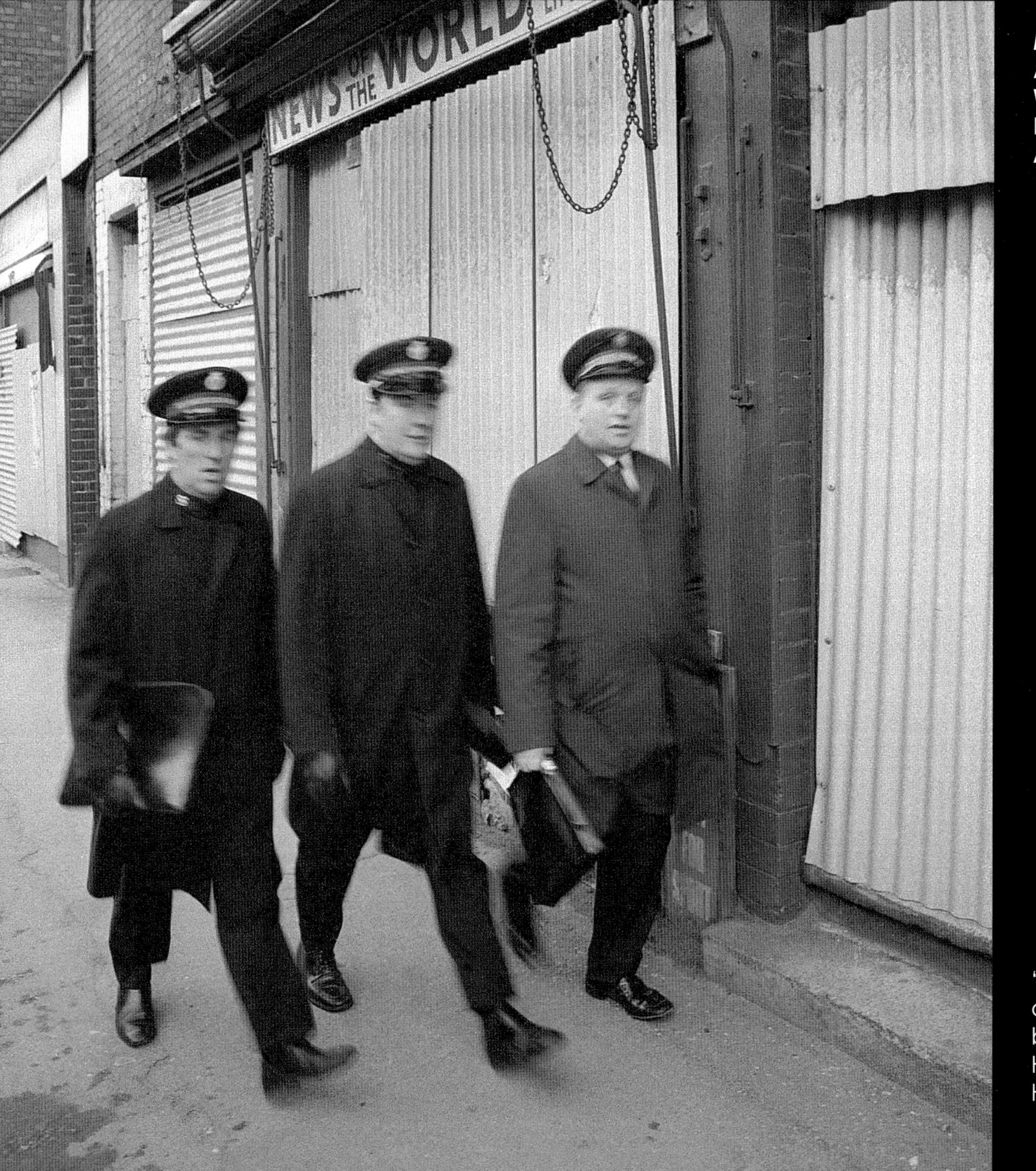

Members of the Salvation Army on the way to the William Booth Memorial Hall at the bottom of St Ann's Well Road

"We hurried to get dressed, to follow the band down to Kingdom Hall, at the bottom of Huntingdon Street."

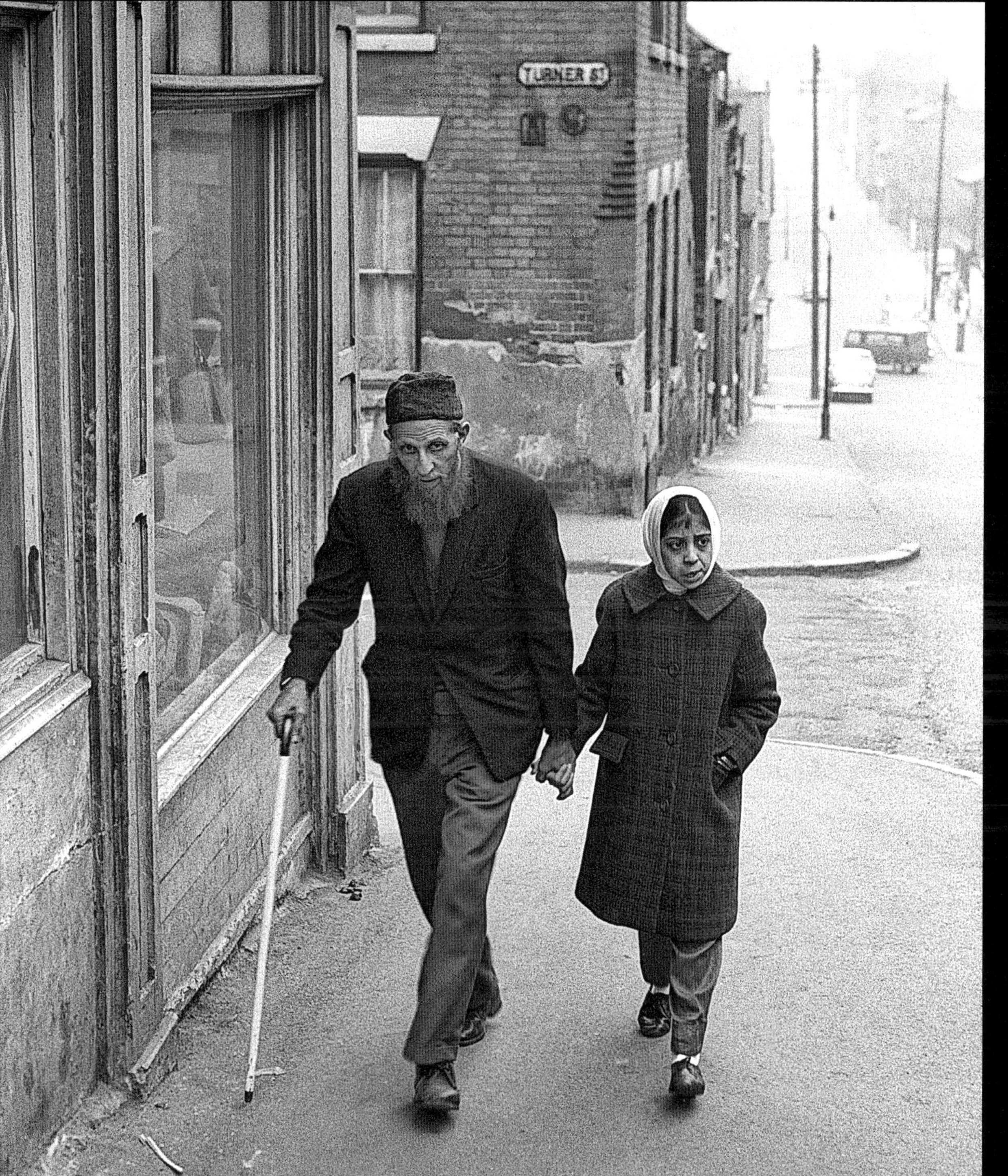

Junction of Pym Street and Turner Street

Elderly man and young girl walking up Pym Street from St Ann's Well Road at the bottom of the hill.

"I lived first at 7 Turner Street, which was my grandma's house, and when it got a bit crowded we moved to 3 Turner Street, next door to the shop. I had friends living at the shop, we used to chat to each other over the fence, played together round the streets..."

Anne Binns

33

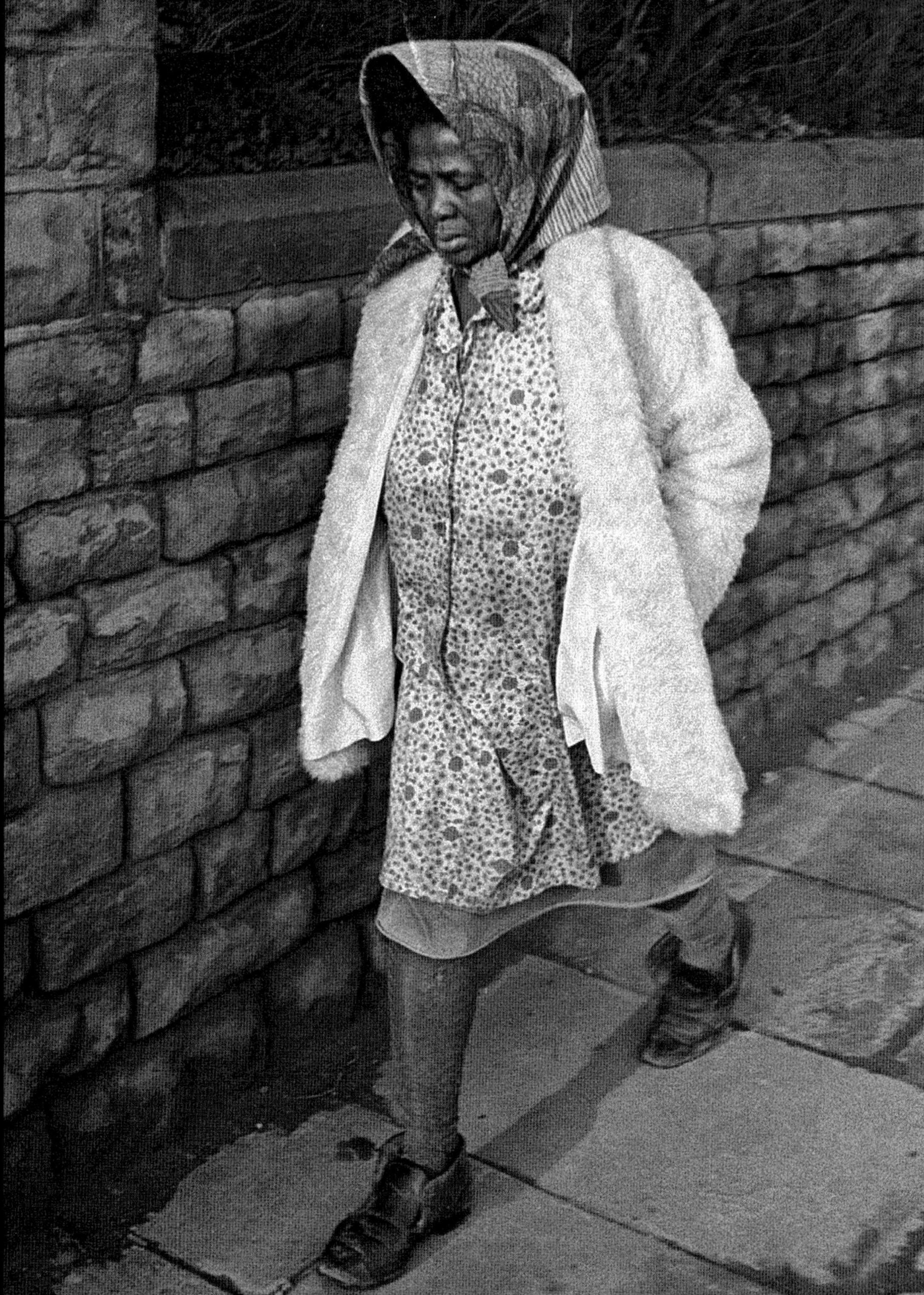

Woodborough Road

Elderly lady wearing a work smock and headscarf. Hats and scarves were the order of the day for most people – cloth caps for men and woollen hats with hatpins for women.

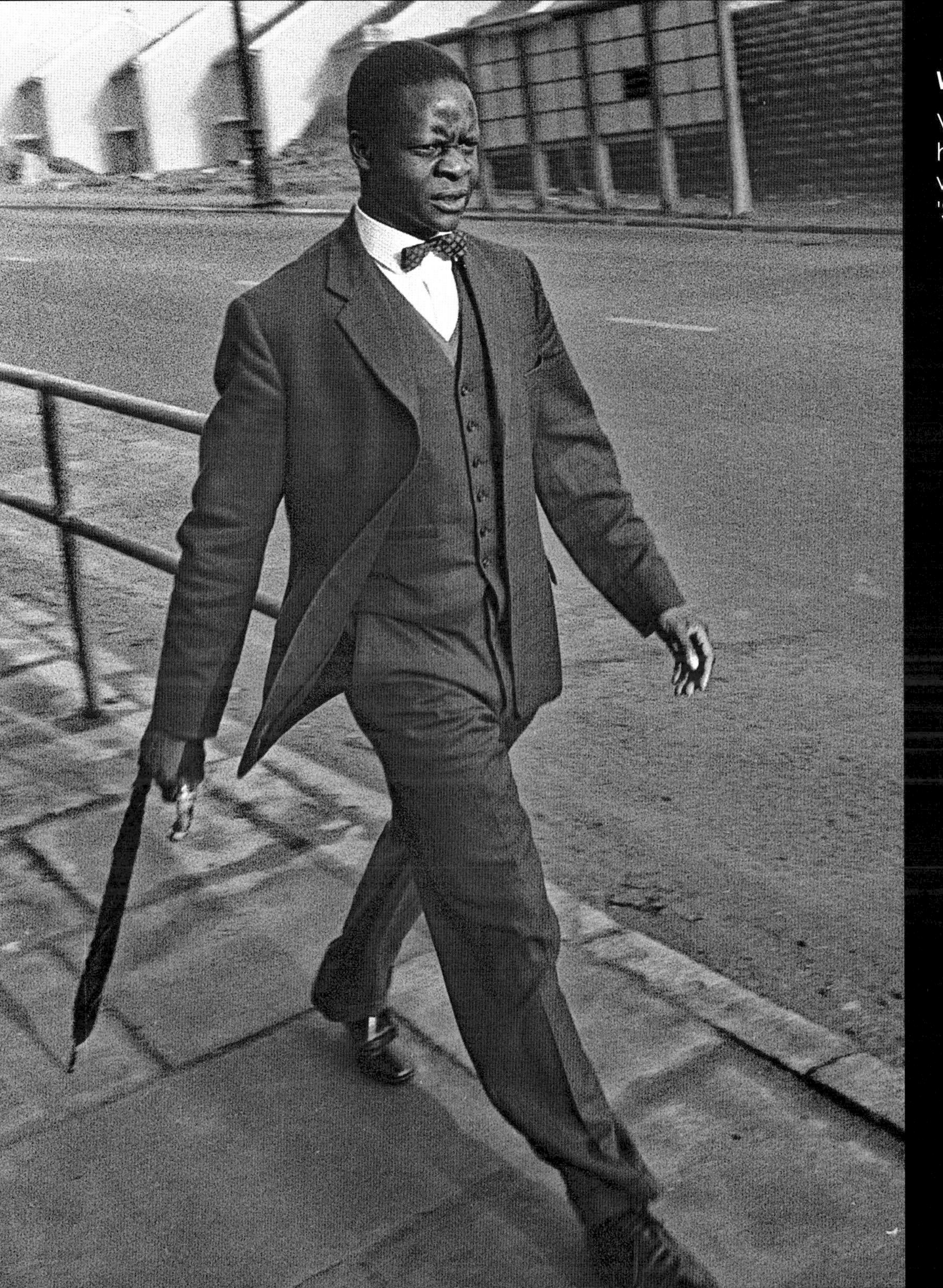

Very smart man, probably on his way to church. People would always put on their 'Sunday best' for church.

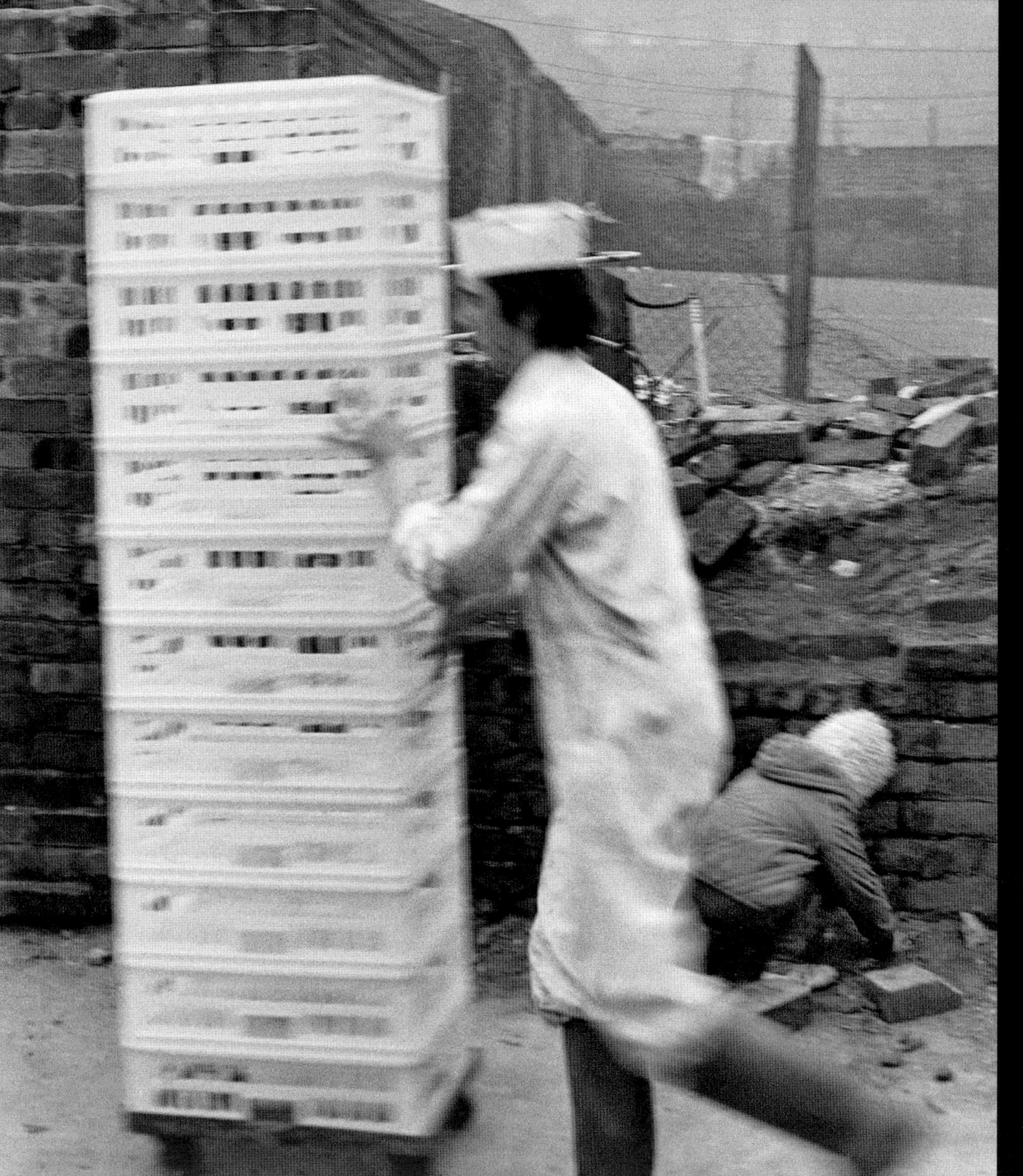

Work and play goes
on as usual during the
demolition

Children play amongst the rubble as workers go about their daily duties

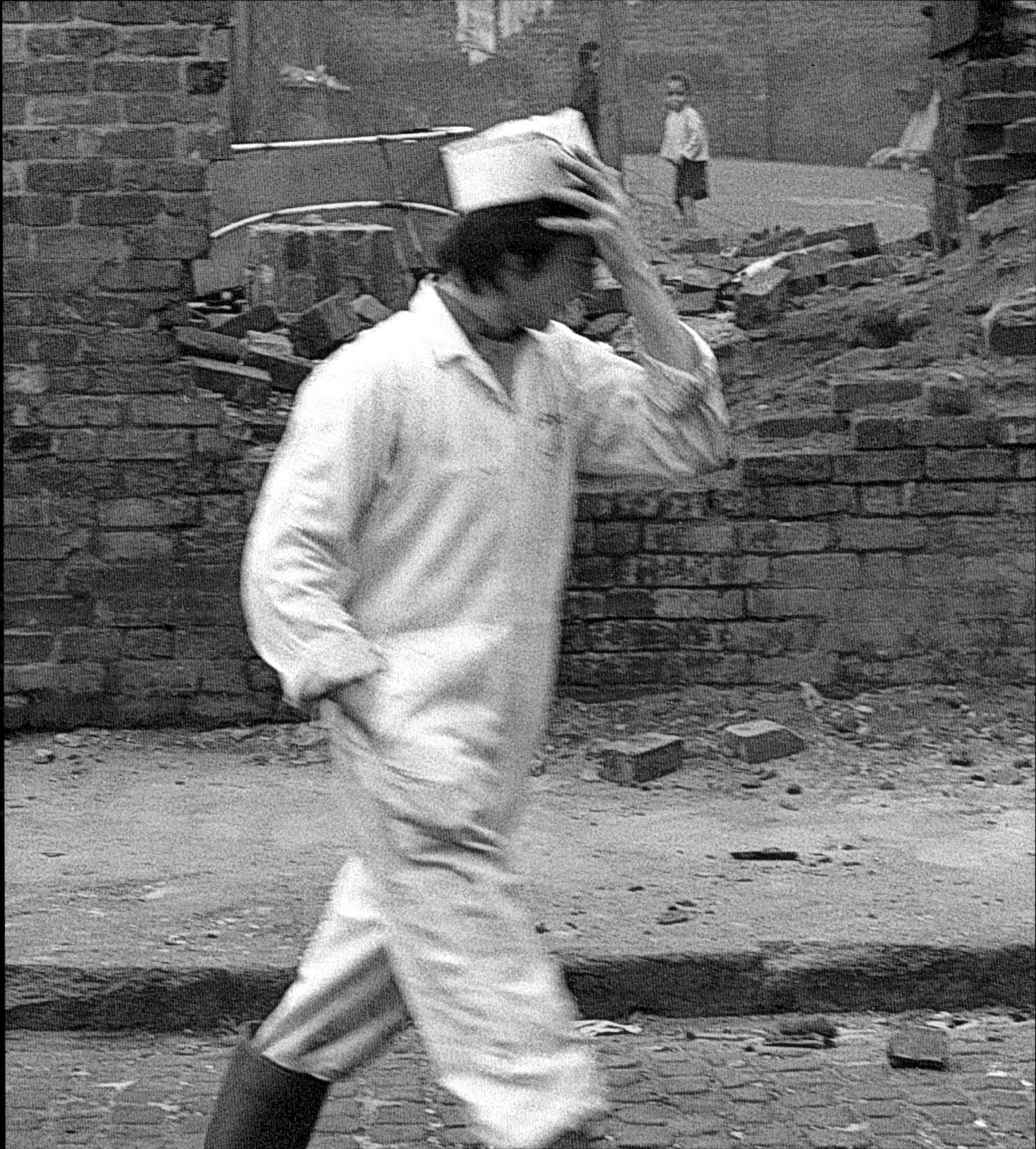

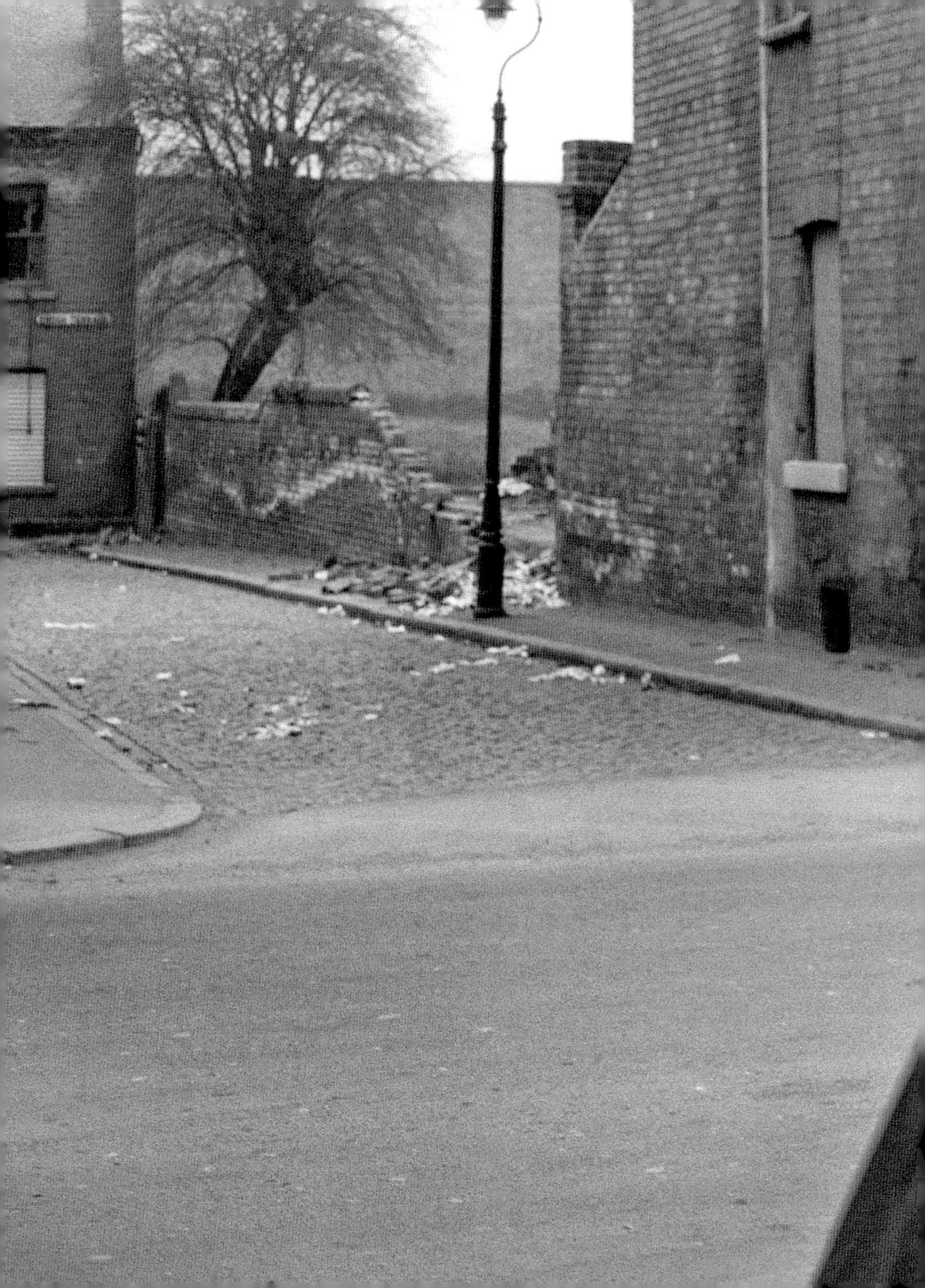

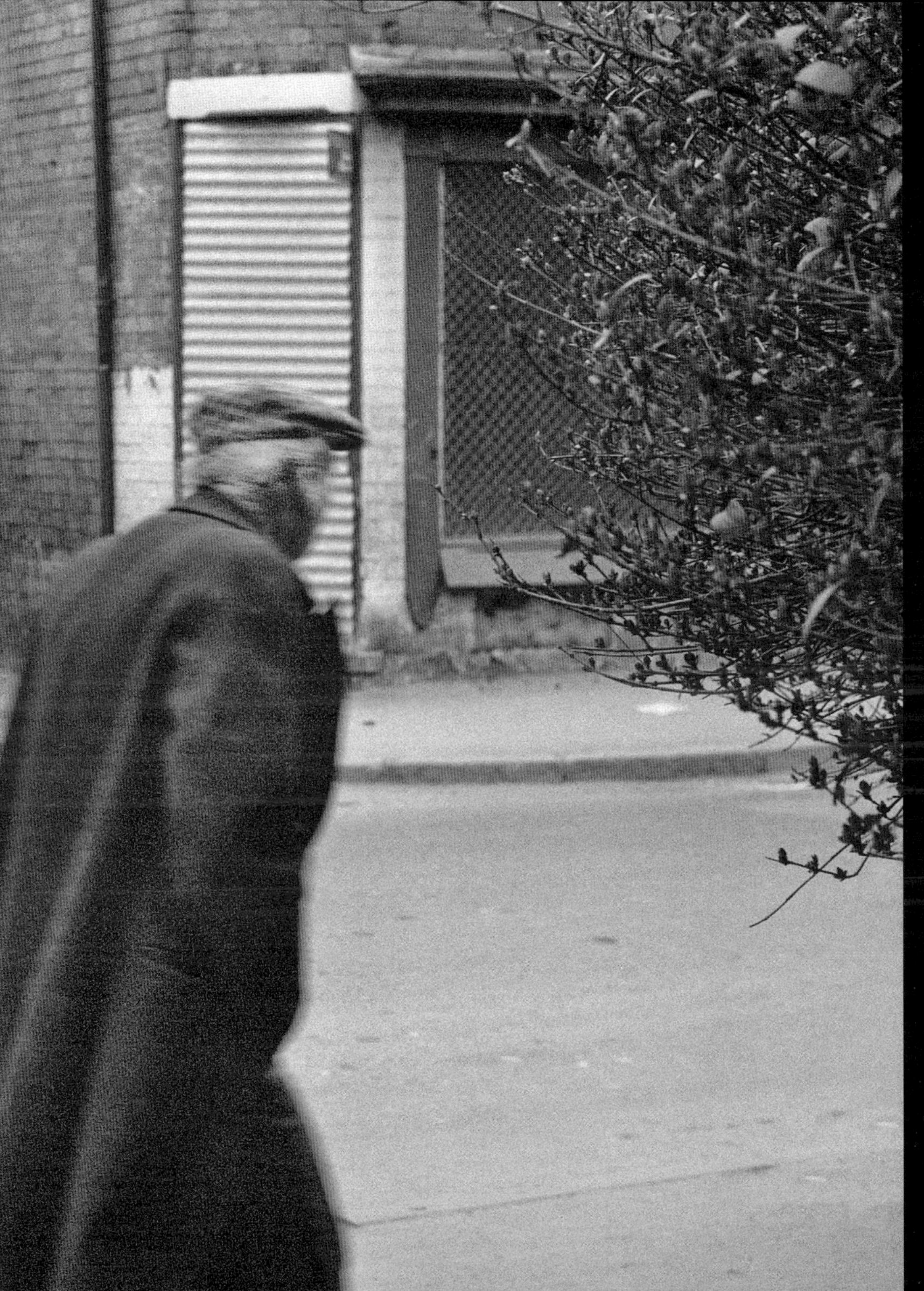

"I remember when I first started working and told a chap who lived in West Bridgford how friendly the neighbours in St Ann's were. He was fascinated. He said his neighbours hardly spoke. We took all that for granted. We might not have had a lot of money, but we was rich in friendship and spirit."

Ken Wood

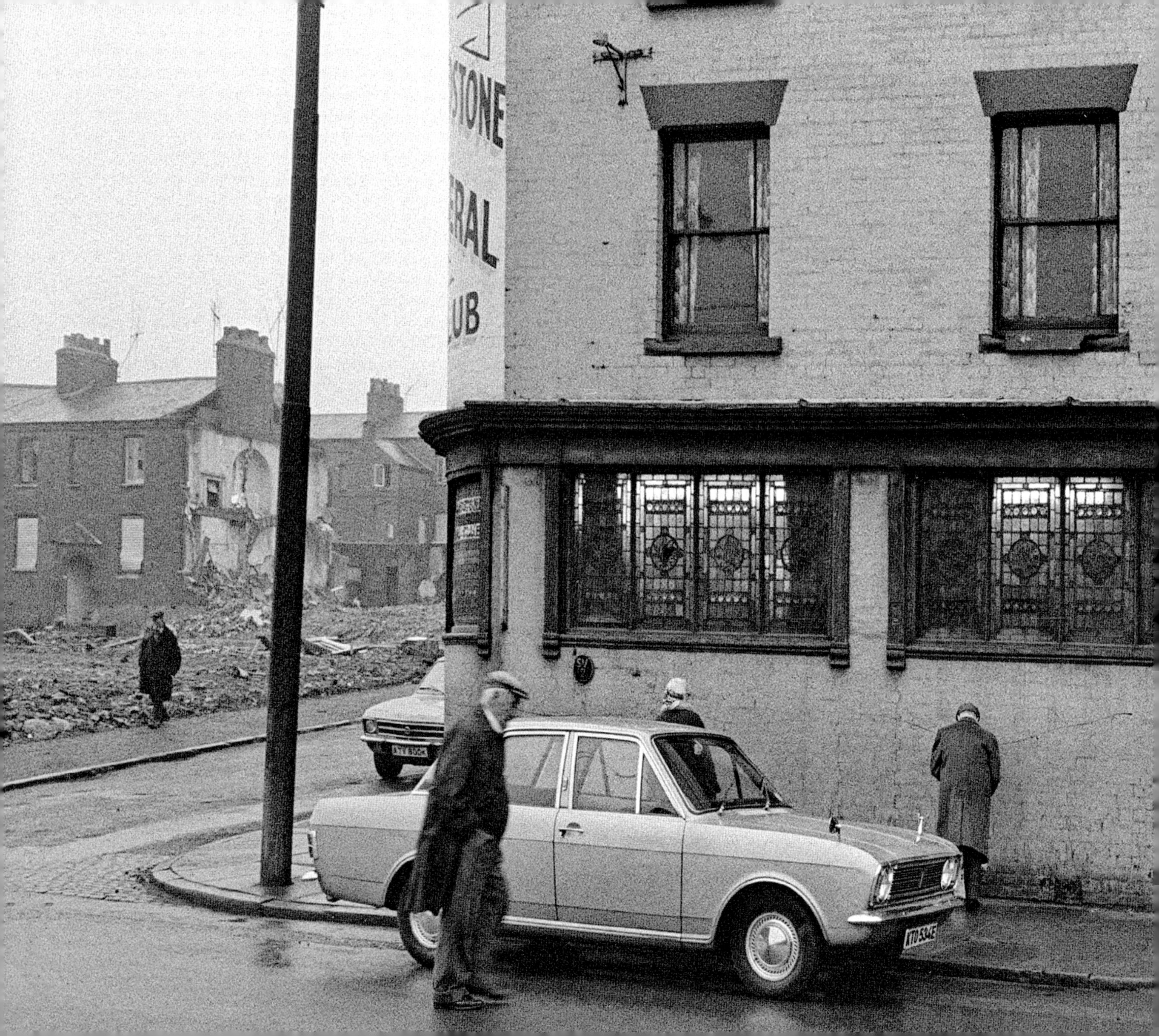
STONE
ERAL
UB

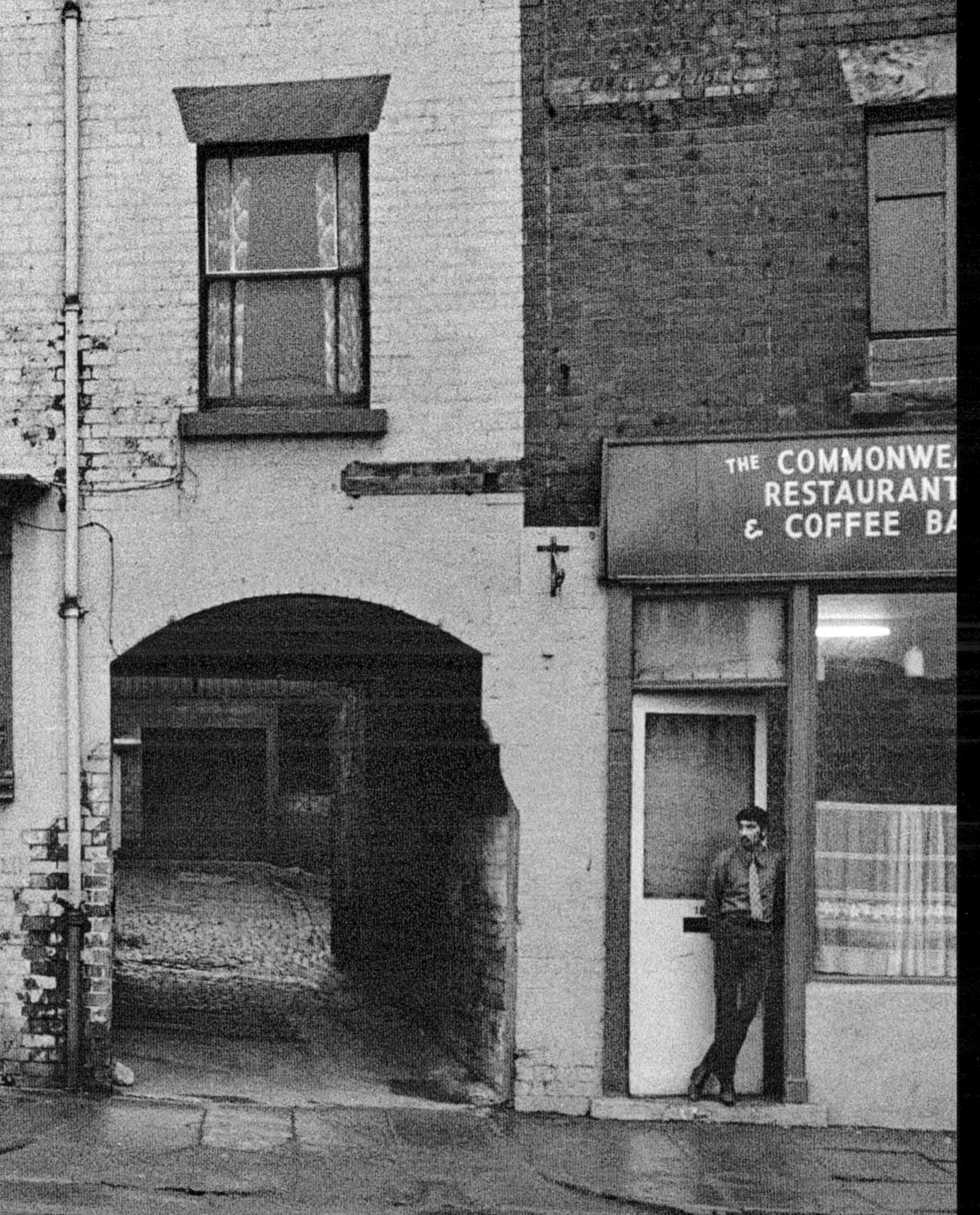

The Gladstone Liberal Club on the corner of St Ann's Well Road and Lamartine Street

"We got married in 1965 and had our reception at the Gladstone Liberal Club. I remember the family doing the conga, they came out of the club, went down St Ann's Well Road to the zebra crossing at the Locarno, stopping all the cars. It must have taken about three-quarters of an hour as we had about 100 people at the reception.

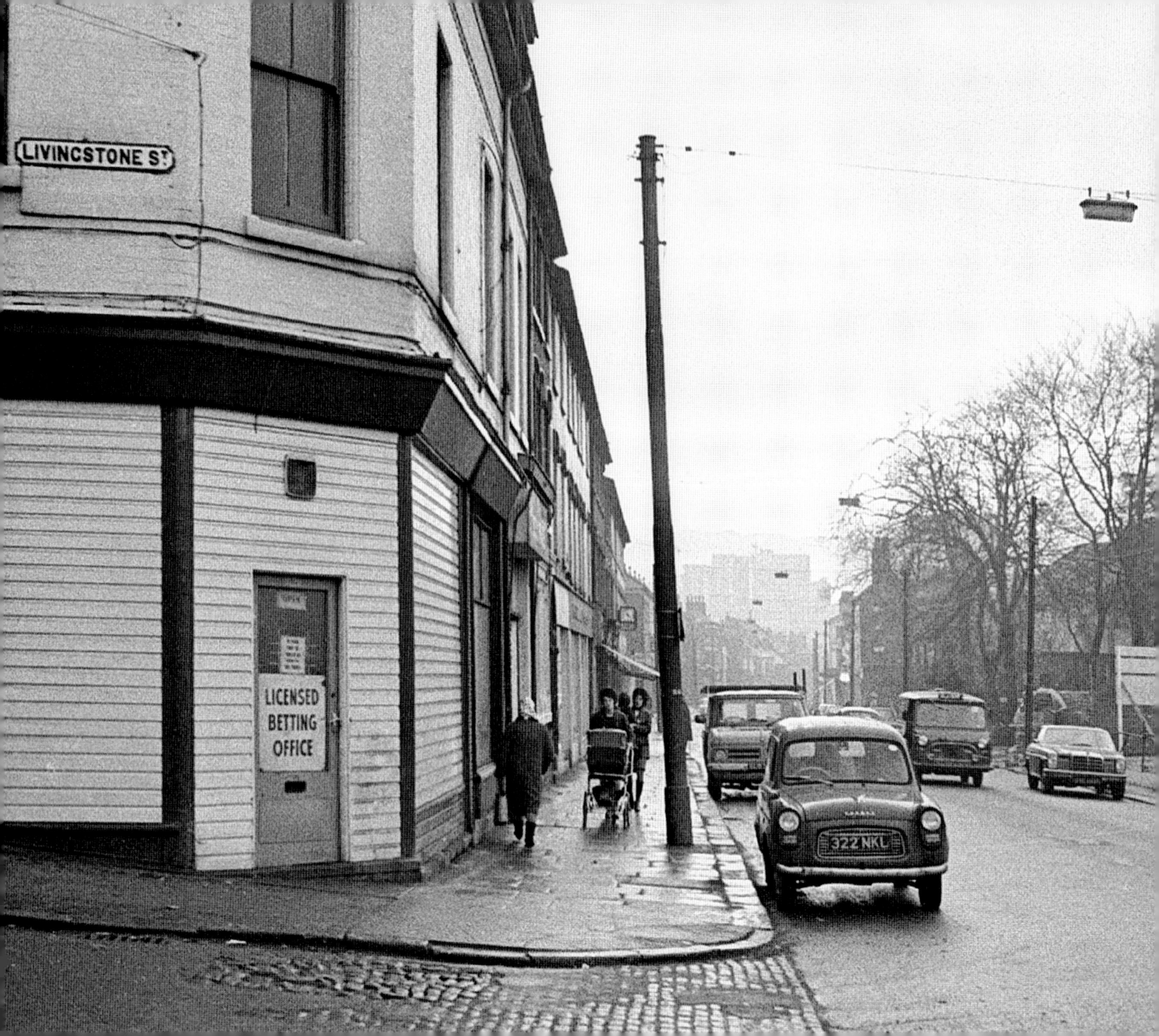

LIVINGSTONE ST.
LICENSED BETTING OFFICE
322 NKL

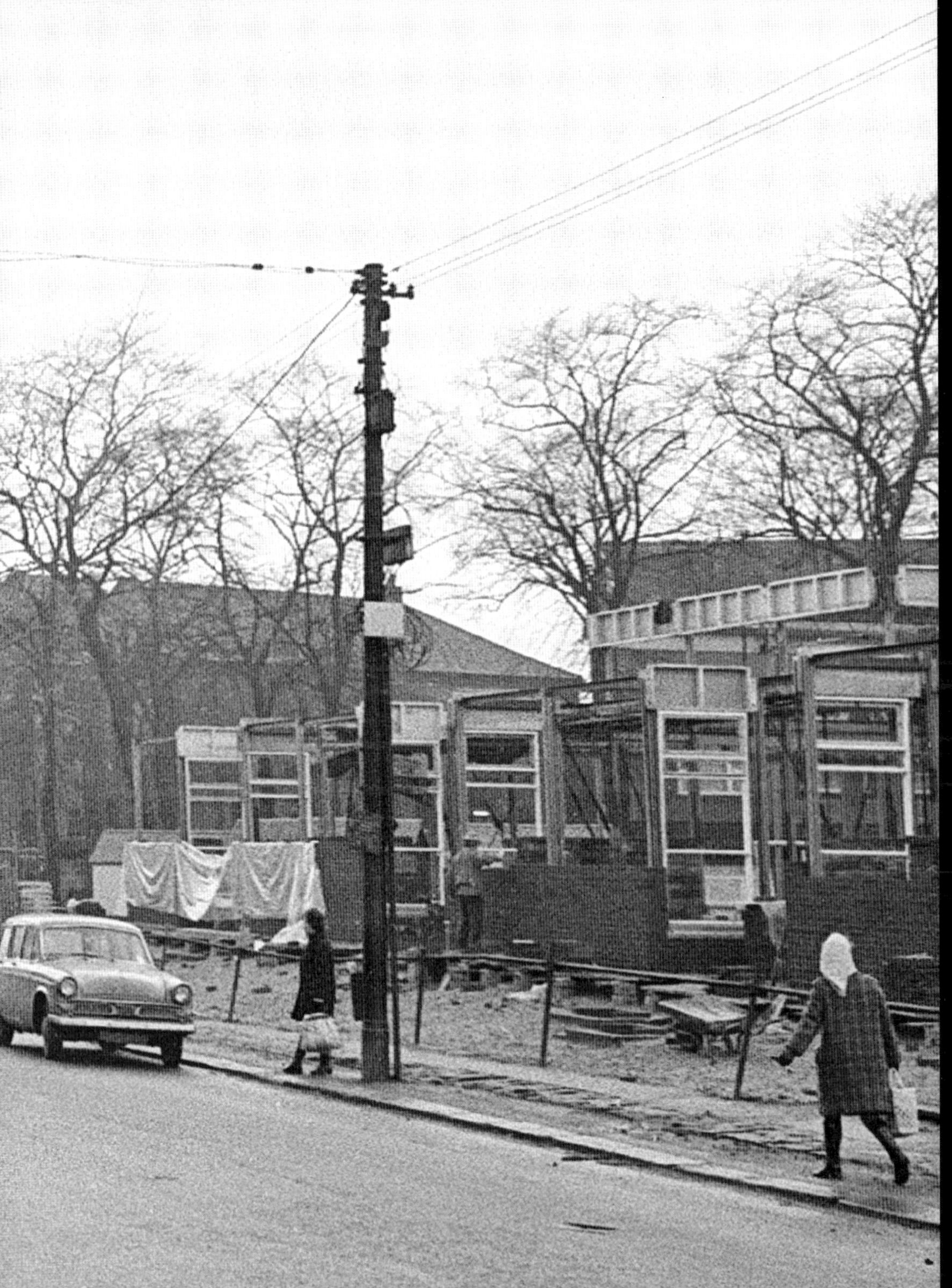

St Ann's Well Road and Livingstone Street Junction

Looking down the road heading towards the city centre. Note the new building work being carried out on the right hand side of the road.

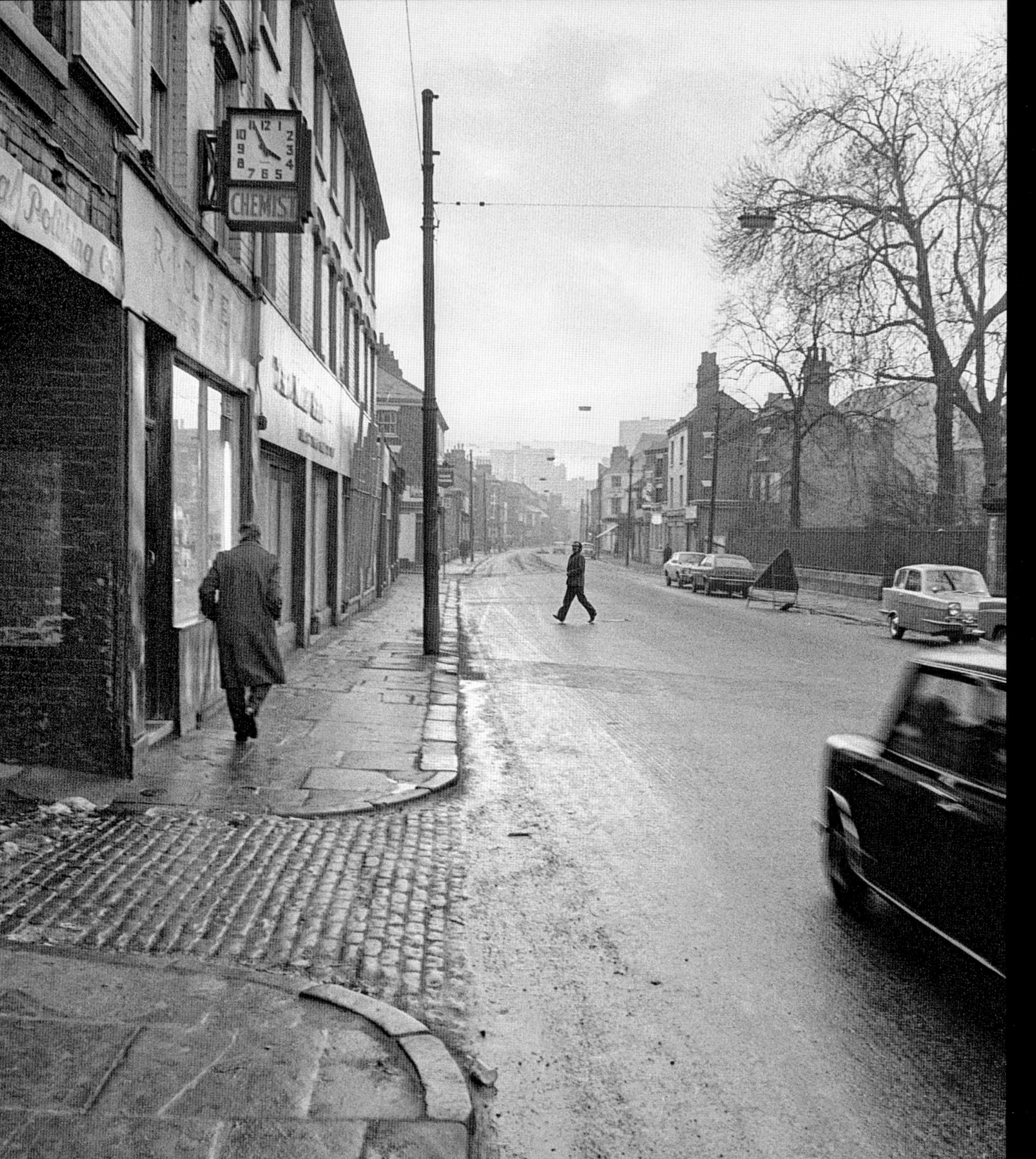

St Ann's Well Road

Ronald Clarke's chemist shop, with a large clock mounted above. The cobbled entrance to St Ann's Mews (depicted on page 62) is just next to the shop.

St Ann's Well Road

Woman in knee-length white boots, which were very fashionable at the time. In the distance the Victoria Centre can be seen under construction. Note the muddy road due to the demolition and building work being carried out.

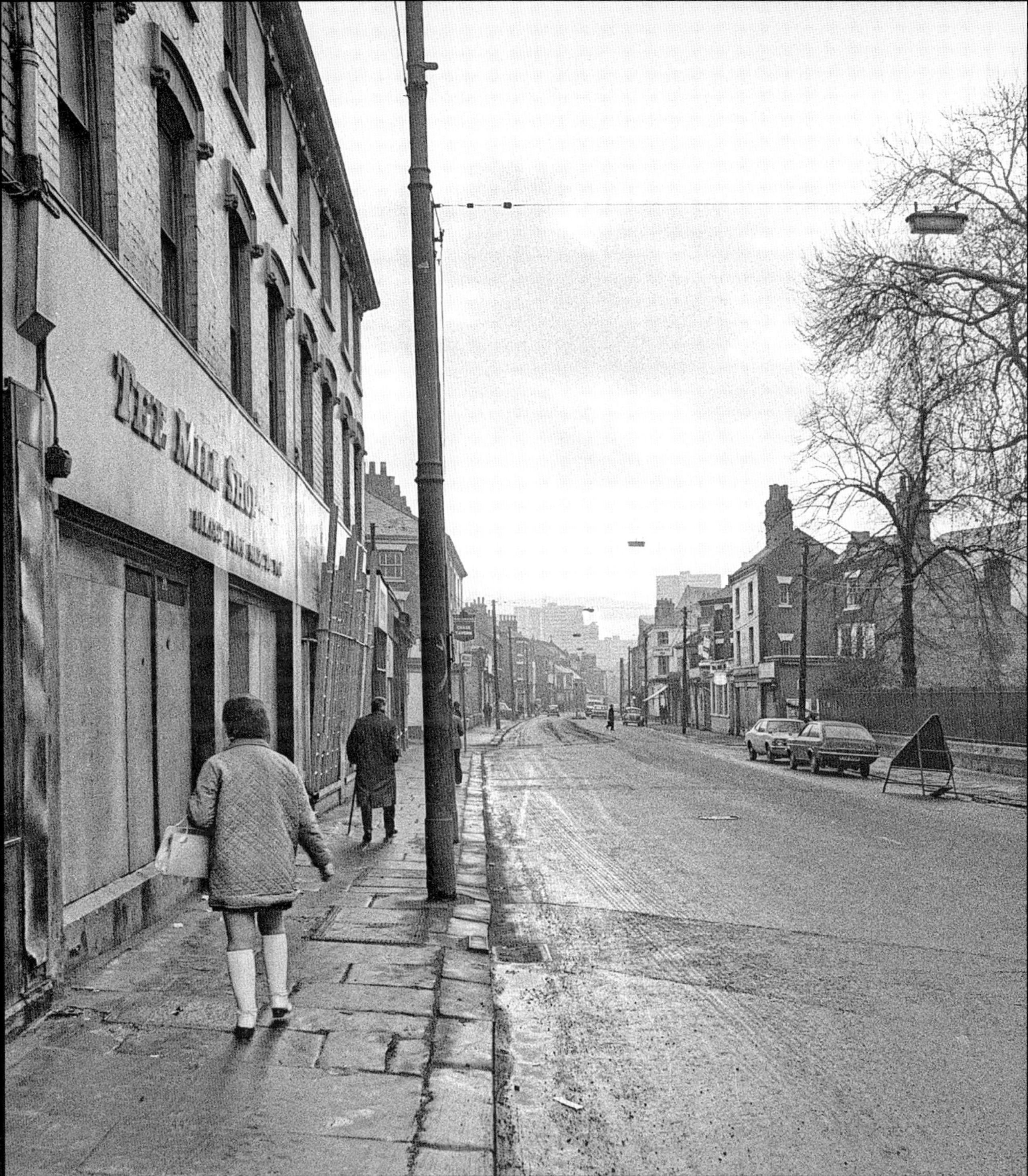

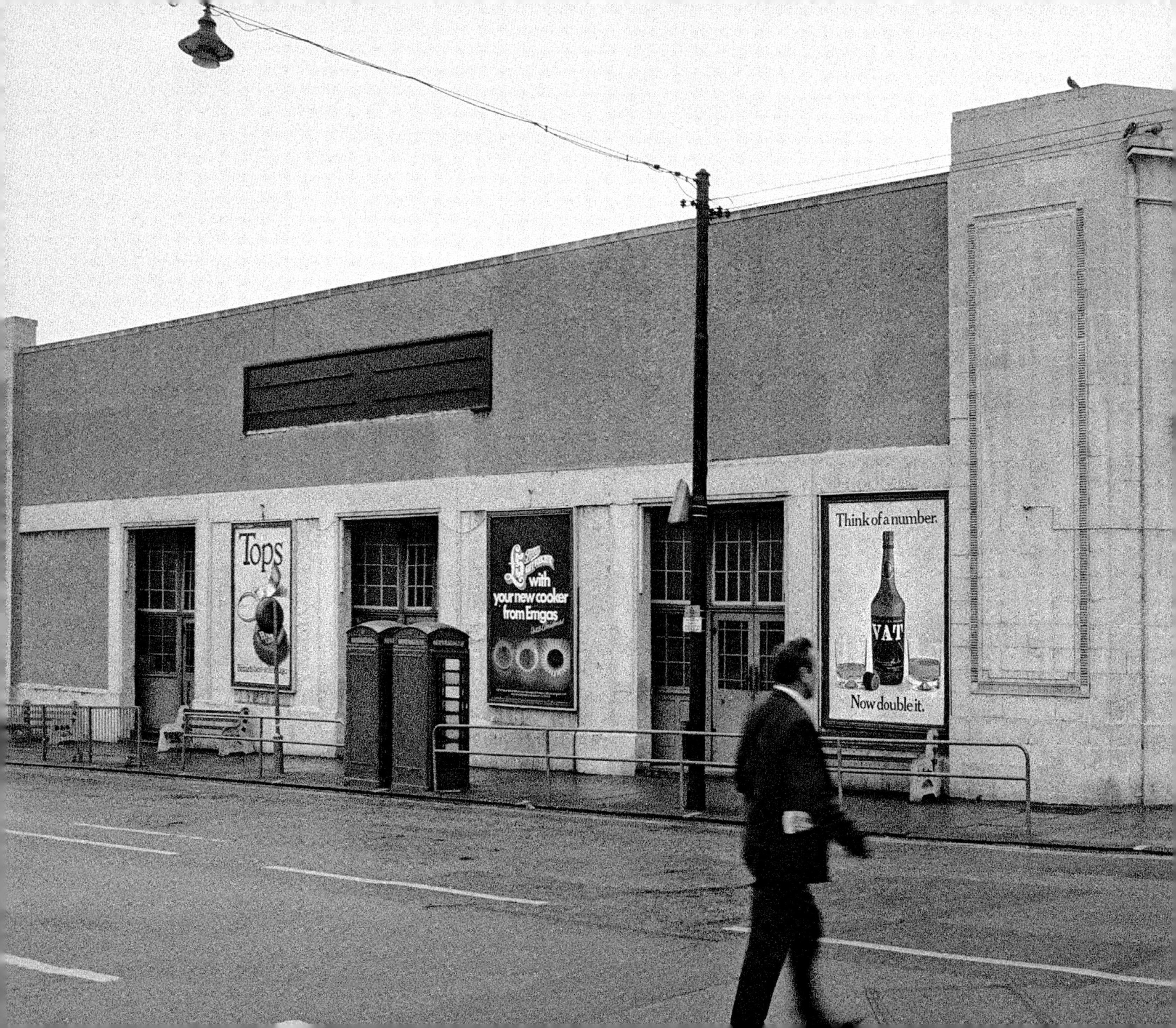

Tops
Think of a number.
VAT
Now double it.
£5 with your new cooker from Emgas

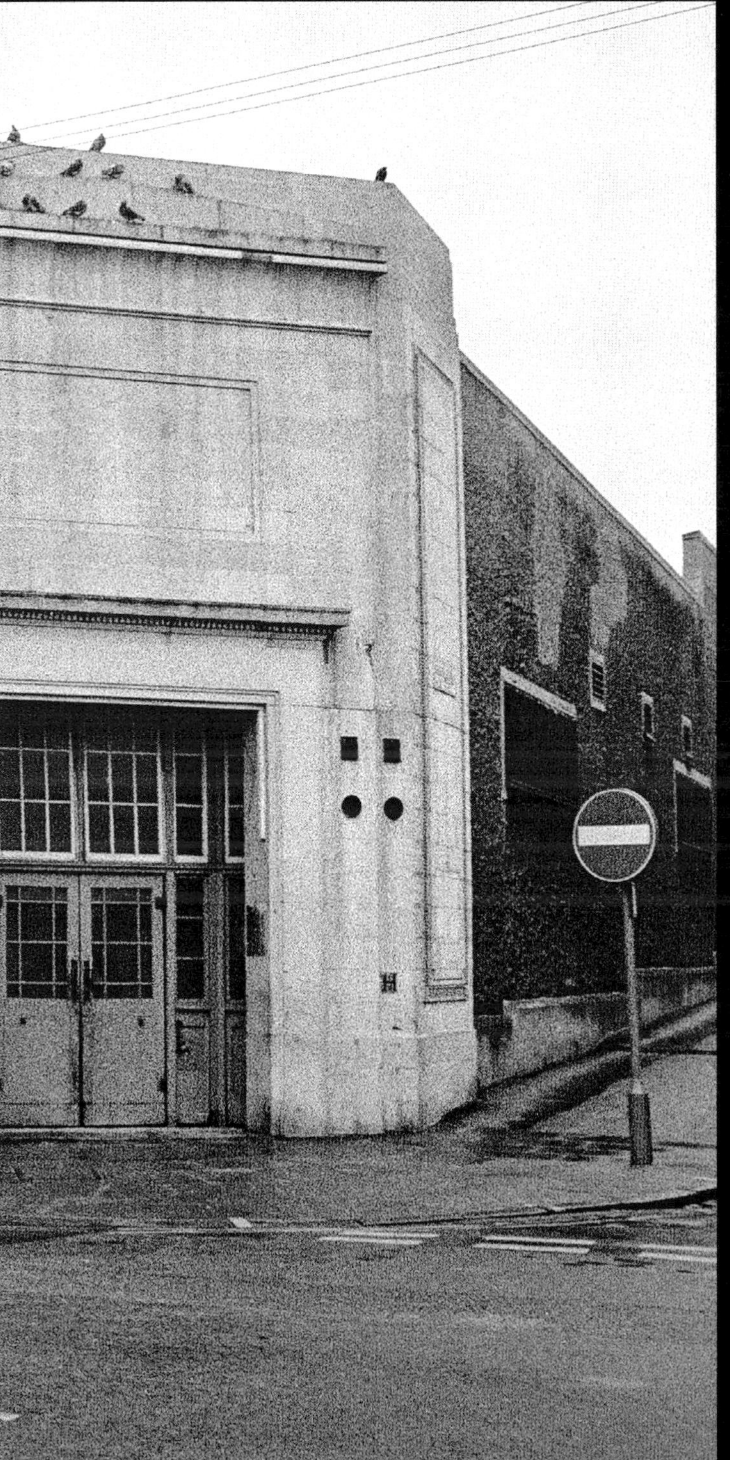

"Can smell the wet fish now, oh the memories. Peas, mint sauce, and I loved the pet stall and Arthur the second-hand record man. I once spent all my £3/12/6 wages there on Motown records that someone had brought in to sell. I think I got about a dozen at 2/6 each or less!! That was about 1968-ish!"

"The shop on the corner of the Central Market was a Cake and Biscuit shop. Mum would send me there to get half a pound of "Broken Biscuits". There was never half a pound when I got back home."

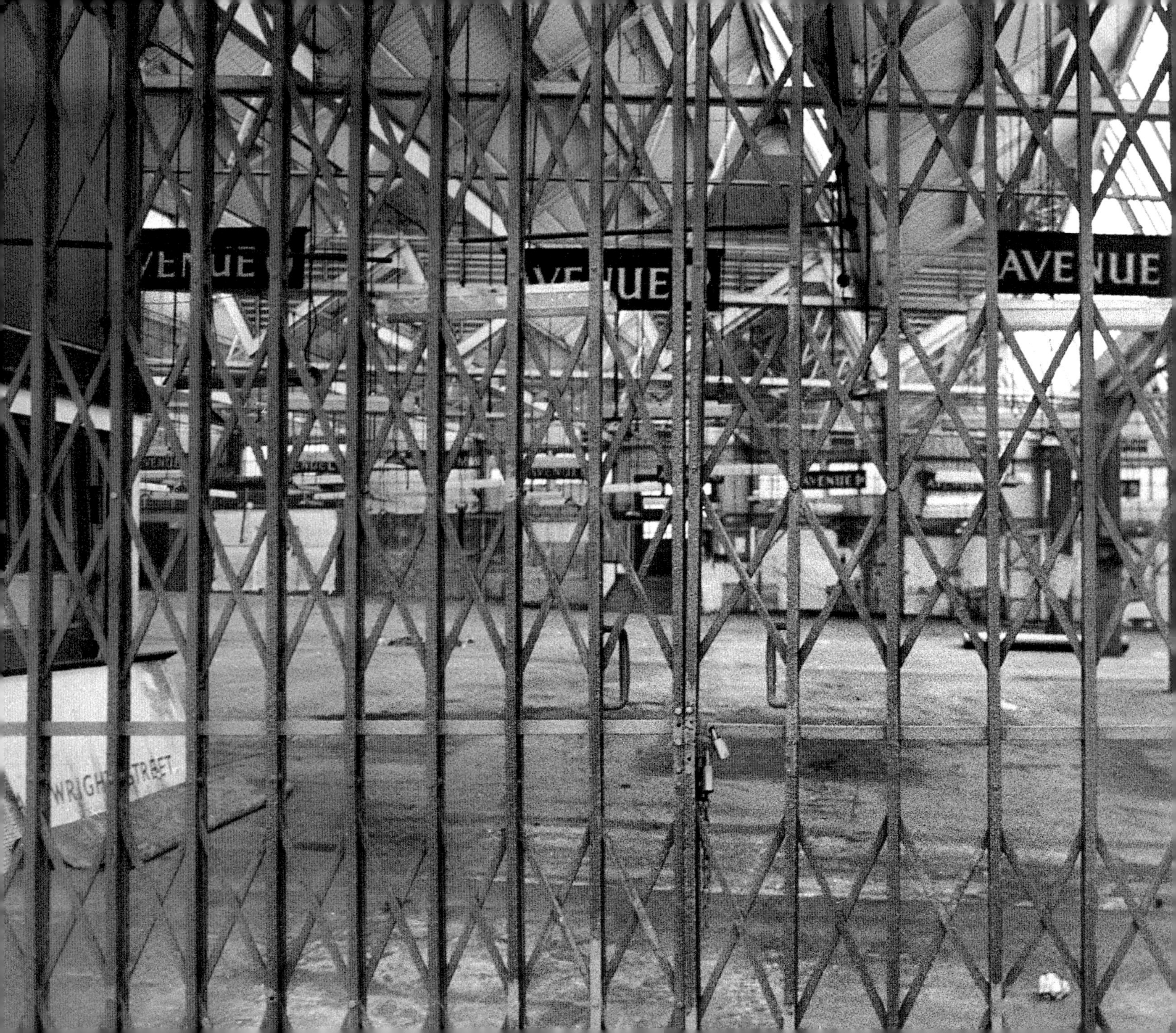
AVENUE
AVENUE
AVENUE
WRIGHT STREET

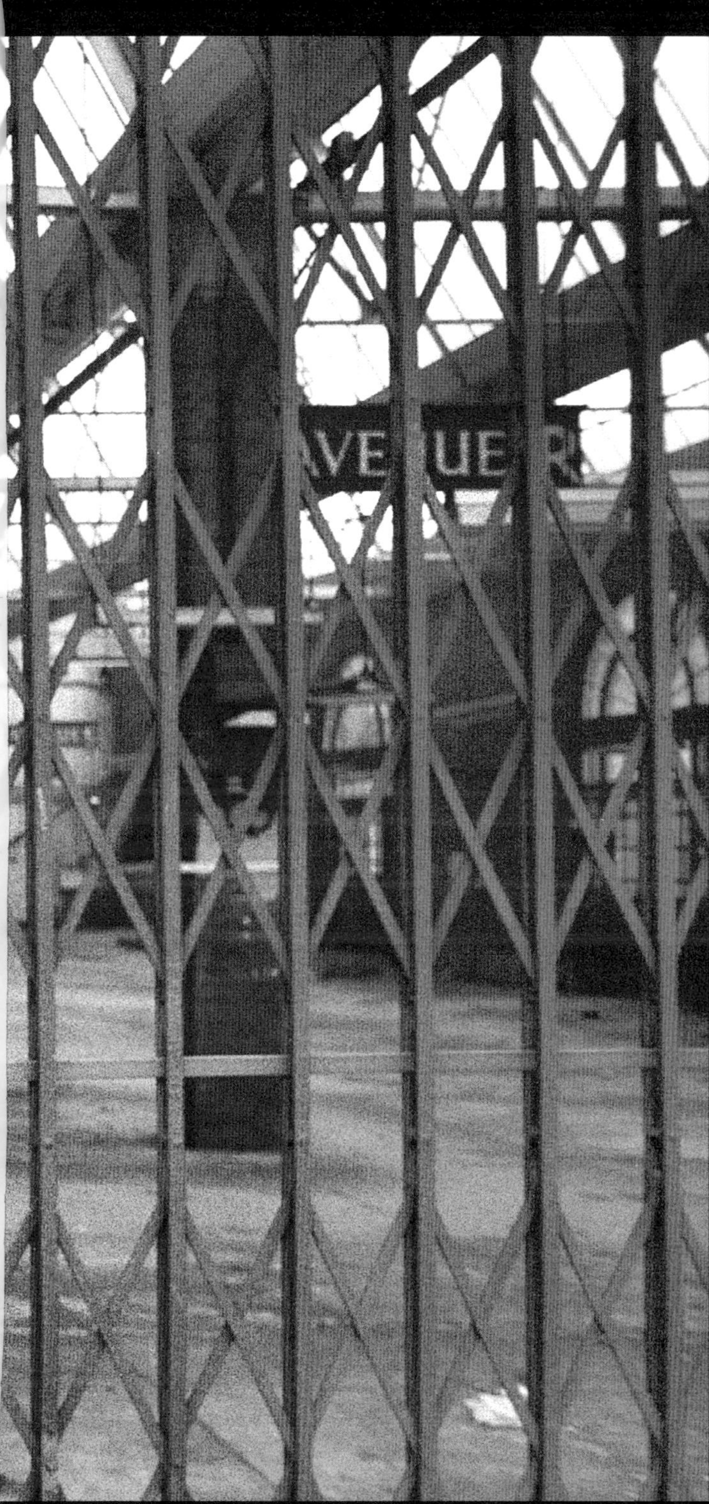

Central Market. Avenues O,P,Q and R

These Avenues were mainly greengrocers, fruiterers, flower-sellers and market gardening stalls.

"My wife Ann had a Saturday job on the market as a girl. She started to work at Middup's Fruit & Veg, market gardeners from Woodborough, at the age of thirteen and worked for Sam and Elsie Middup right up to when we got married in 1964. We first started courting when Ann was fourteen and I was sixteen. I used to take her out to the pictures Saturday nights... she was always tired, worn out and smelt of potatoes."

Tony Miller

Derelict Buildings and Streets

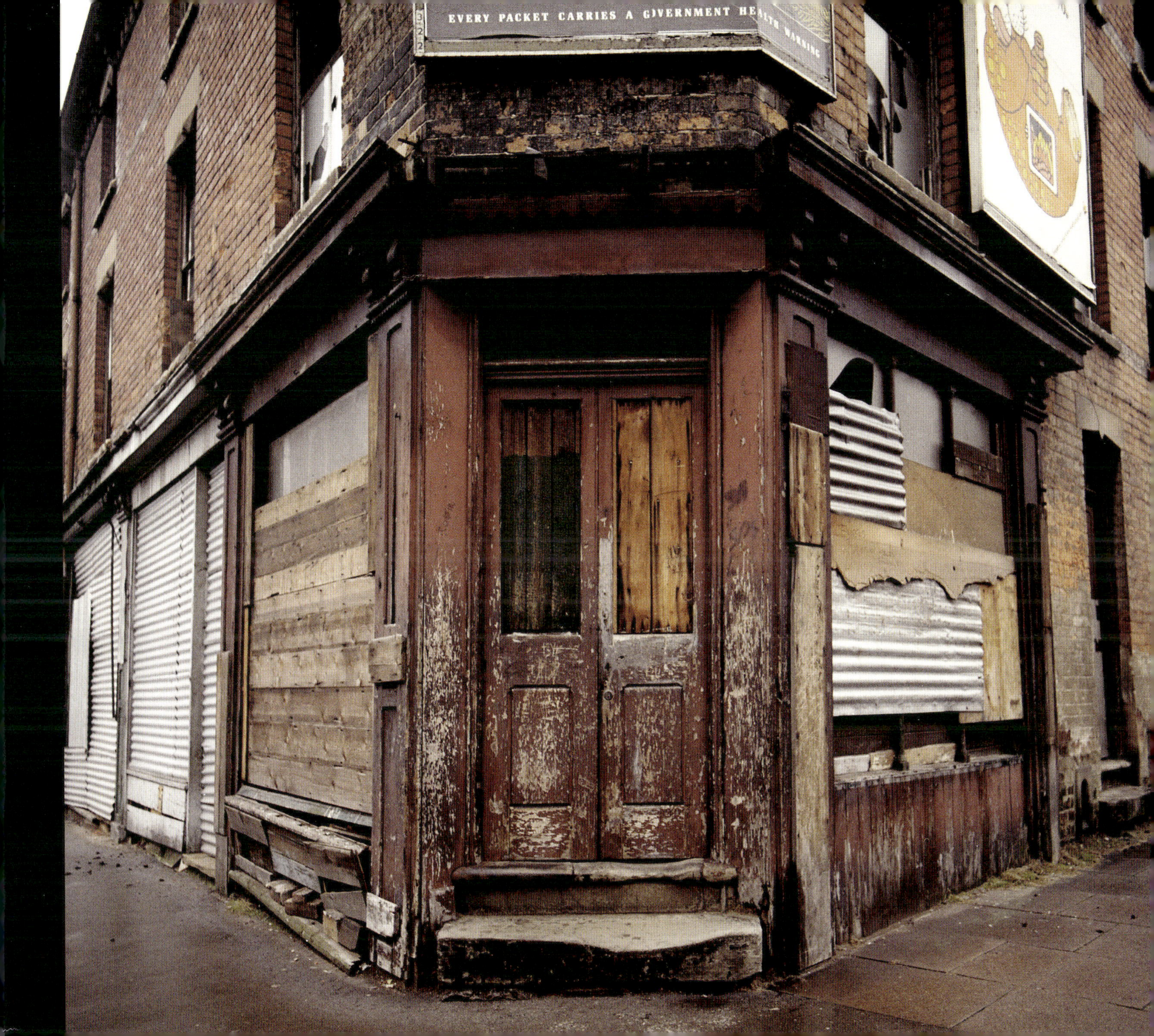
EVERY PACKET CARRIES A GOVERNMENT HEALTH WARNING

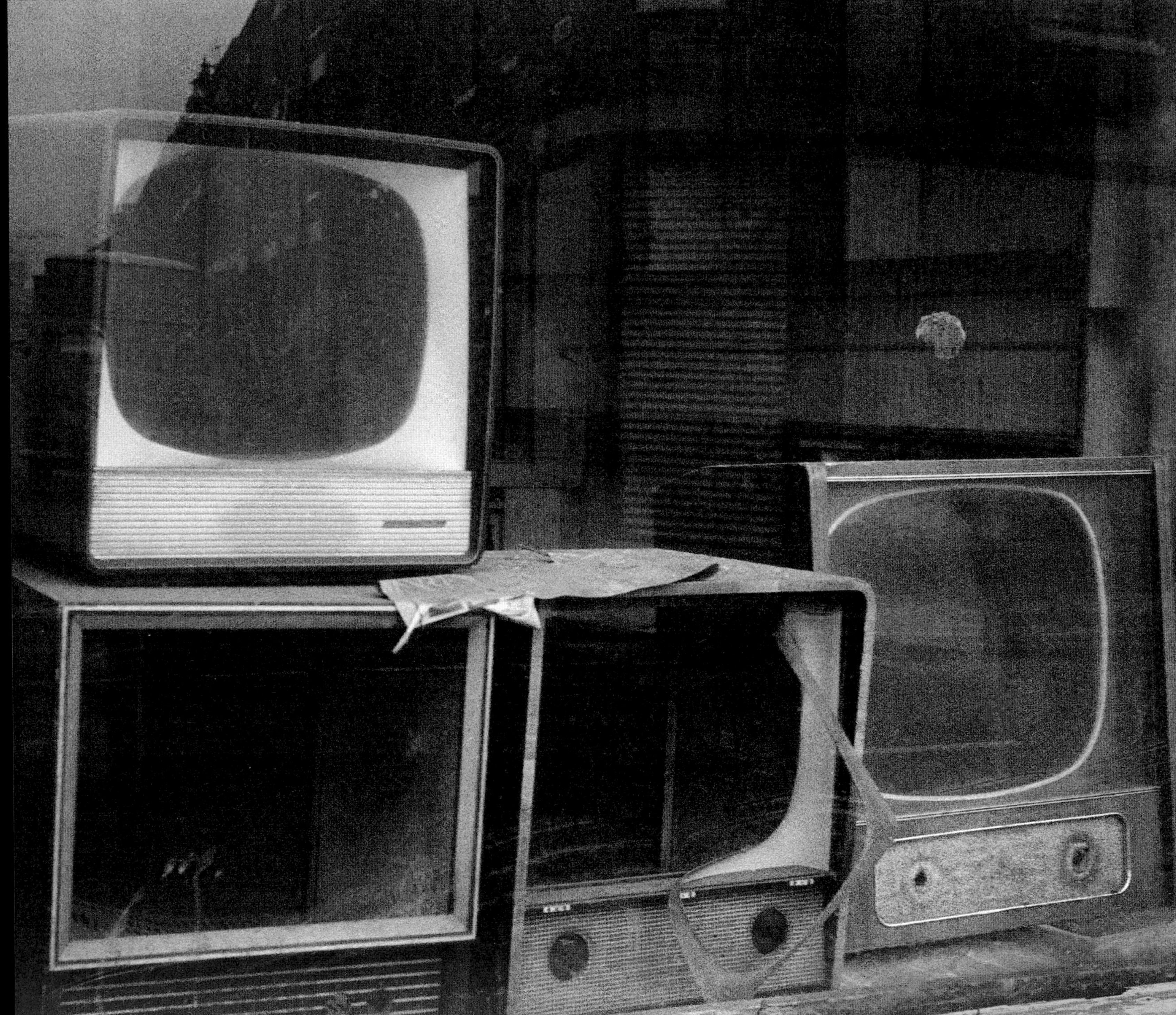

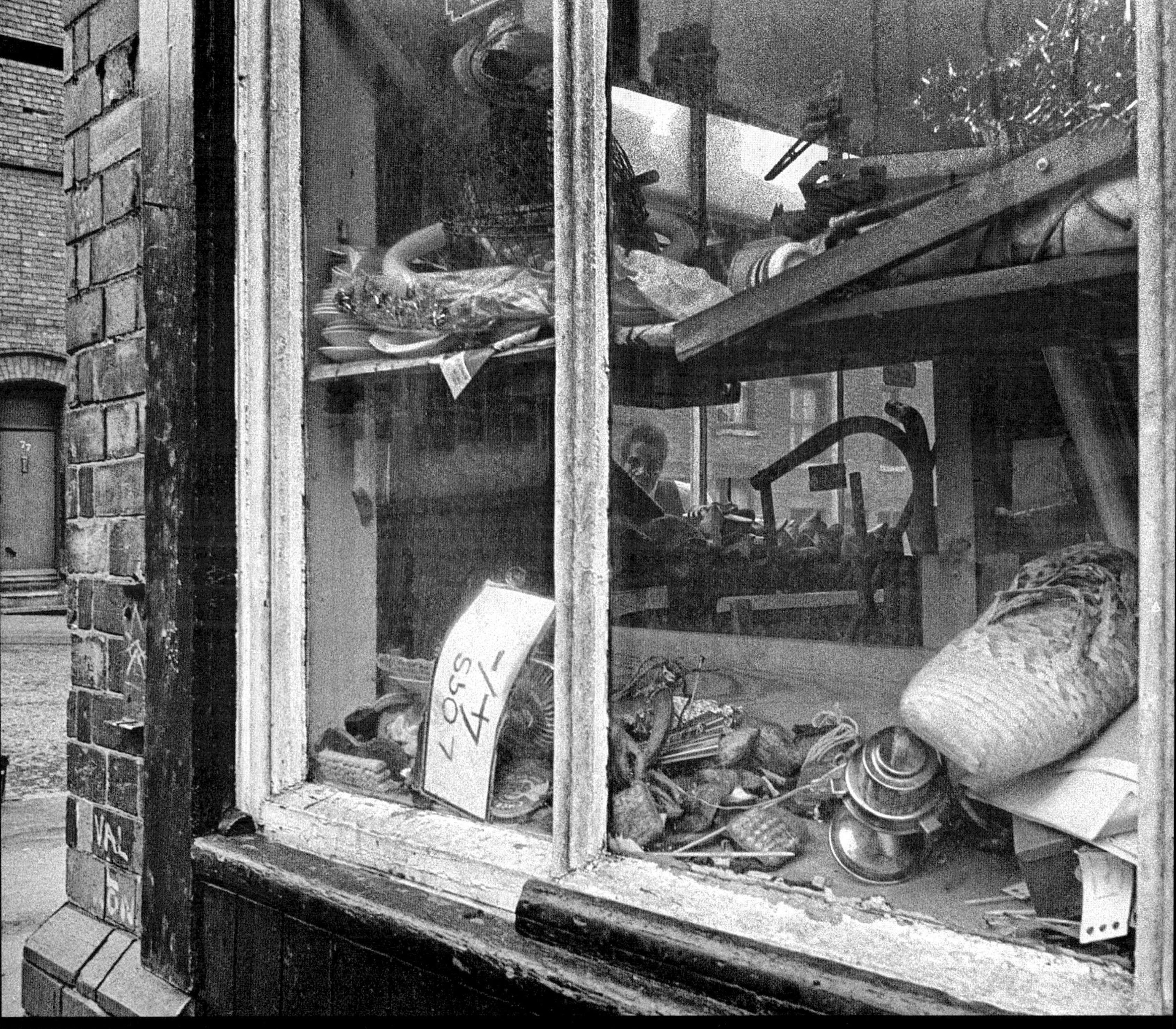
LOGS
4/-

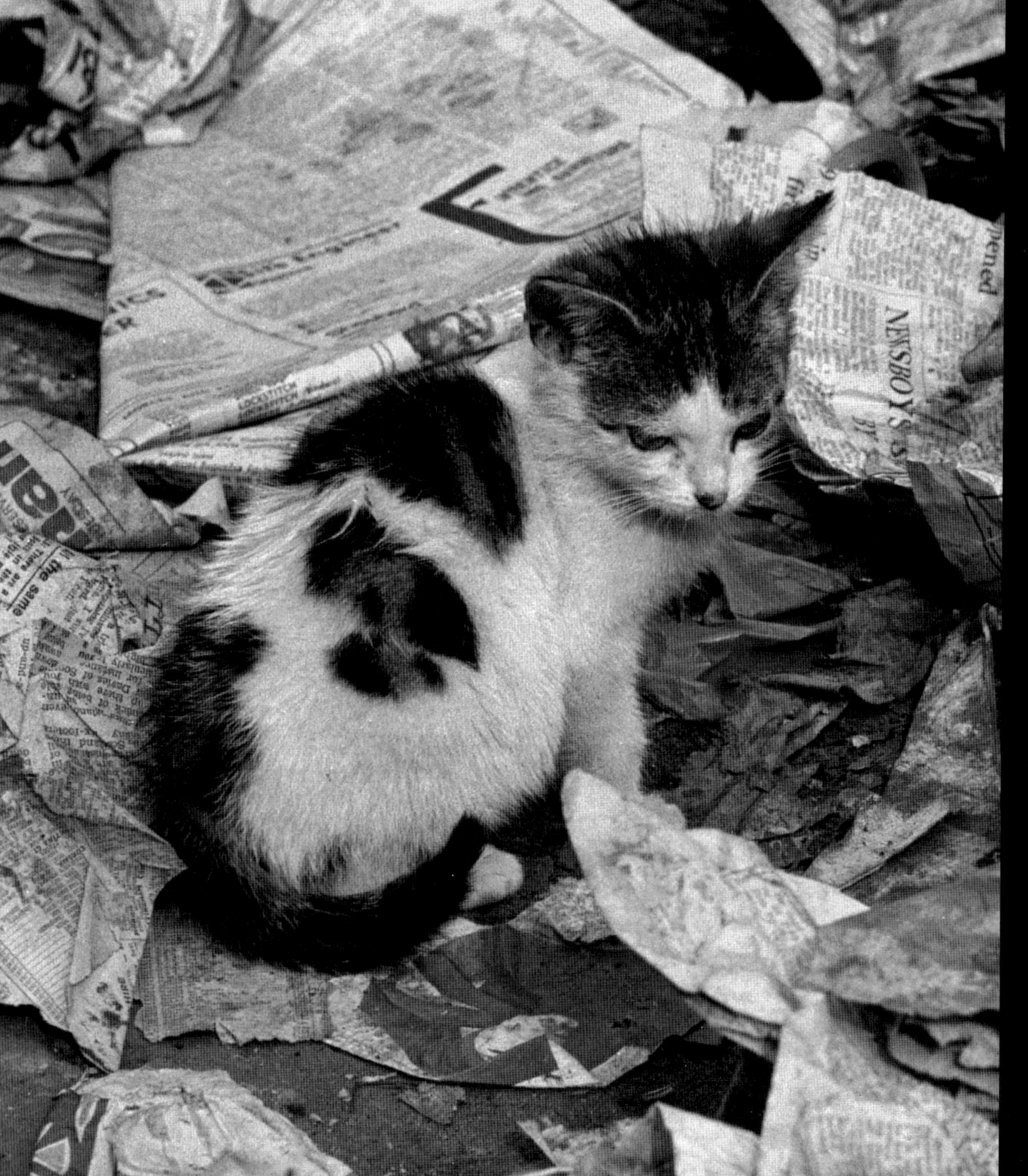

Pets wander freely on the deserted streets of empty houses and shops

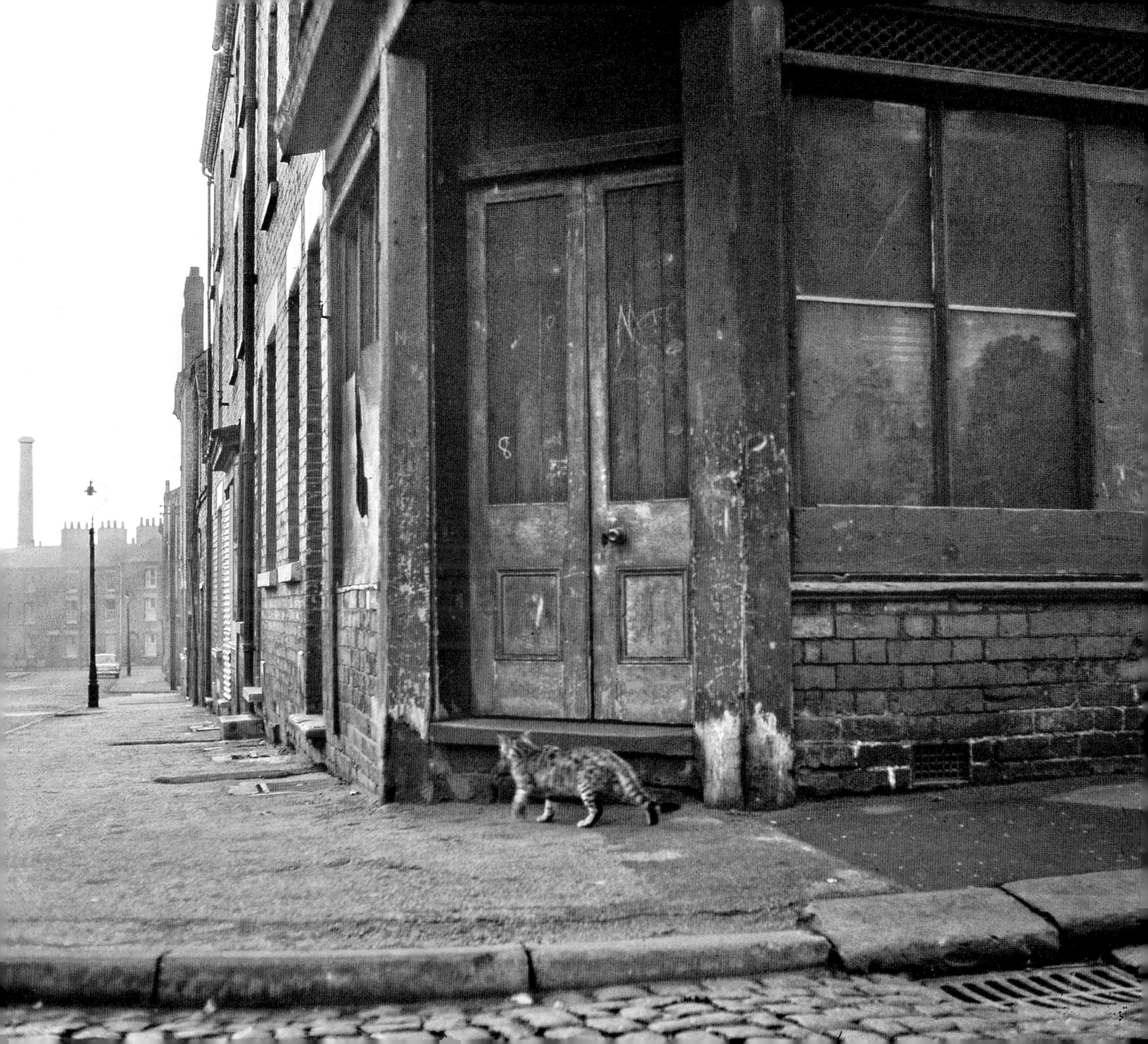

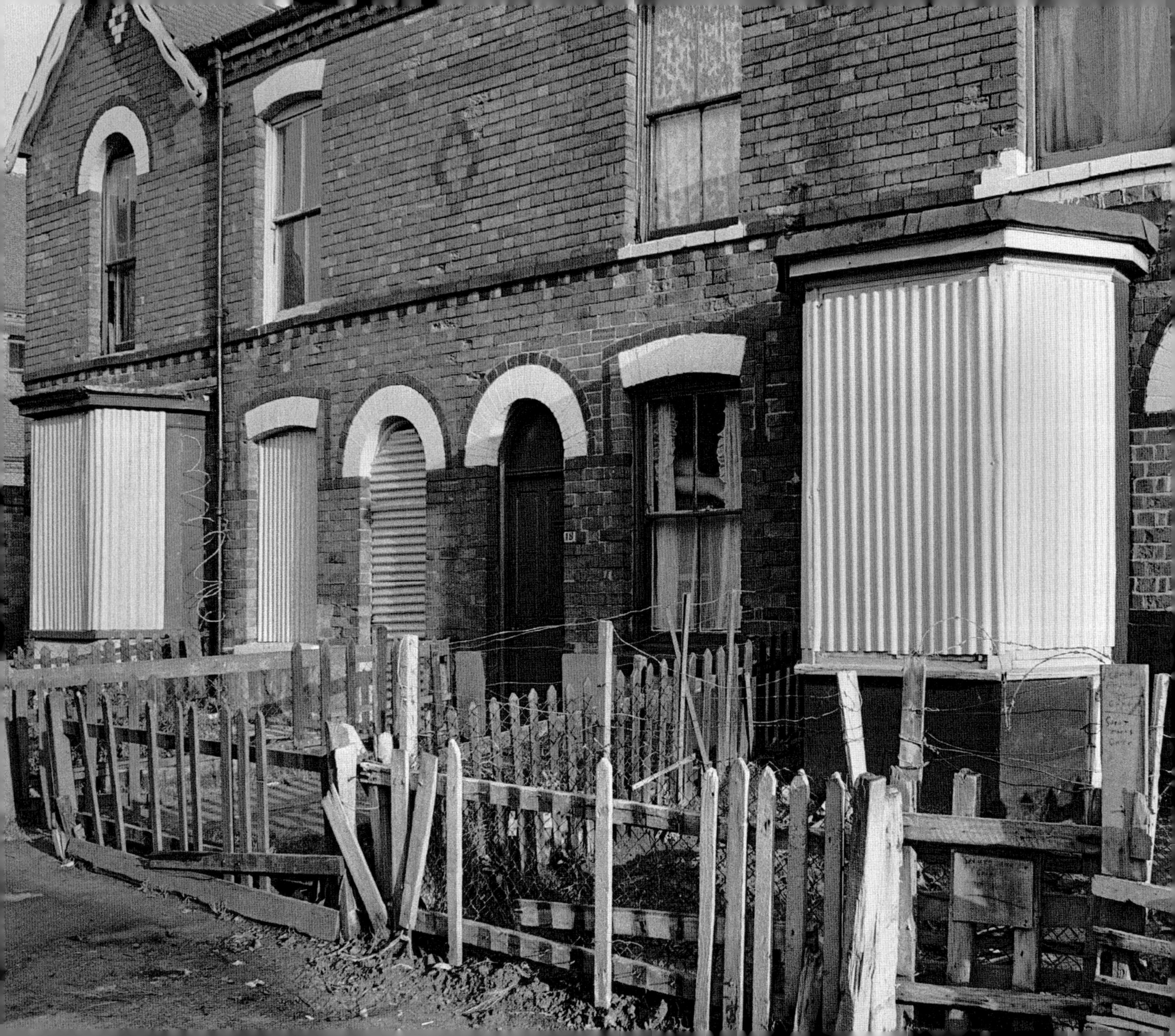

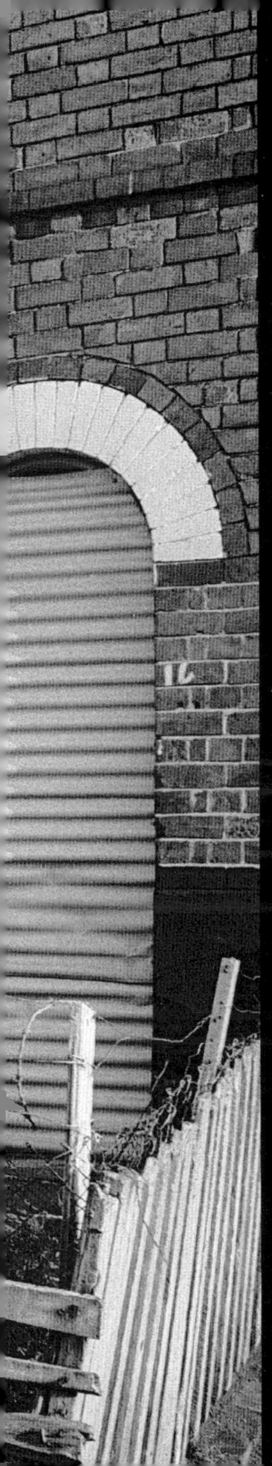

Should all the houses have been demolished?

Note the ornate brickwork, arched windows and doorways and beautiful barge board on the houses in this row. Many people thought that the better buildings should have been retained and modernised. Some of the houses that were built to replace such houses as these have themselves already been demolished.

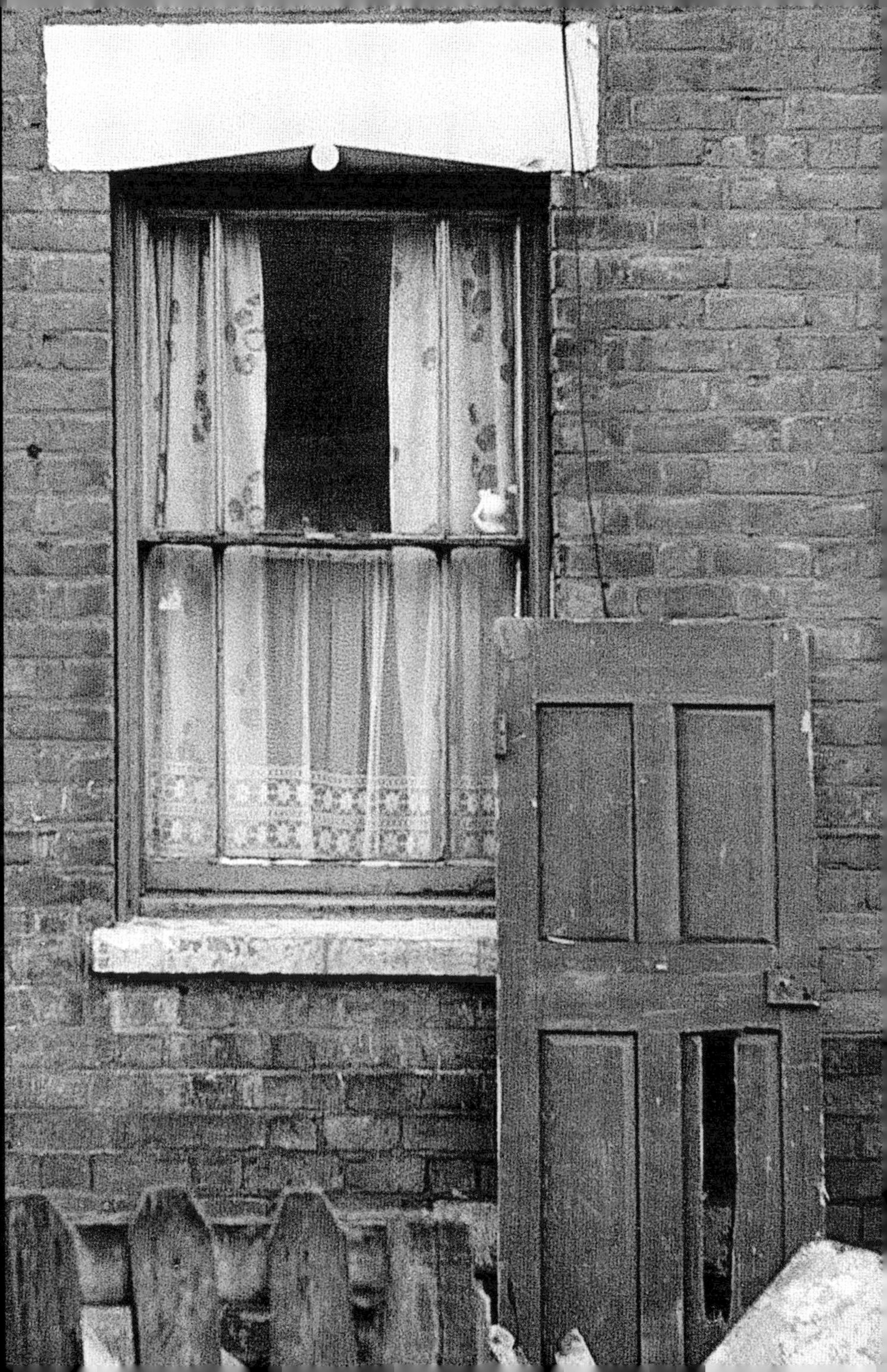

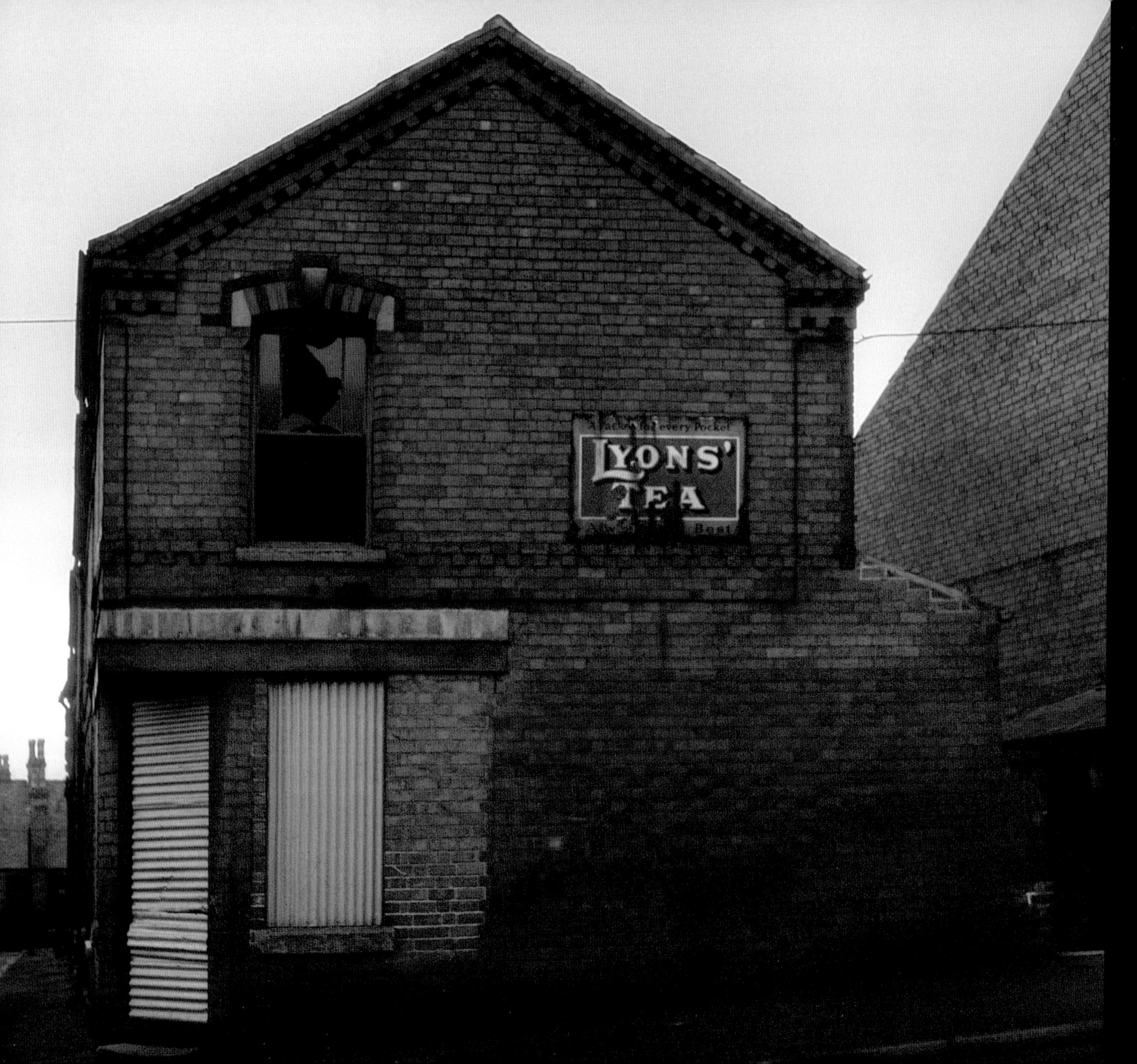
A ration in every Pocket
LYONS'
TEA
At their Best

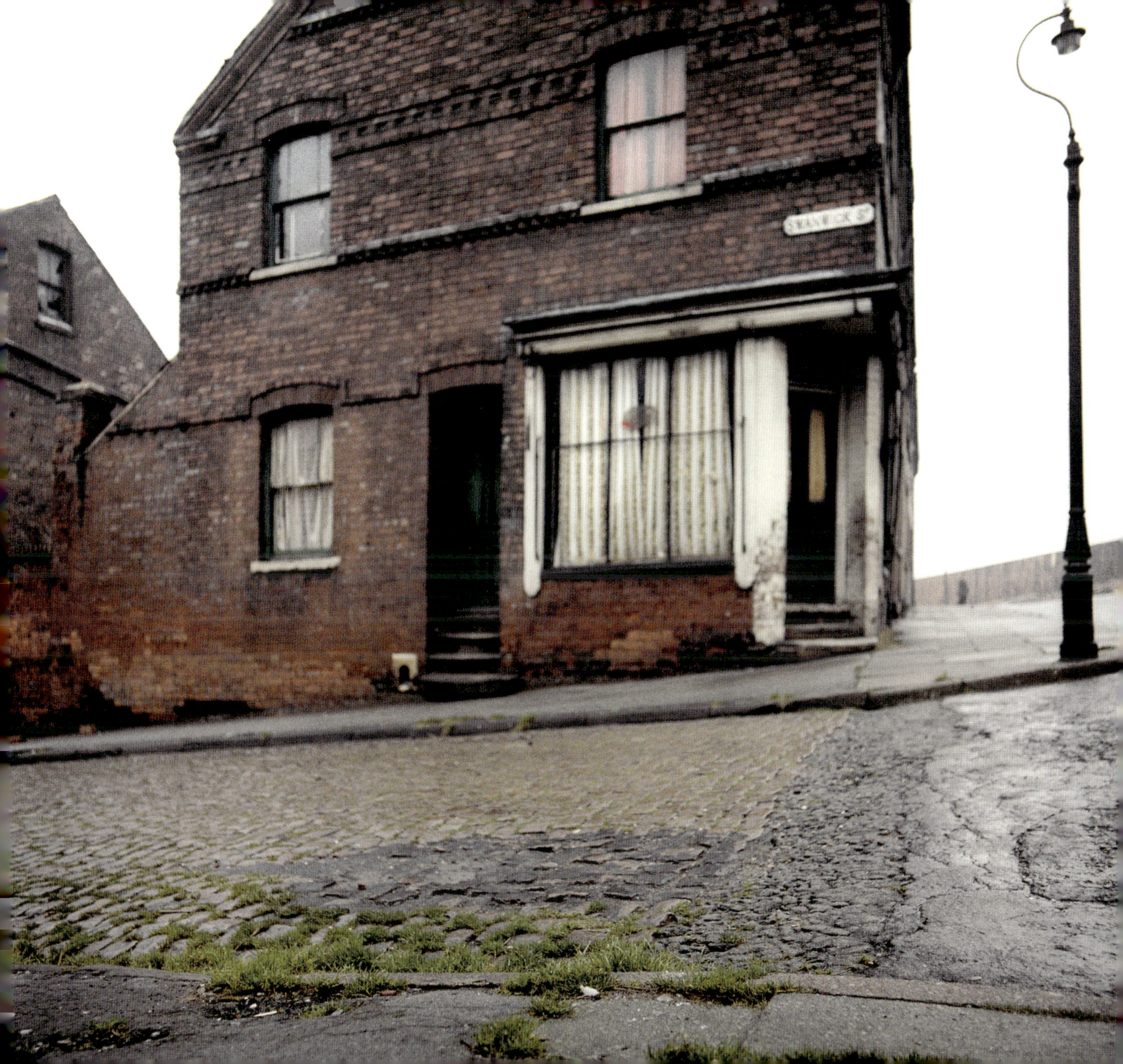

SWANWICK ST

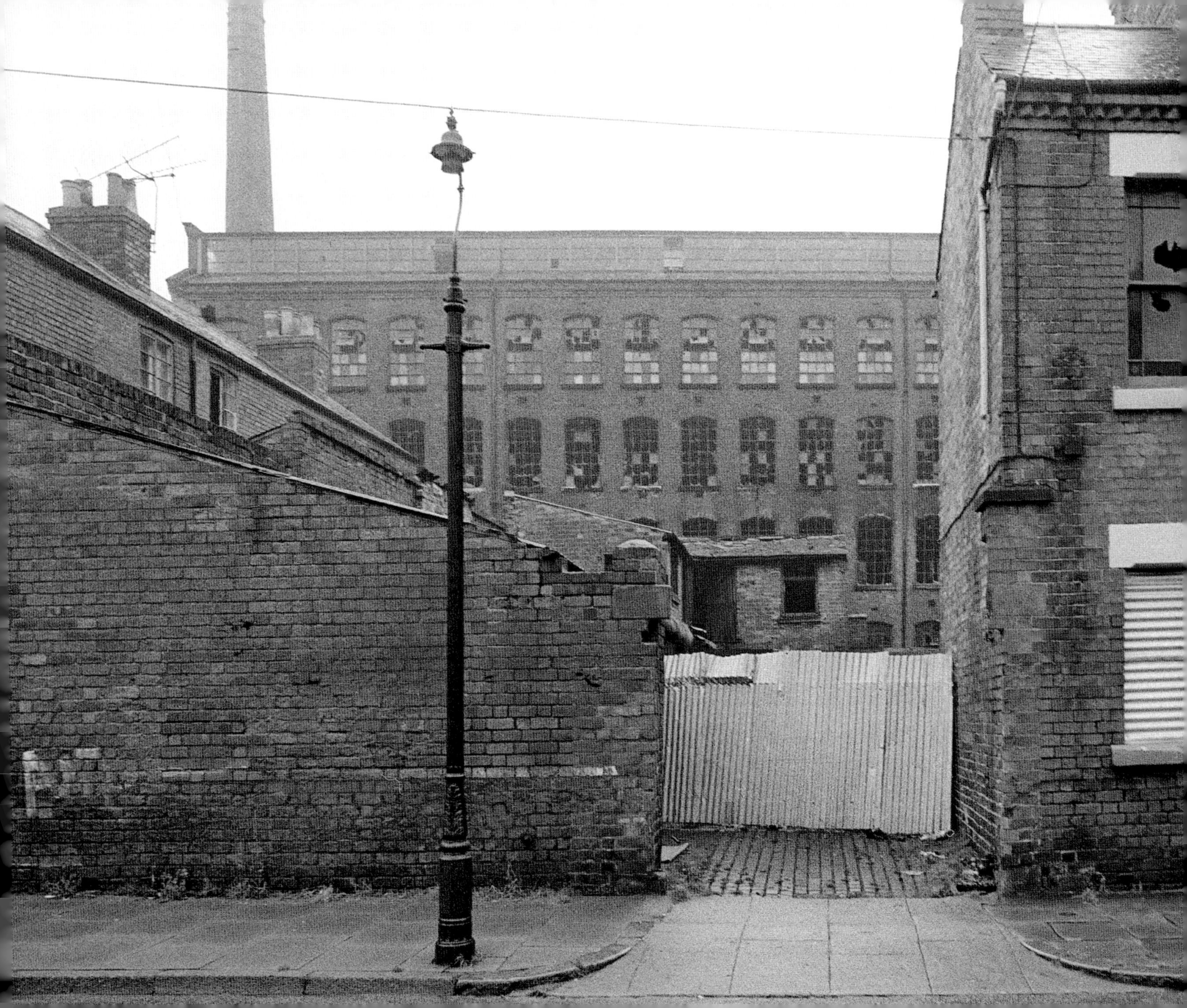

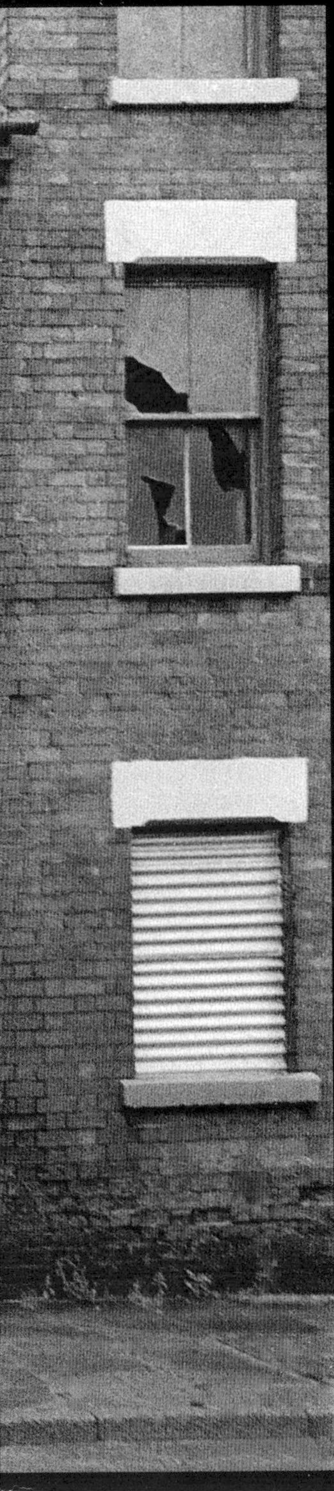

Vandalised factories and houses

Factories and houses were built side by side so the workers didn't need to travel. Many of the factories were related to the lace and hosiery industries for which Nottingham was famous.

The factory in the background is possibly the William Bancroft Building, where blouses were manufactured.

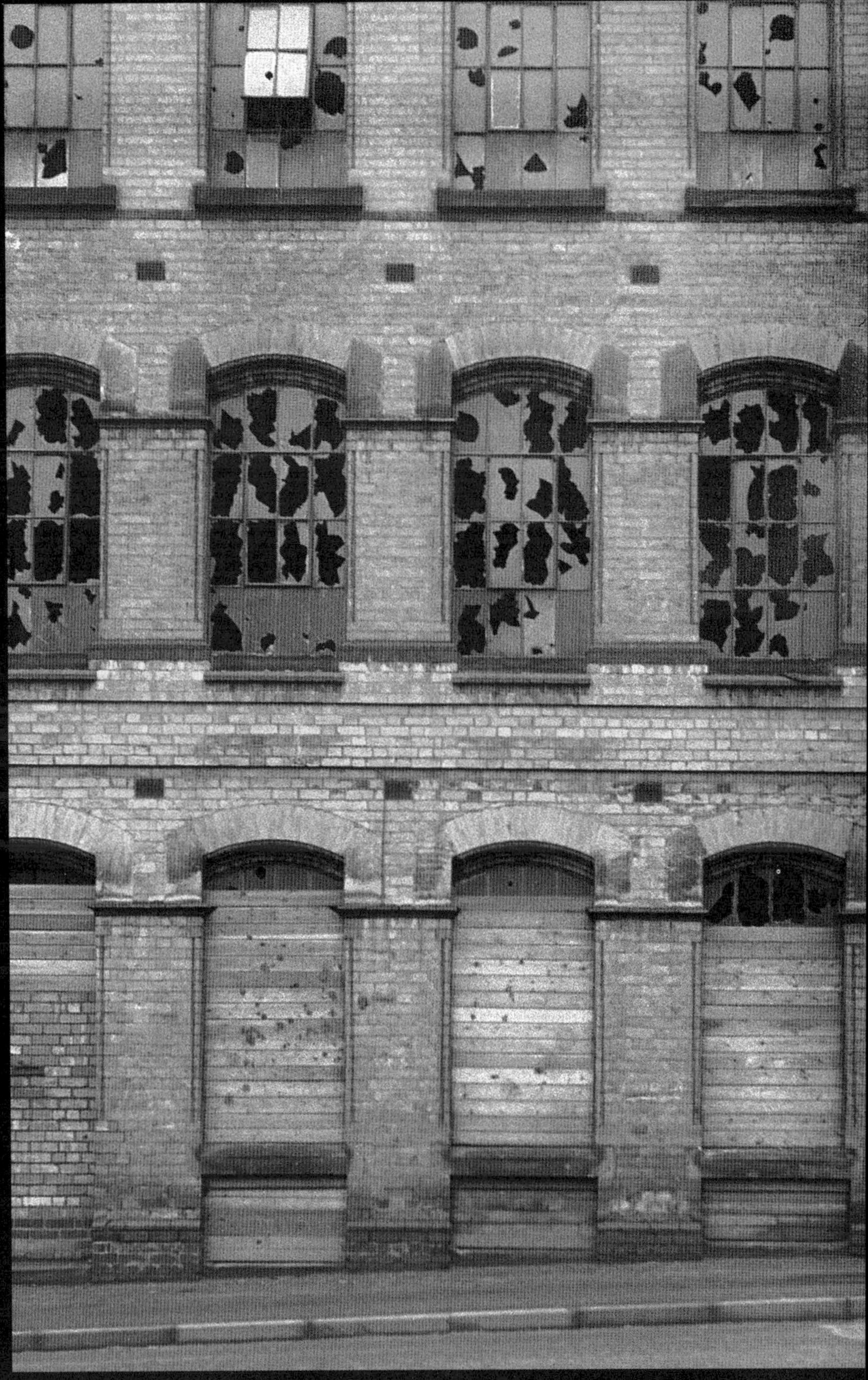

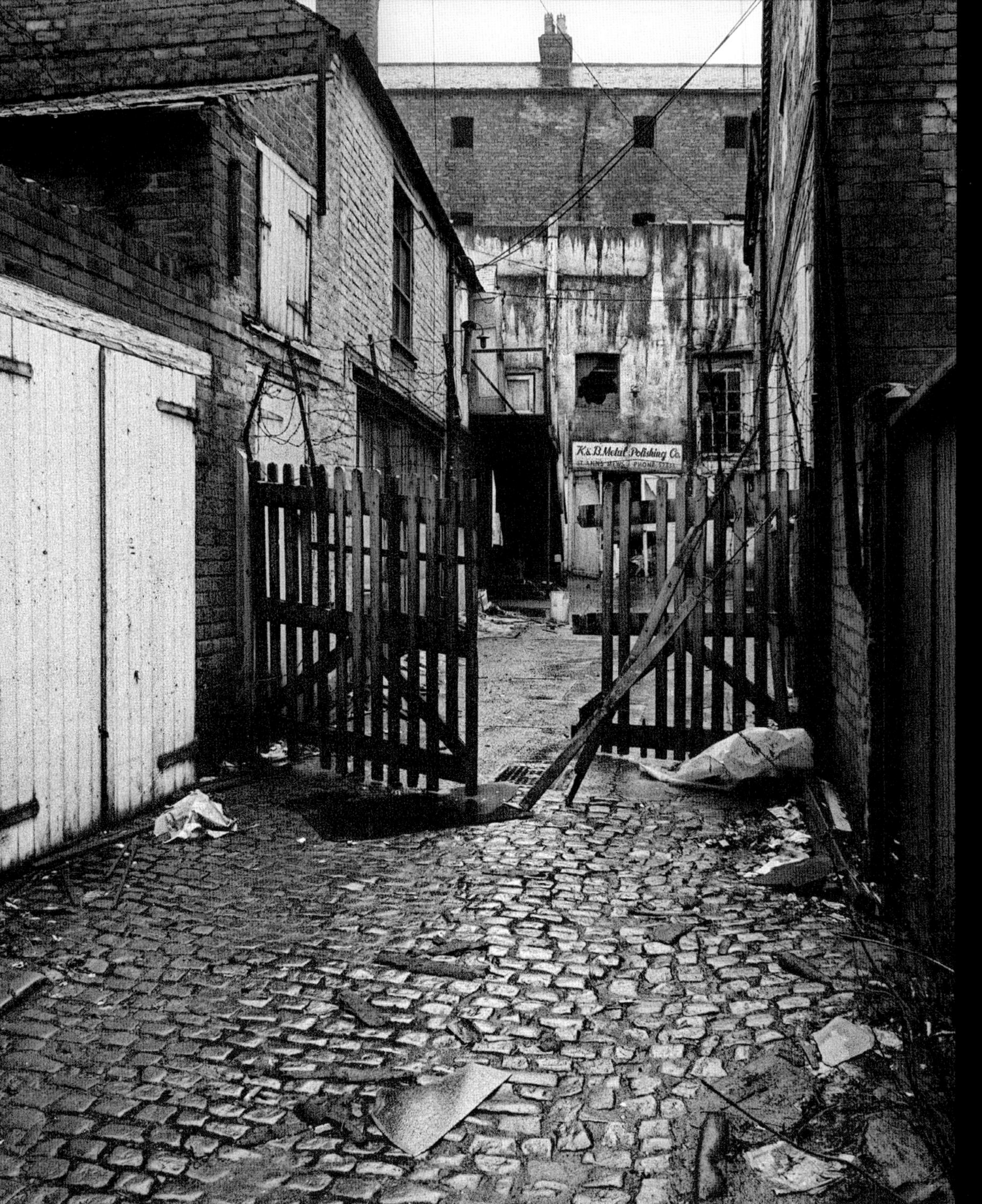

Business premises of K & B Metal Polishing Co., St Ann's Mews, off St Ann's Well Road

Many streets had entrances to yards, workshops and even stables at the rear of the properties.

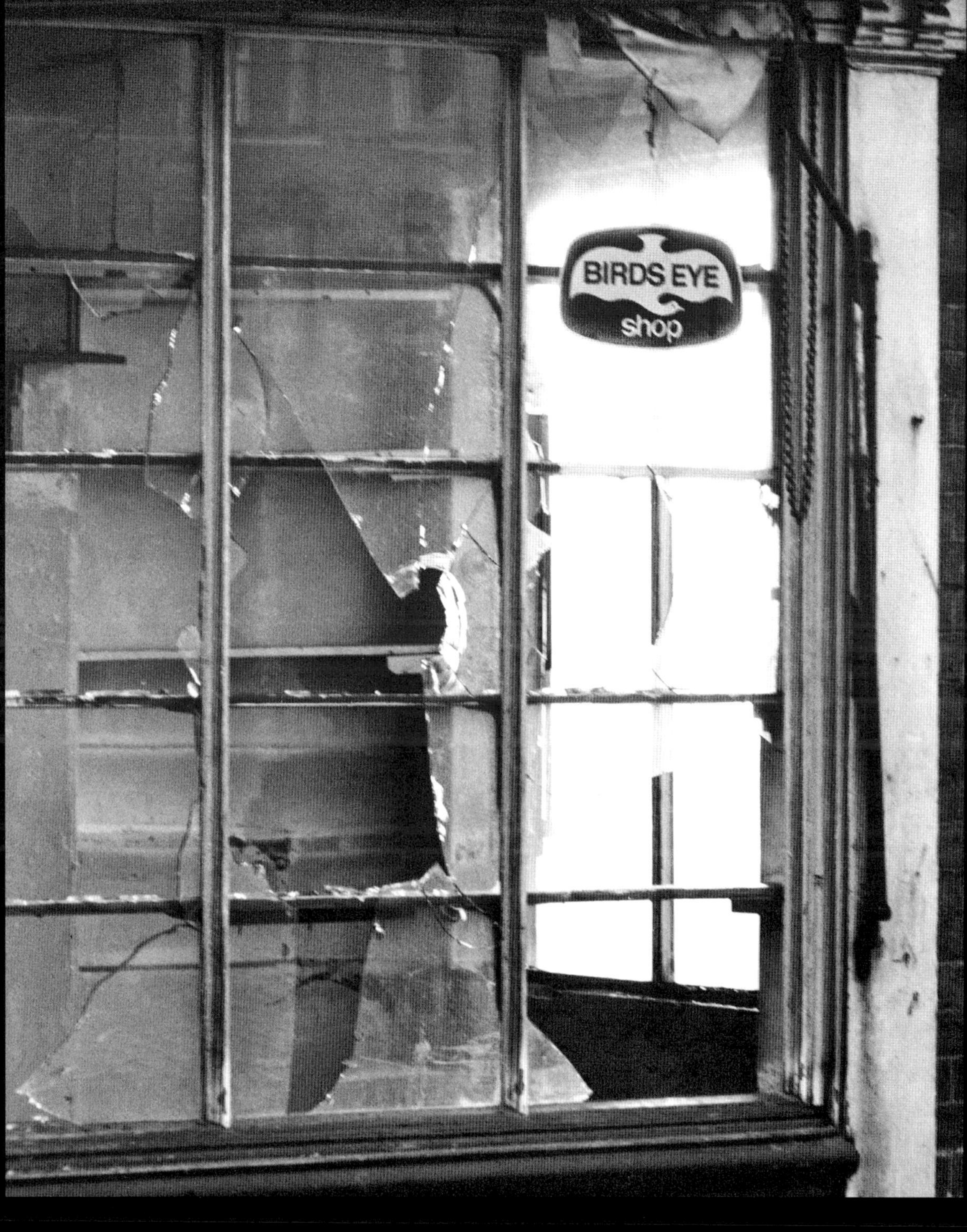

Empty shop with broken windows

Old shelving and the Birds Eye shop sign indicate it was probably a general corner shop.

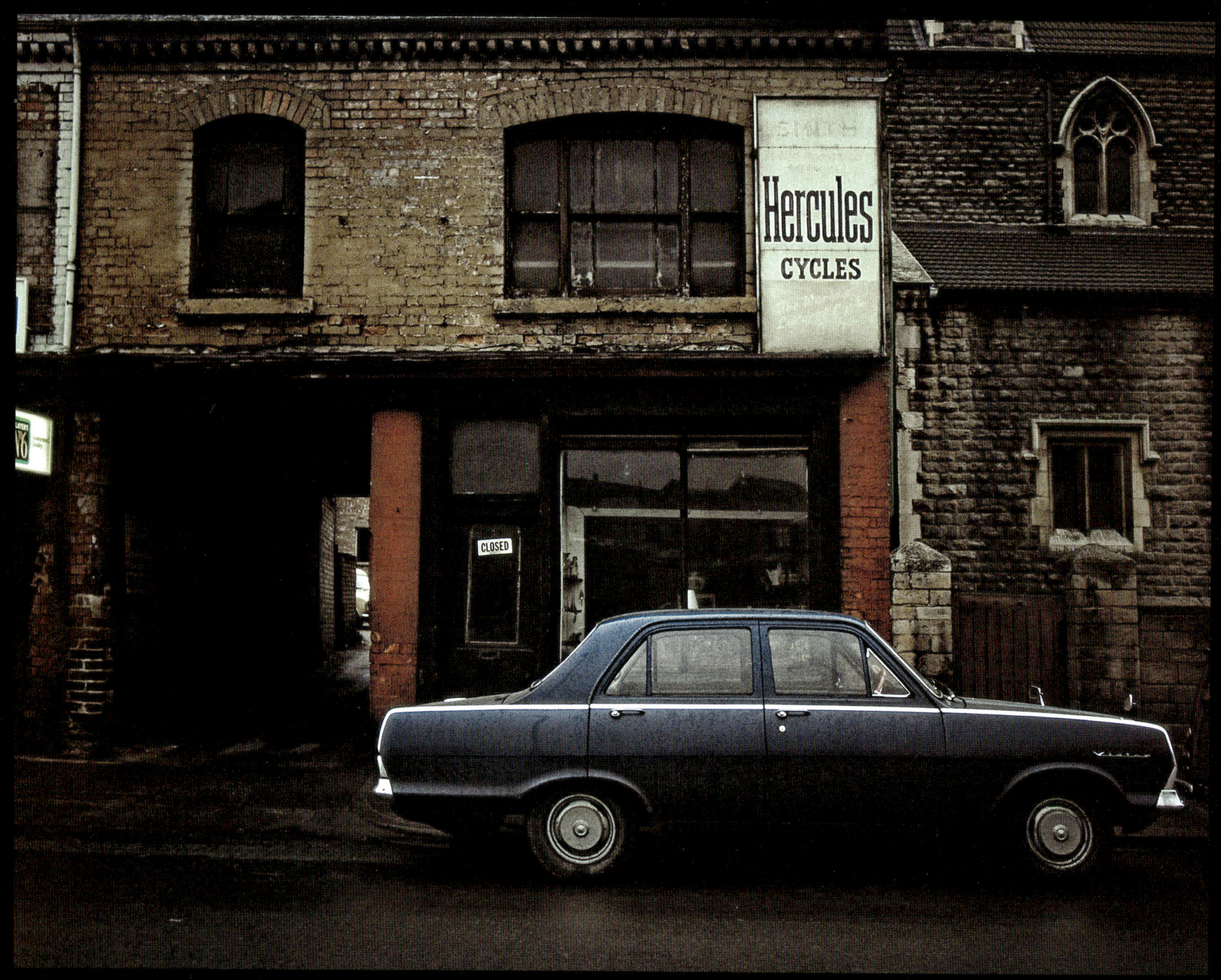

Example of an entrance to workshops, storage and business premises at the rear of shops and houses

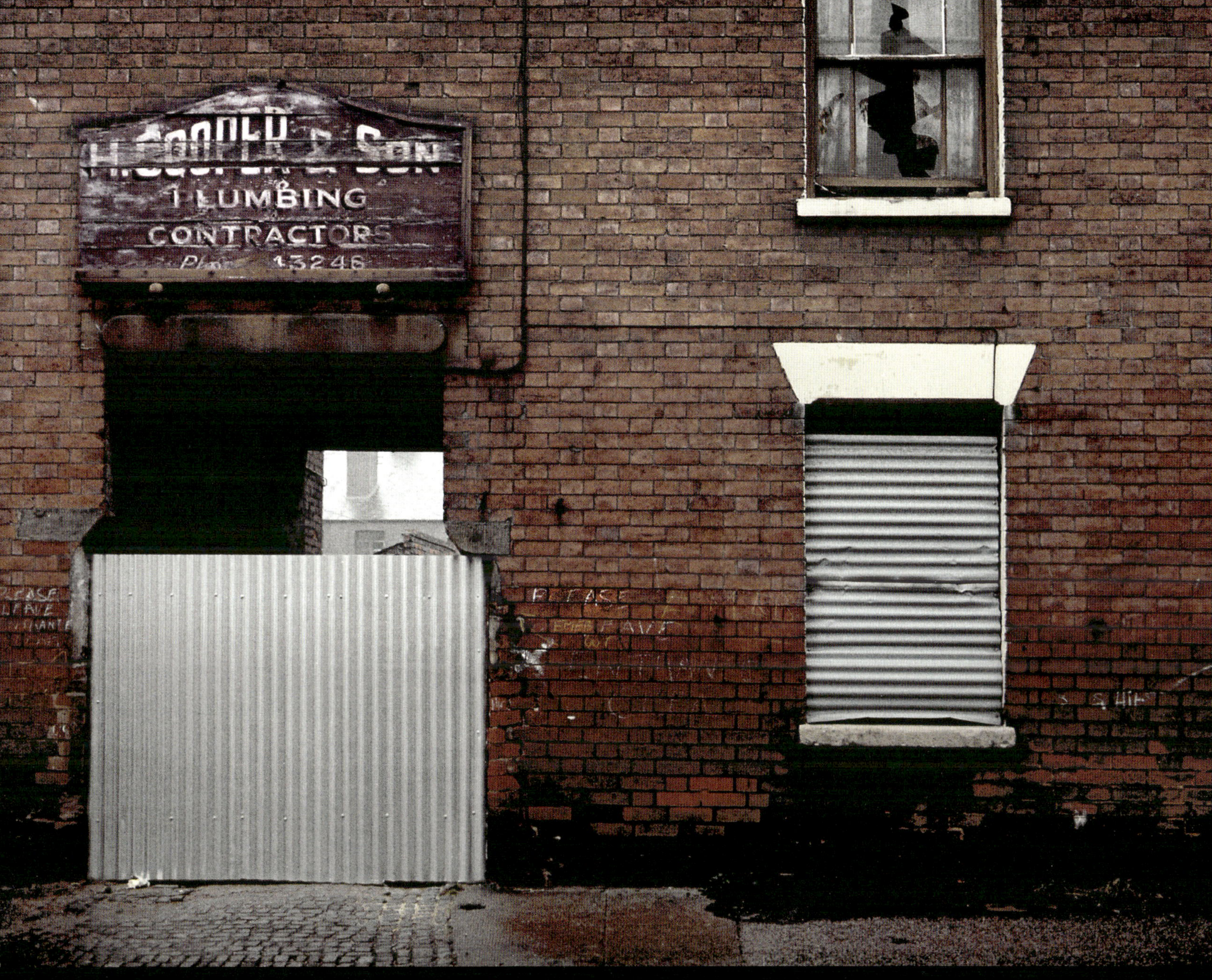

Hawkridge Street   Shuttered up entrance to a plumber's yard.

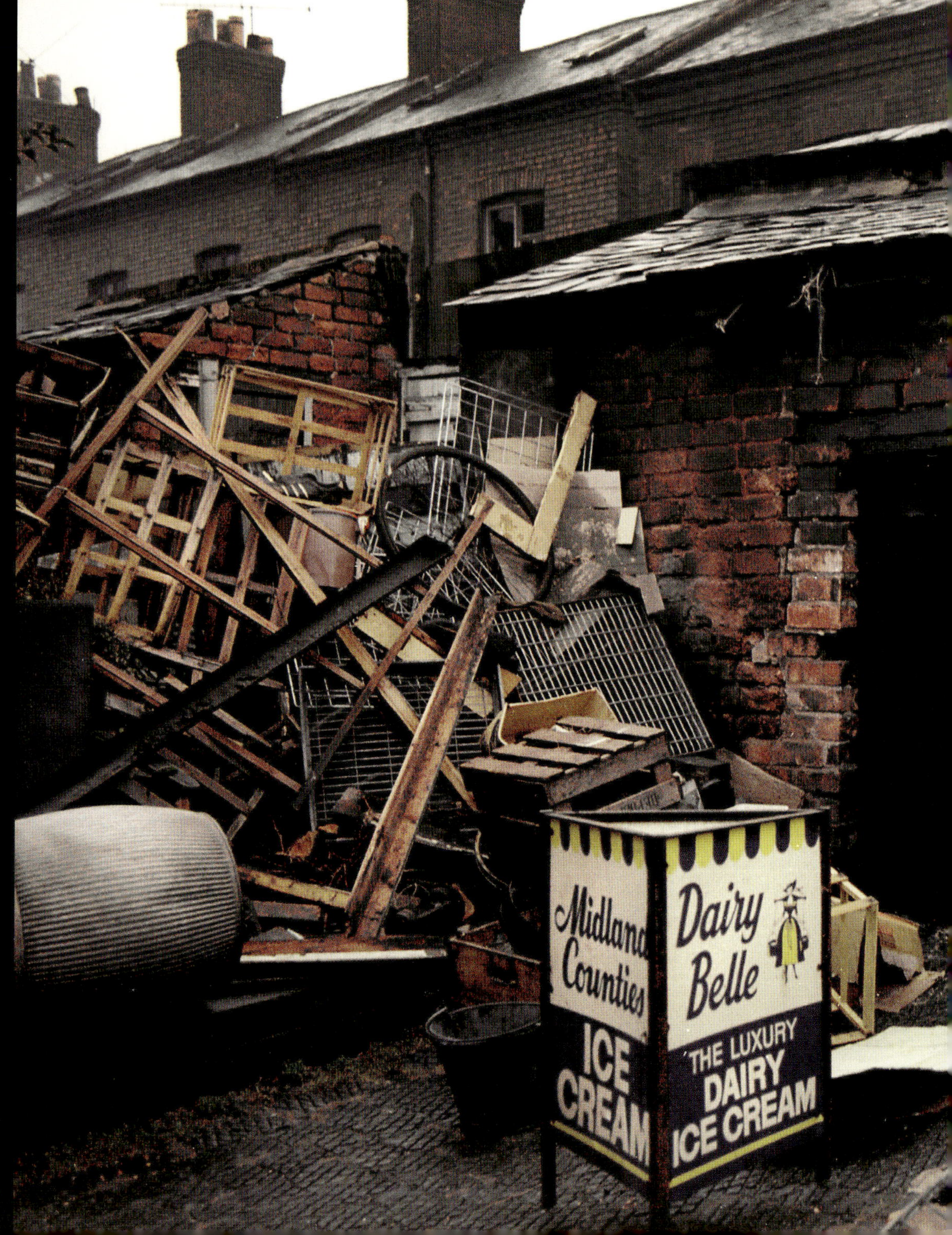
Midland
Counties
Dairy
Belle
ICE
CREAM
'THE LUXURY
DAIRY
ICE CREAM

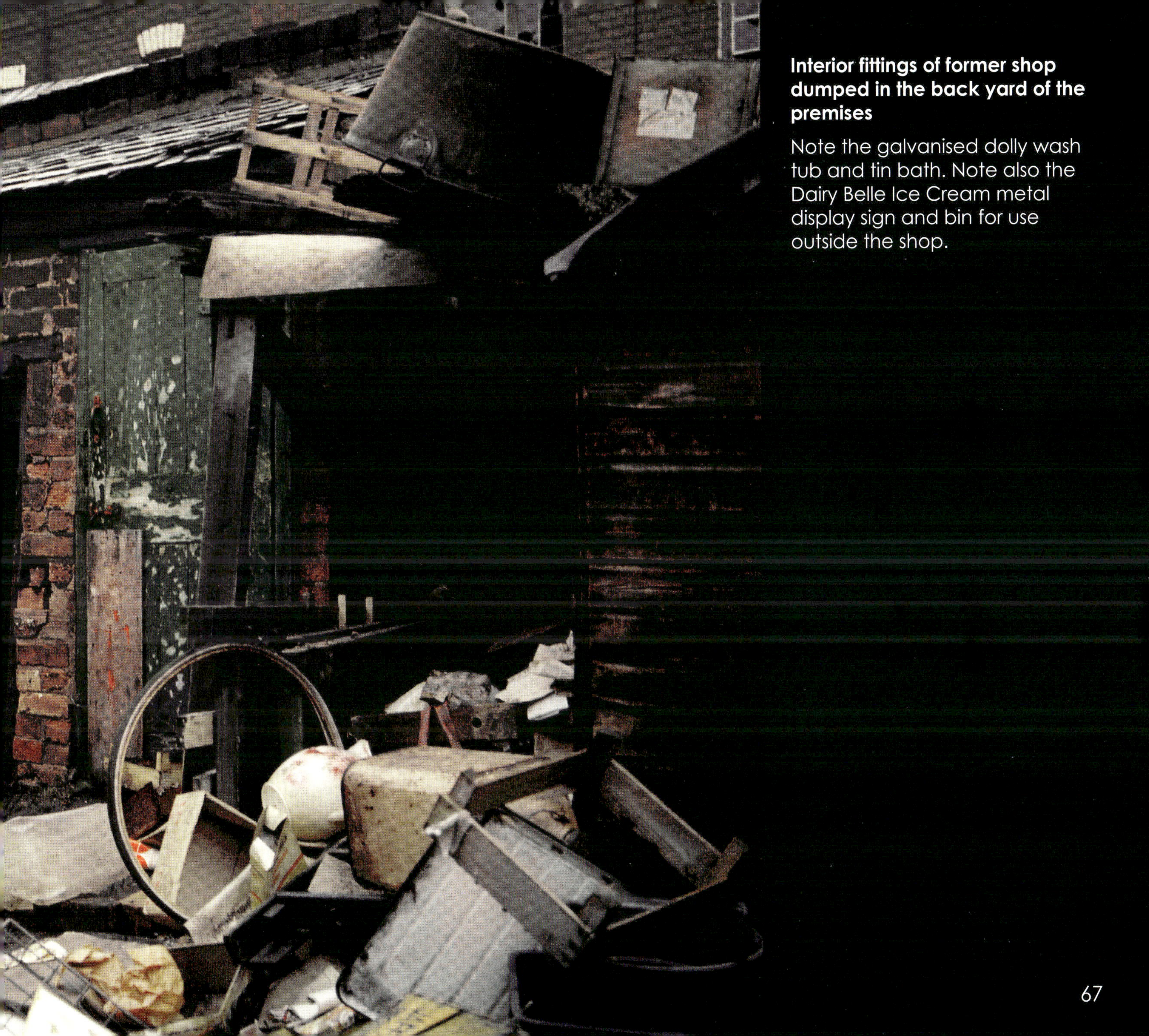

Interior fittings of former shop dumped in the back yard of the premises

Note the galvanised dolly wash tub and tin bath. Note also the Dairy Belle Ice Cream metal display sign and bin for use outside the shop.

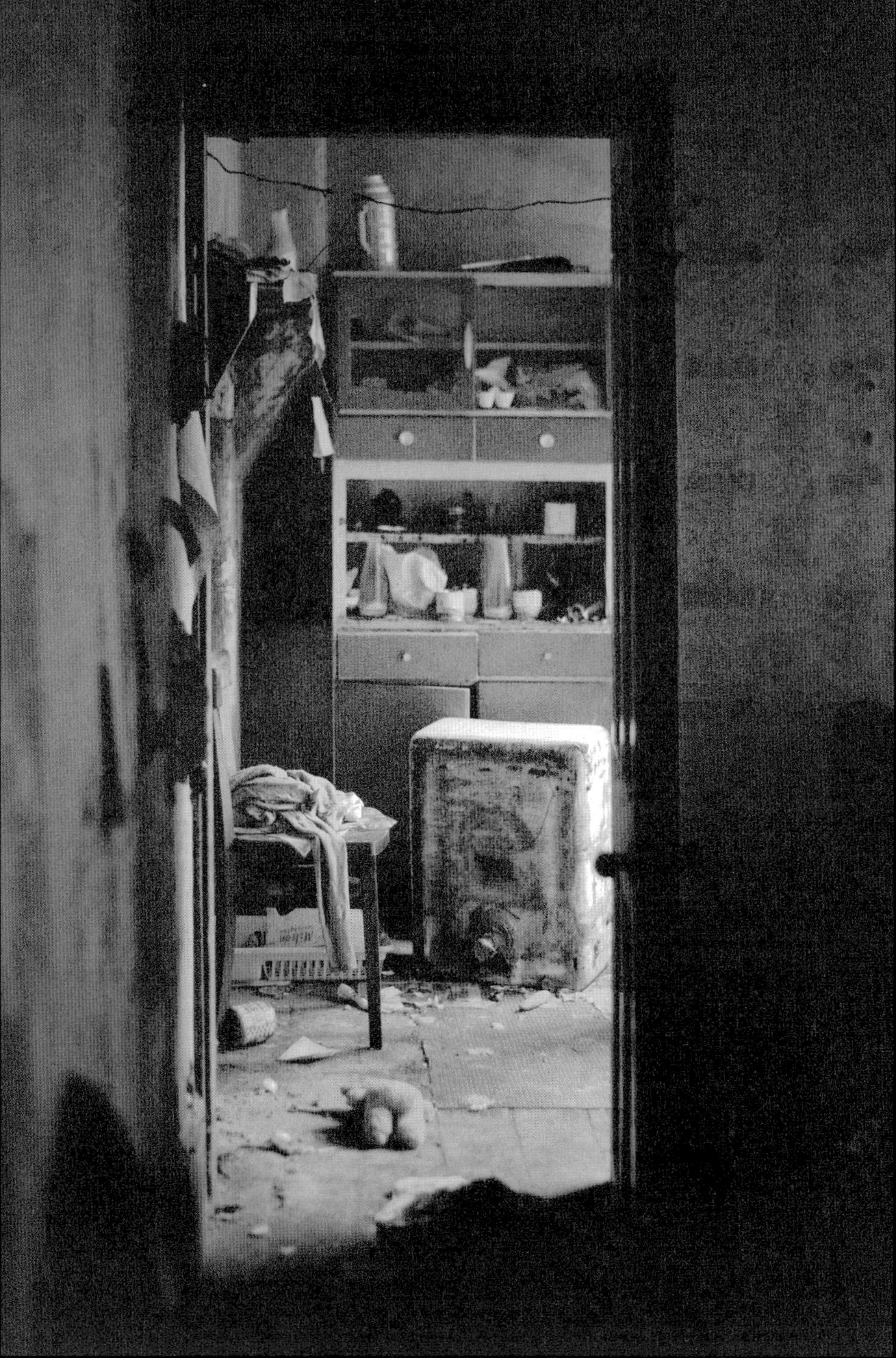

Left: Empty house with an abandoned look

The scullery is left as though the occupants had to leave in a hurry. Half-empty milk bottles, thermos flask, mugs and cups, a tin of Birds custard powder, even a child's teddy bear.

Right: "There was an entry every six or eight houses in the street, and sometimes the entry led to stables or business premises."

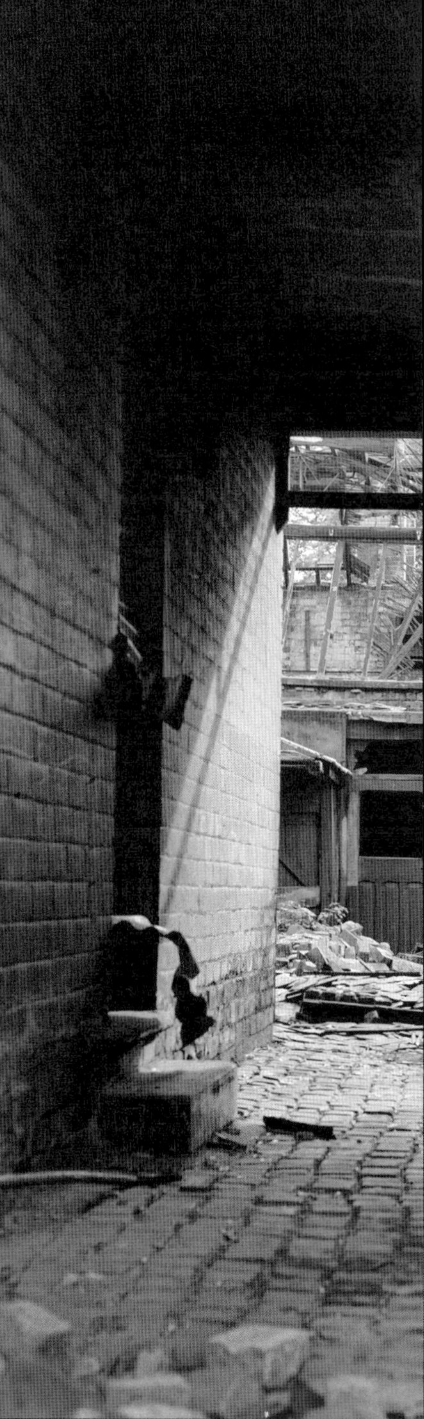

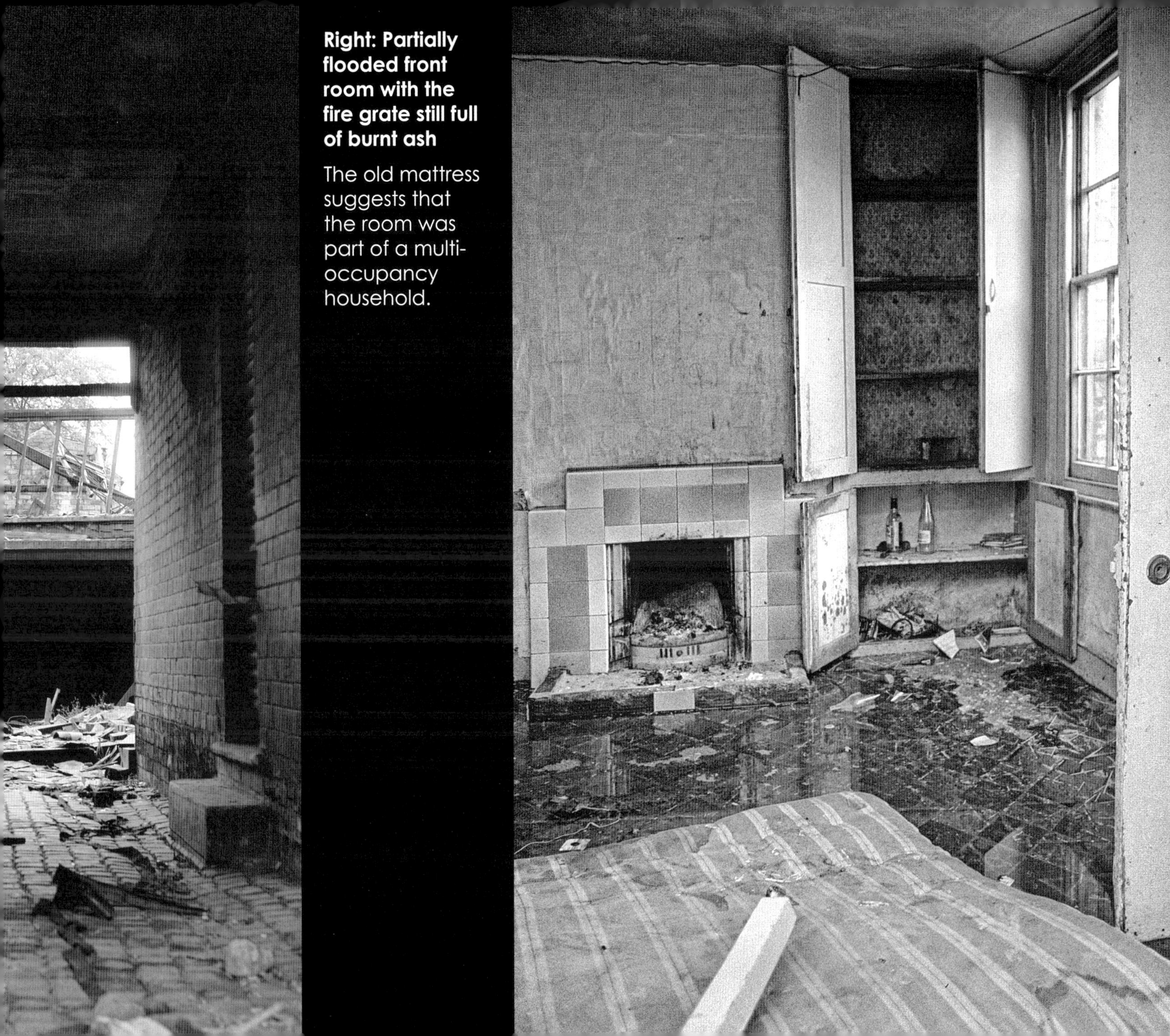

Right: Partially flooded front room with the fire grate still full of burnt ash

The old mattress suggests that the room was part of a multi-occupancy household.

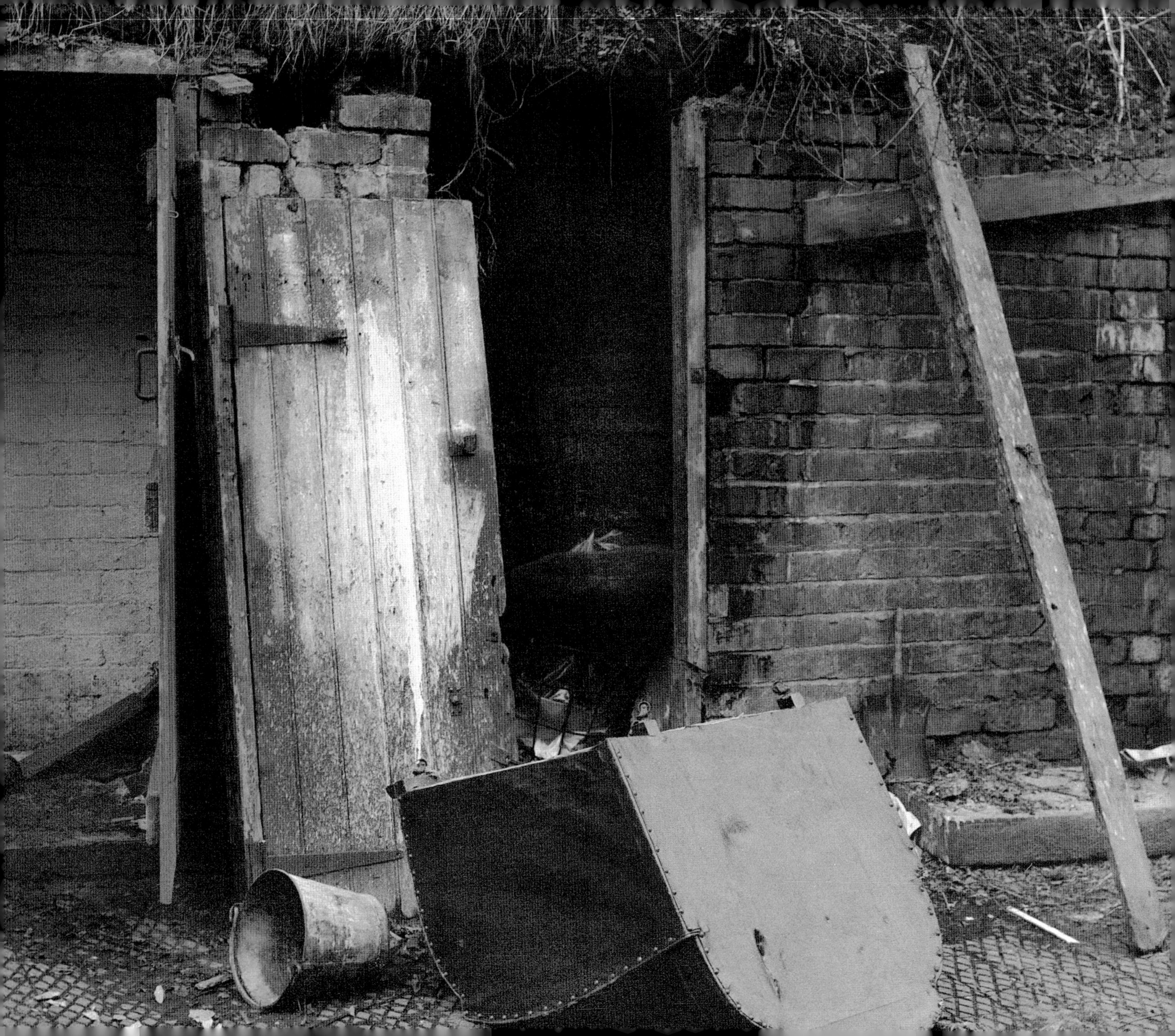

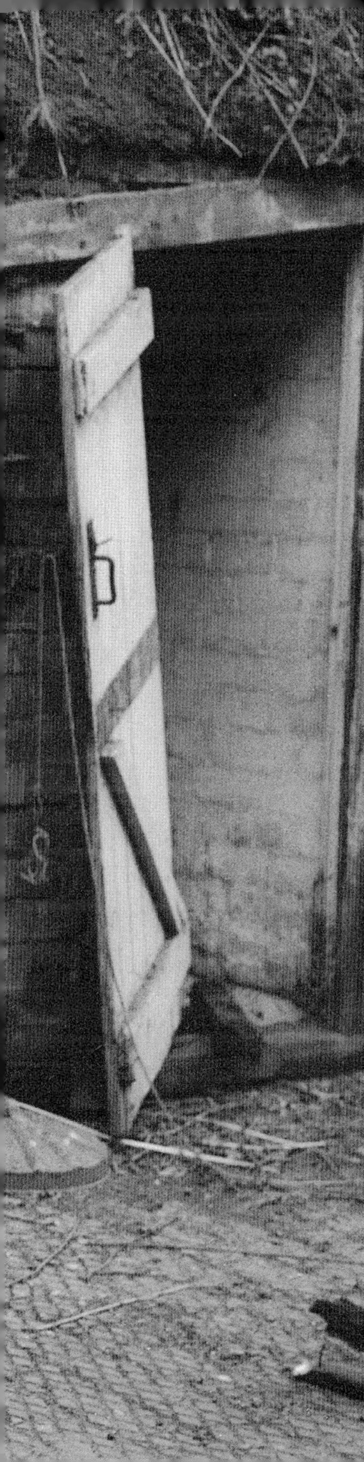

Left: Line of toilets built into an earthen bank

"'To the best of my belief, none of the properties of Robin Hood Street possessed an internal toilet. We had heard that such things were available in posh houses, but that wasn't for us. Ours, along with everyone else's, stood at the end of the back yard. This could be quite inconvenient in the depths of winter."

"Containing neither light nor heat, it was up to each user to decide how best to tackle the problem. Mine was to charge down the yard with a burning brand of newspaper in hand and hope all could be accomplished before the flames reached the end of the paper."

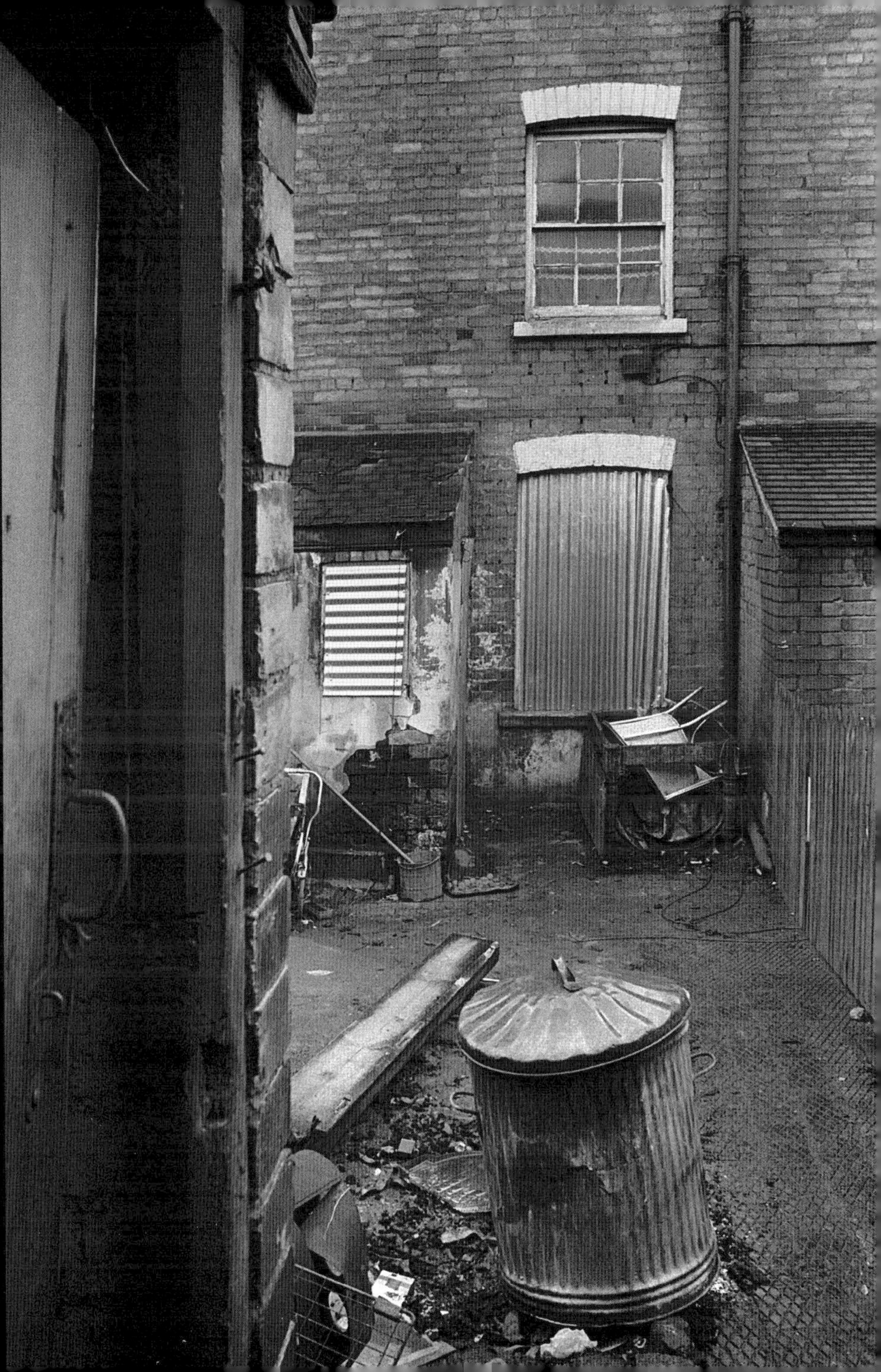

Right: Back yard with Victorian diamond-patterned blue brick floor, outside toilet and a galvanised dustbin

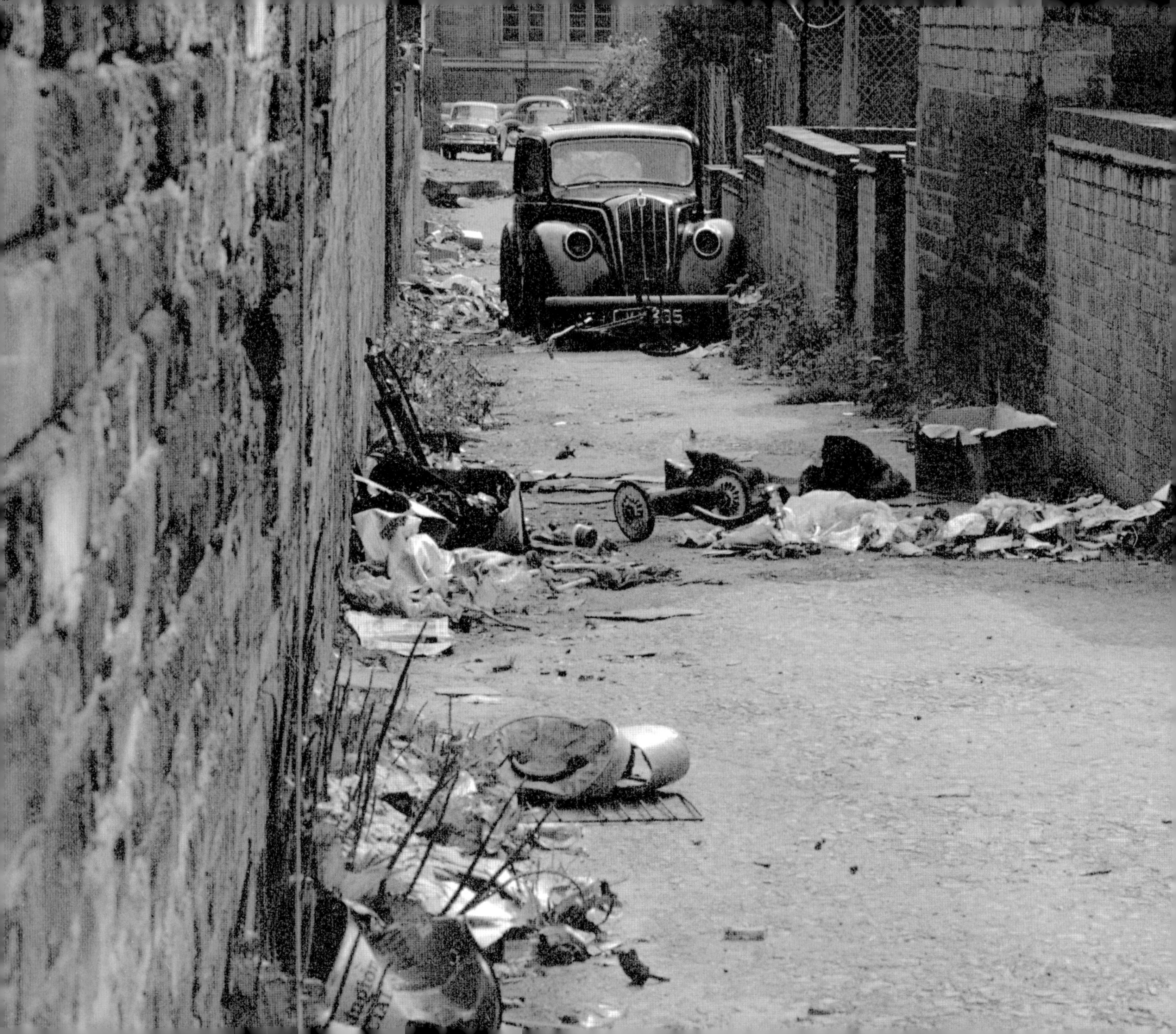

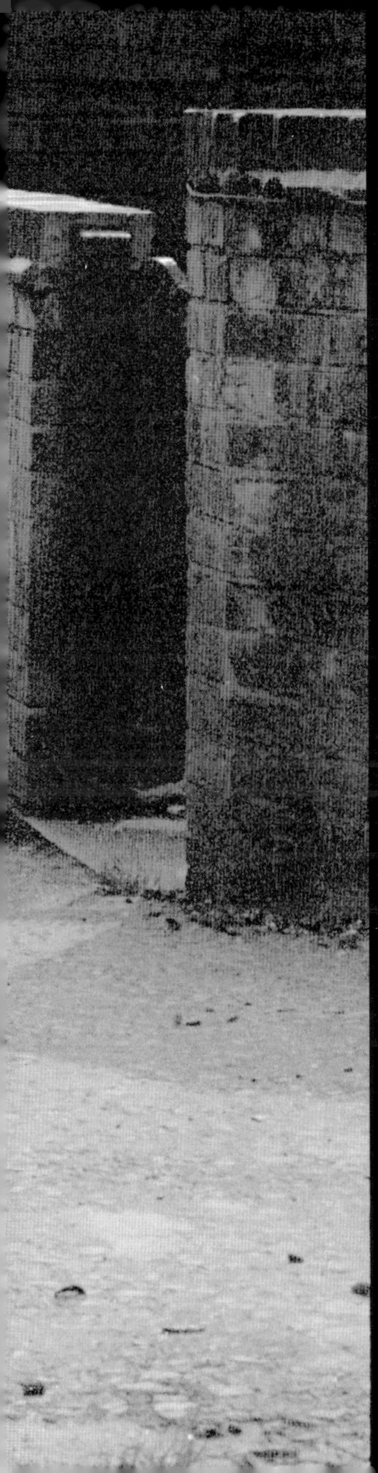

Abandoned cars in the streets

Not many people could afford cars but older ones could be picked up relatively cheaply. They were usually unreliable, and often abandoned because the owners couldn't meet the costs of repair.

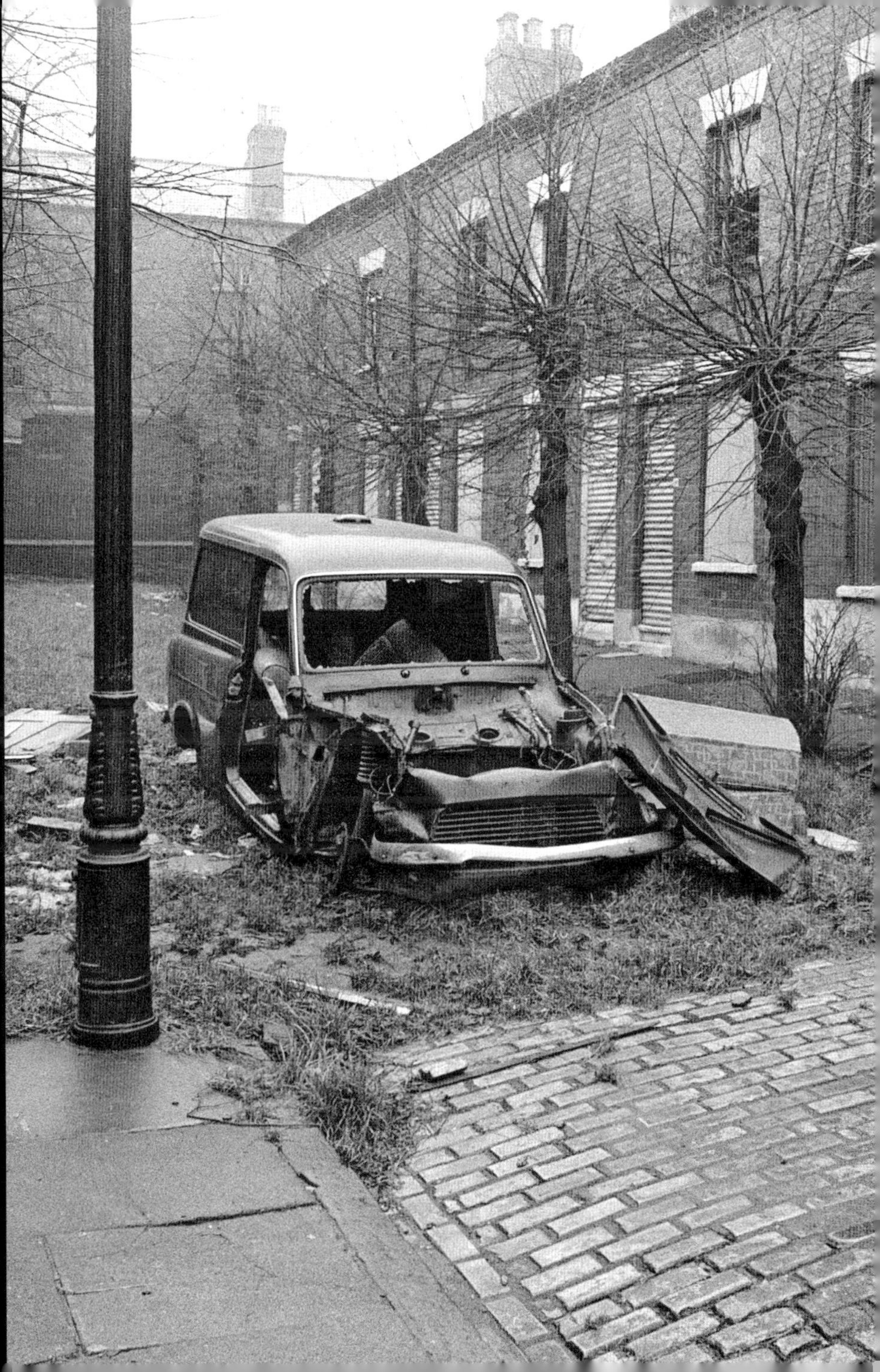

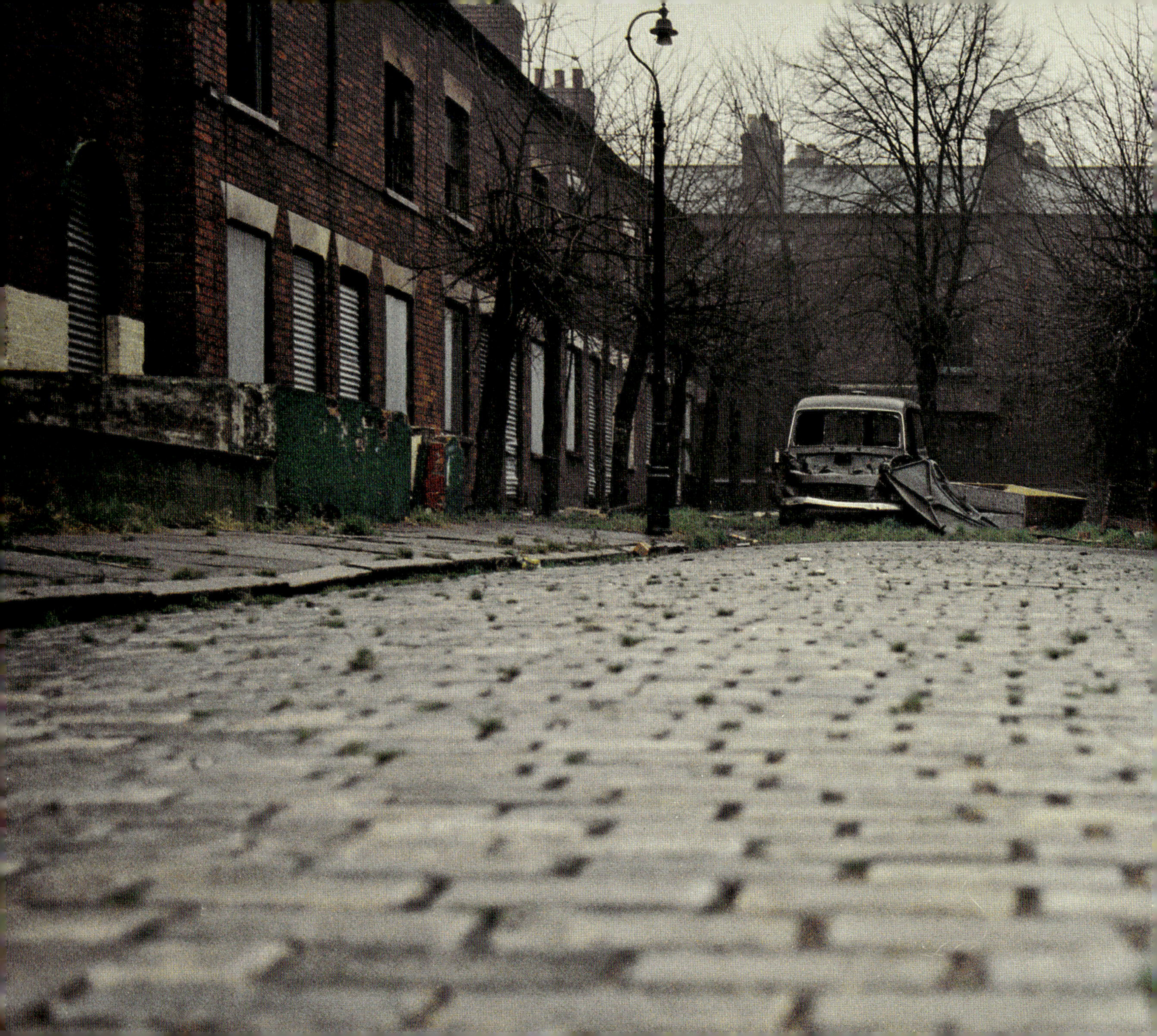

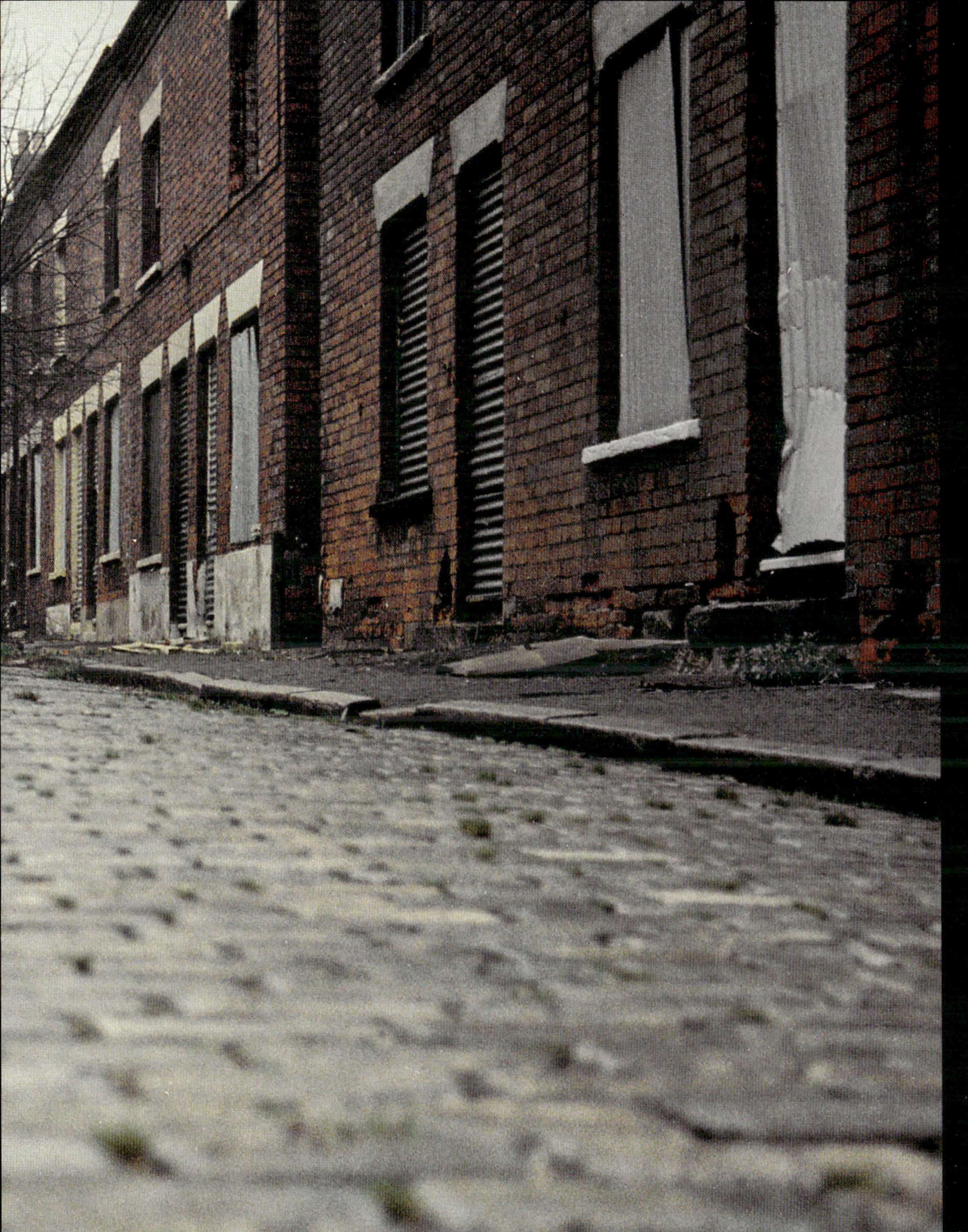

"I was always interested in cars and that, and Manvers School used to have a night school and they had a car in one of the rooms that they used to strip down, and they actually let me attend it before I left school, and my form teacher who had just bought a car, he used to drag me in every morning after the night school and asked me 'What have you learnt? Tell me what this is, tell me what that is?' (laughs) So that was me first time teaching teachers."

Paul Jackson

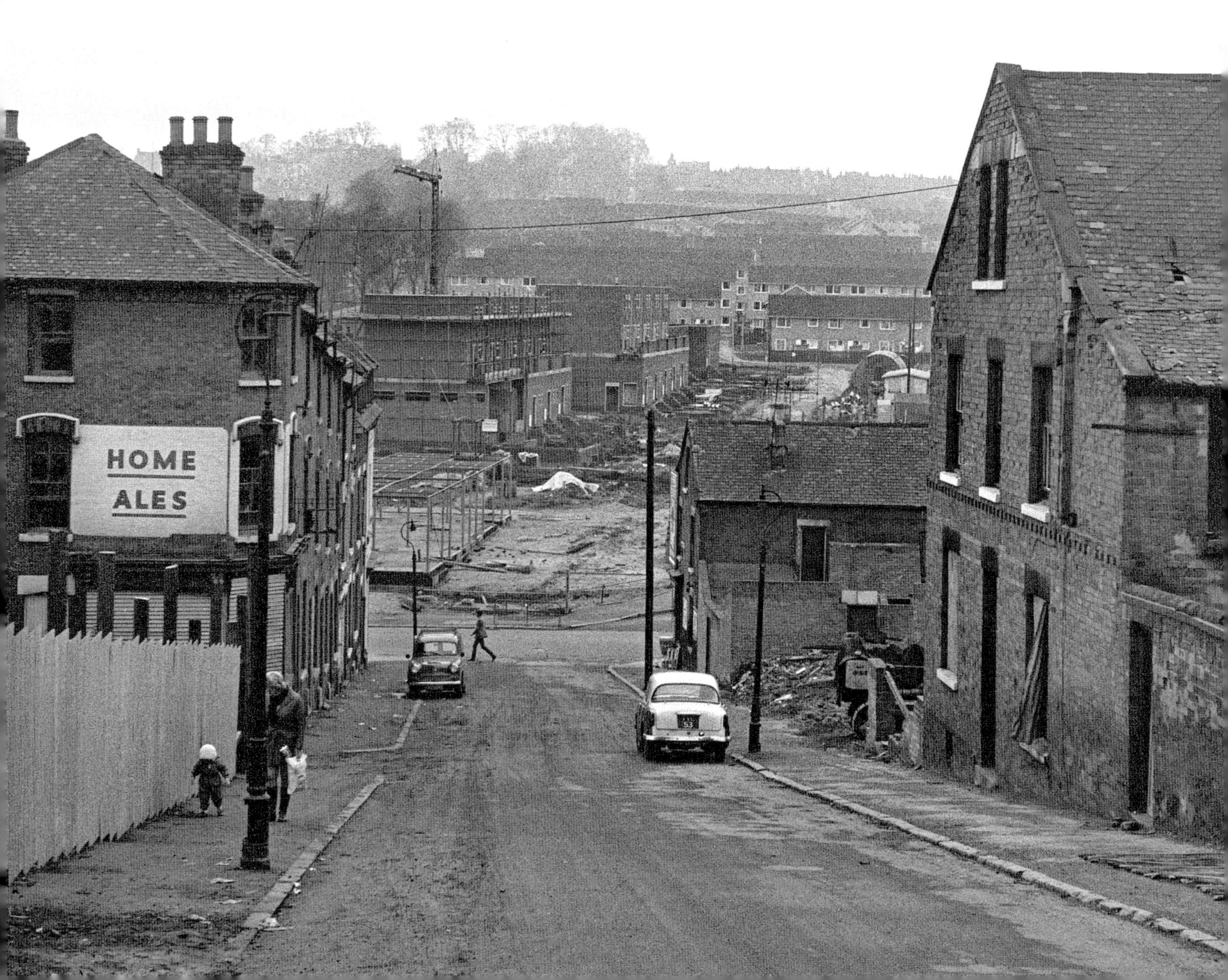

HOME
ALES

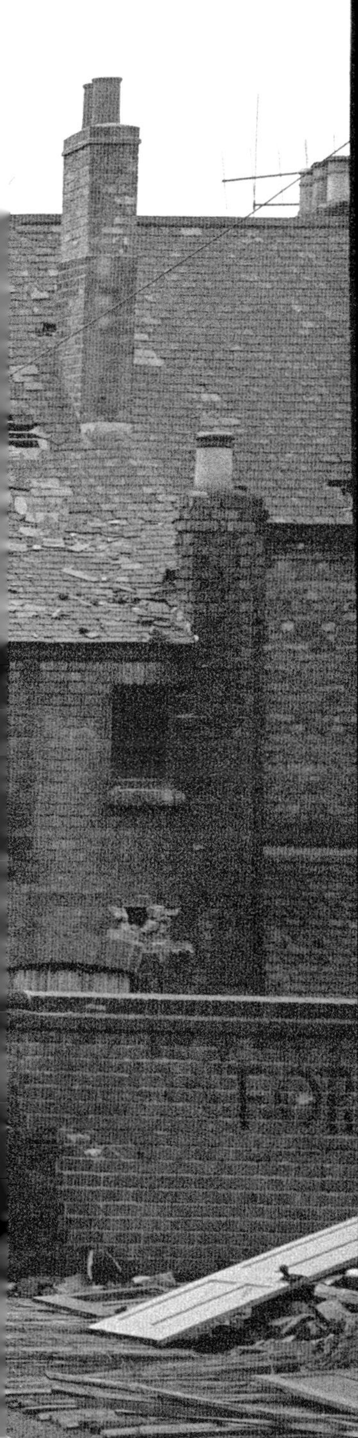

Left: Livingstone Street leading down to St Ann's Well Road

The tree-lined Robin Hood's Chase can be seen to the left of the new builds which are in progress on the opposite side of the road.

Right: Southampton Street leading down to St Ann's Well Road

"I was working for Wimpey and worked on the first houses that Wimpey built to replace them down at the bottom end. The first phase, the first houses I worked on, and I thought you know here I am, they're demolishing the top end and now I'm building at the bottom end."

Dan Cox

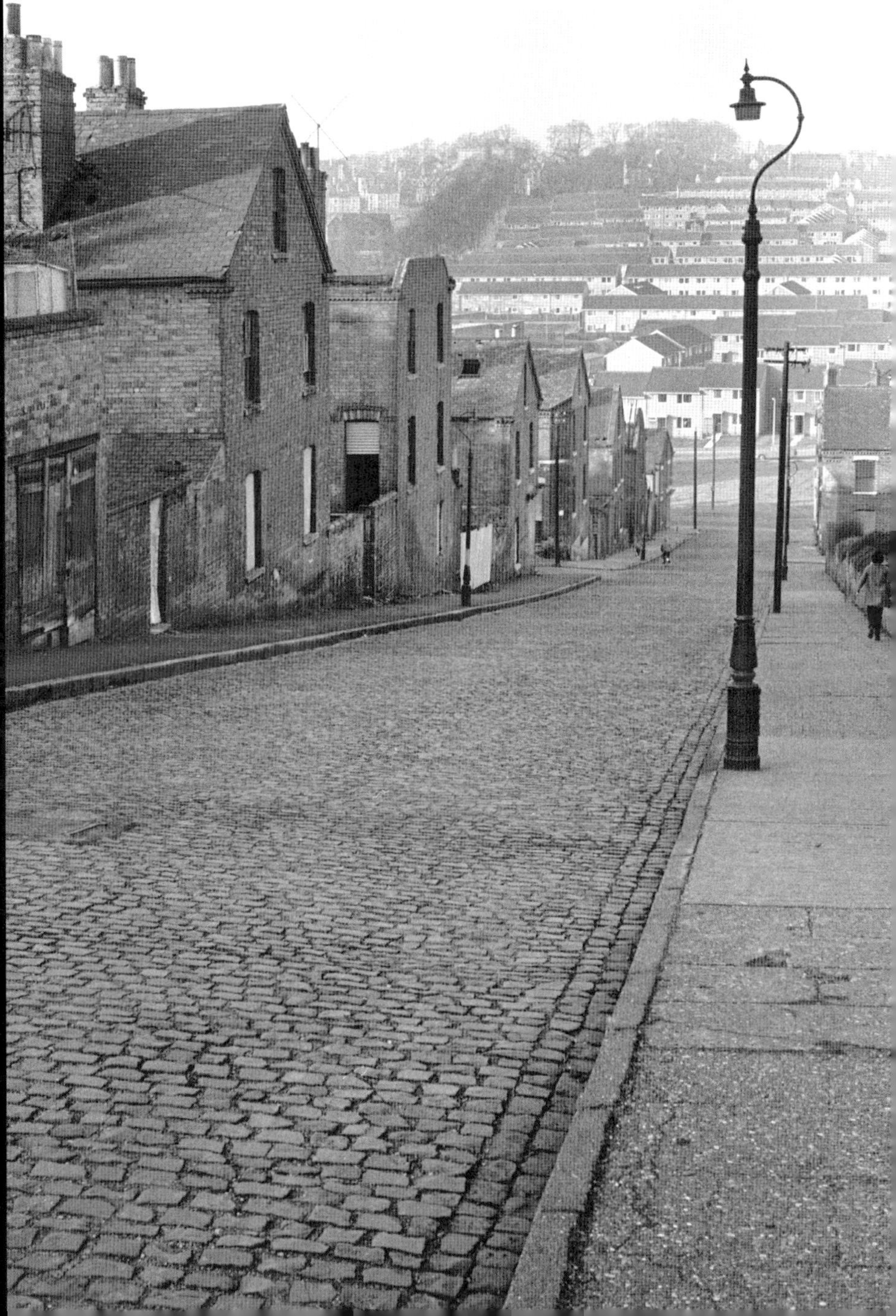

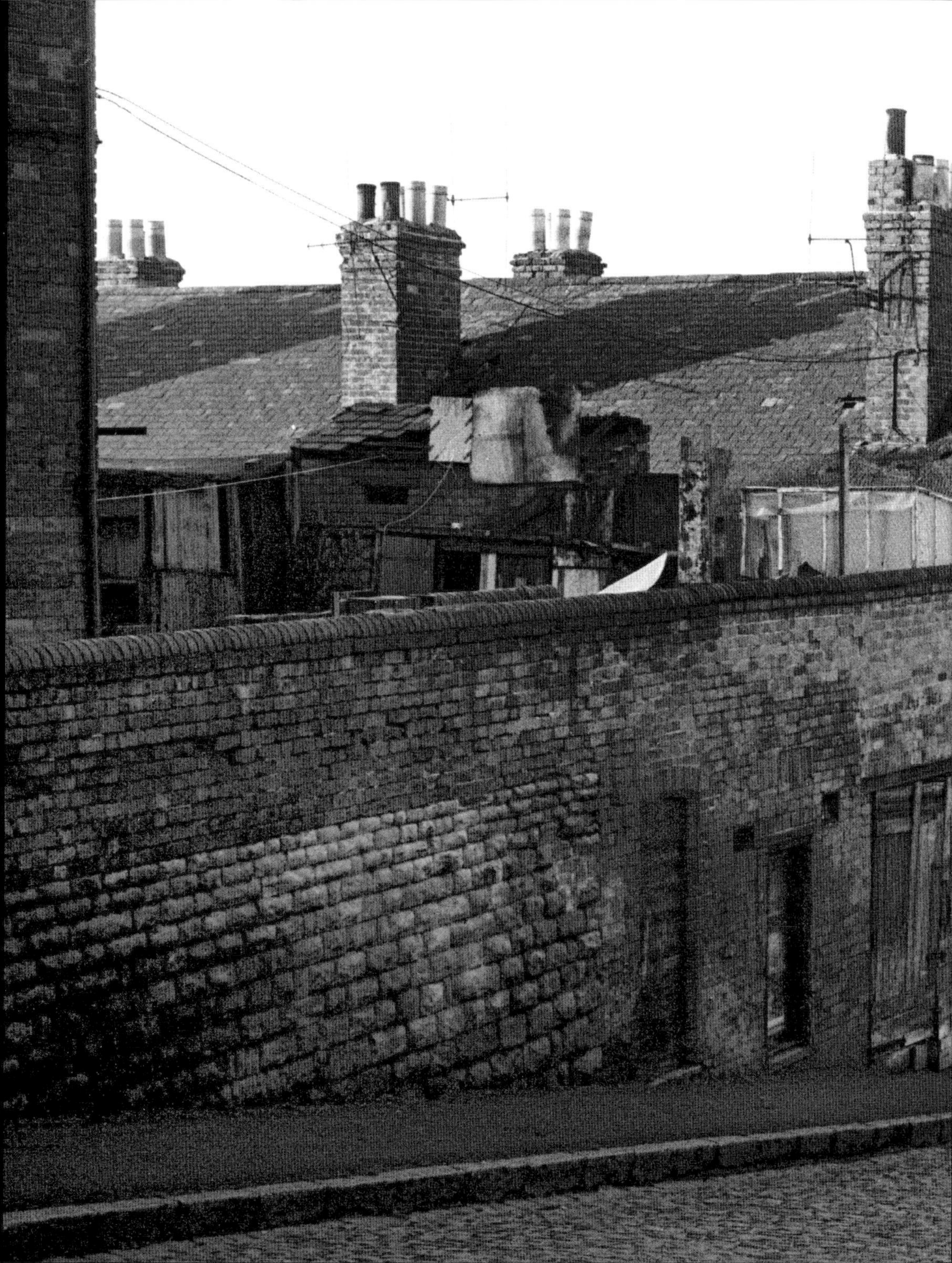

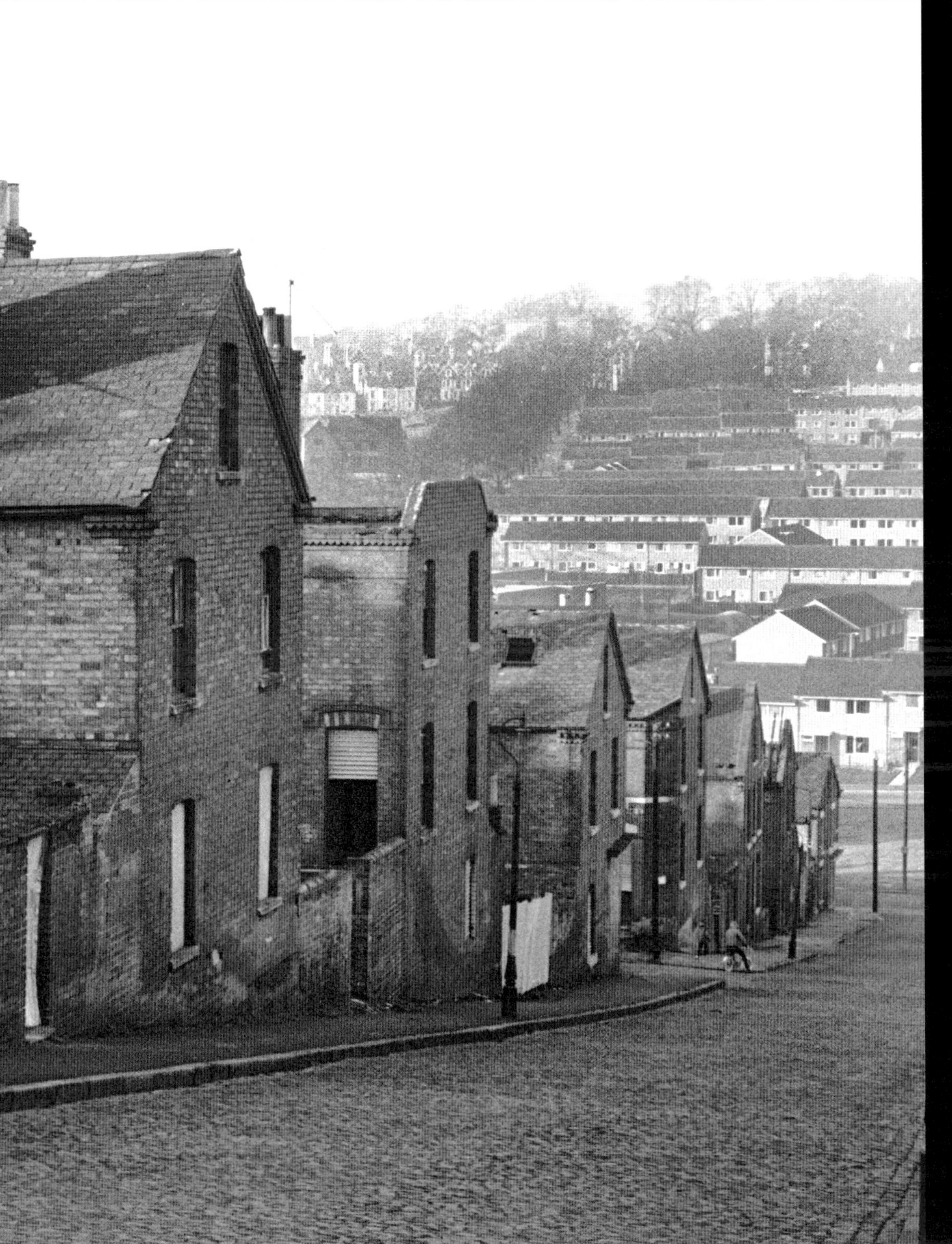

Southampton Street leading down to St Ann's Well Road

Note the new builds under construction to the right of the tree-lined Robin Hood's Chase, on the opposite side of St Ann's Well Road.

Woodborough Road can be seen in the distance at the top of Robin Hood's Chase.

Danger: Demolition

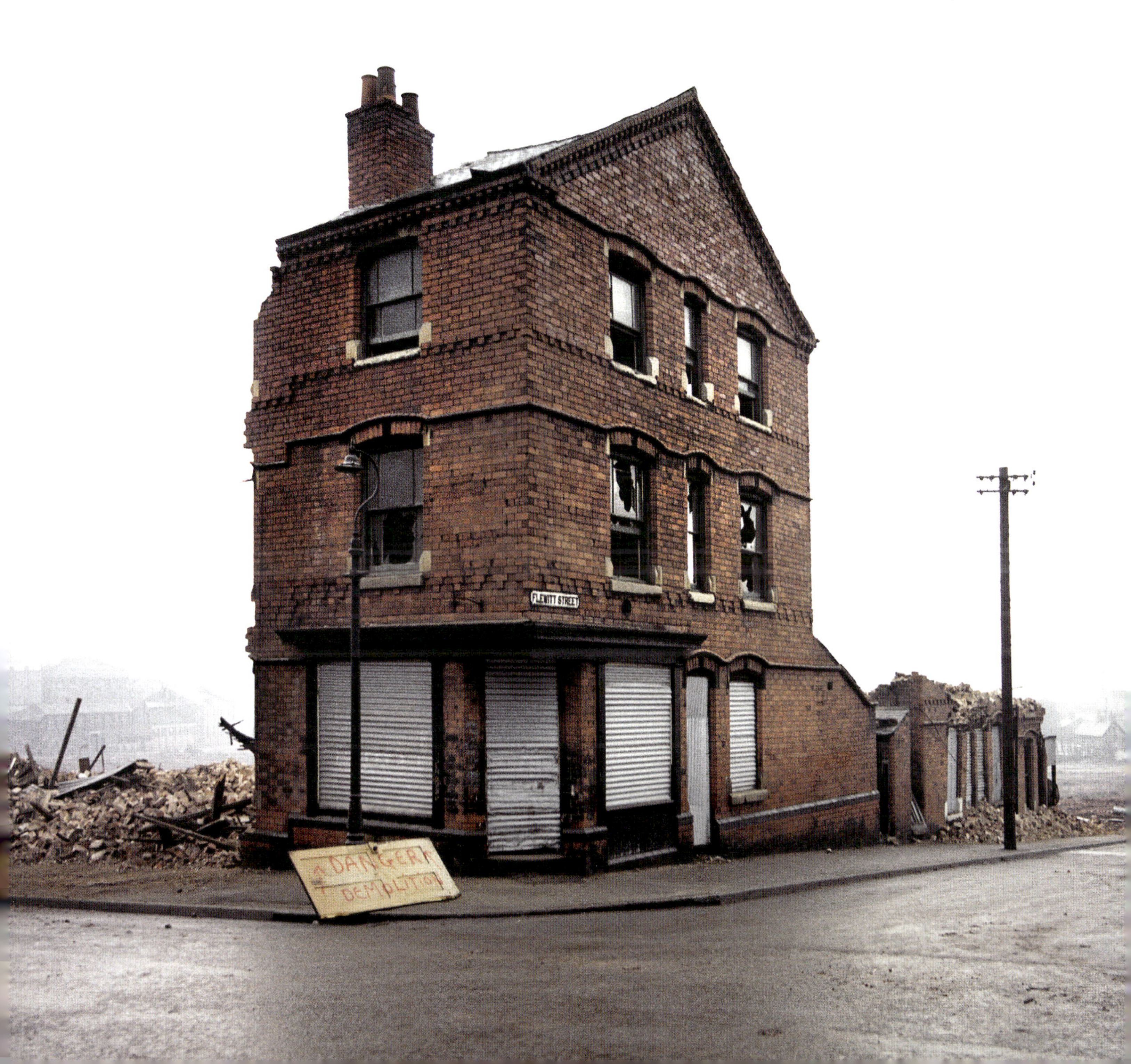

FLEWITT STREET
DANGER
DEMOLITION

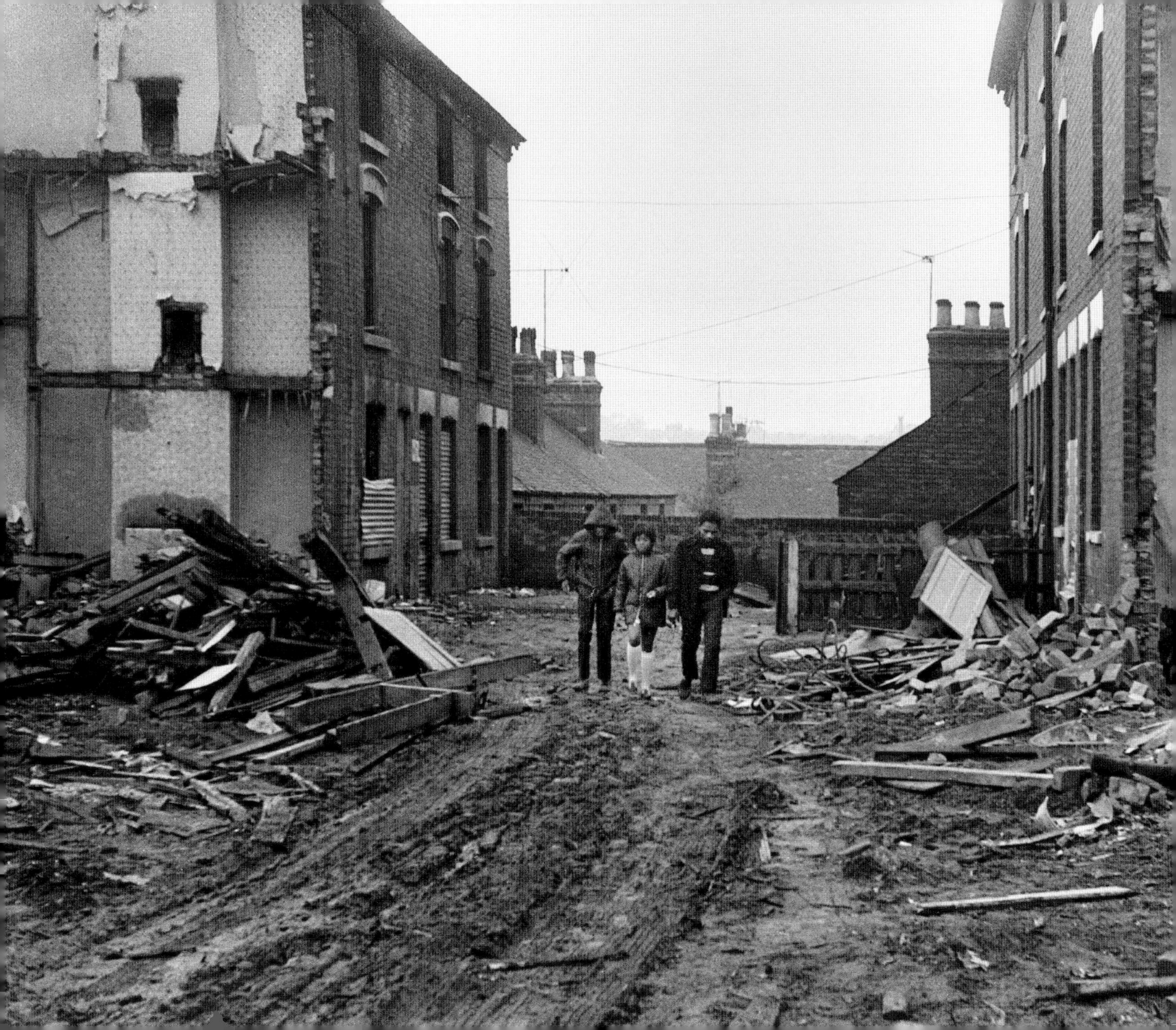

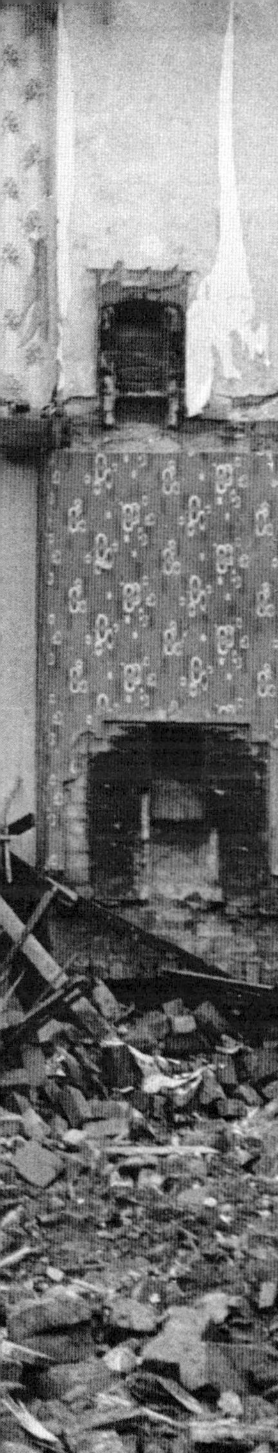

Guy's Terrace off Bluebell Hill Road

Family leaving the house pictured on the right, making their way through the mud and demolition rubble of the houses around them. Note the tin baths in the front yard.

"Her husband had to leap out of bed and scream for the demolition to stop. The conditions were so bad the demolition men did not think people could still be living there and did not think to check."

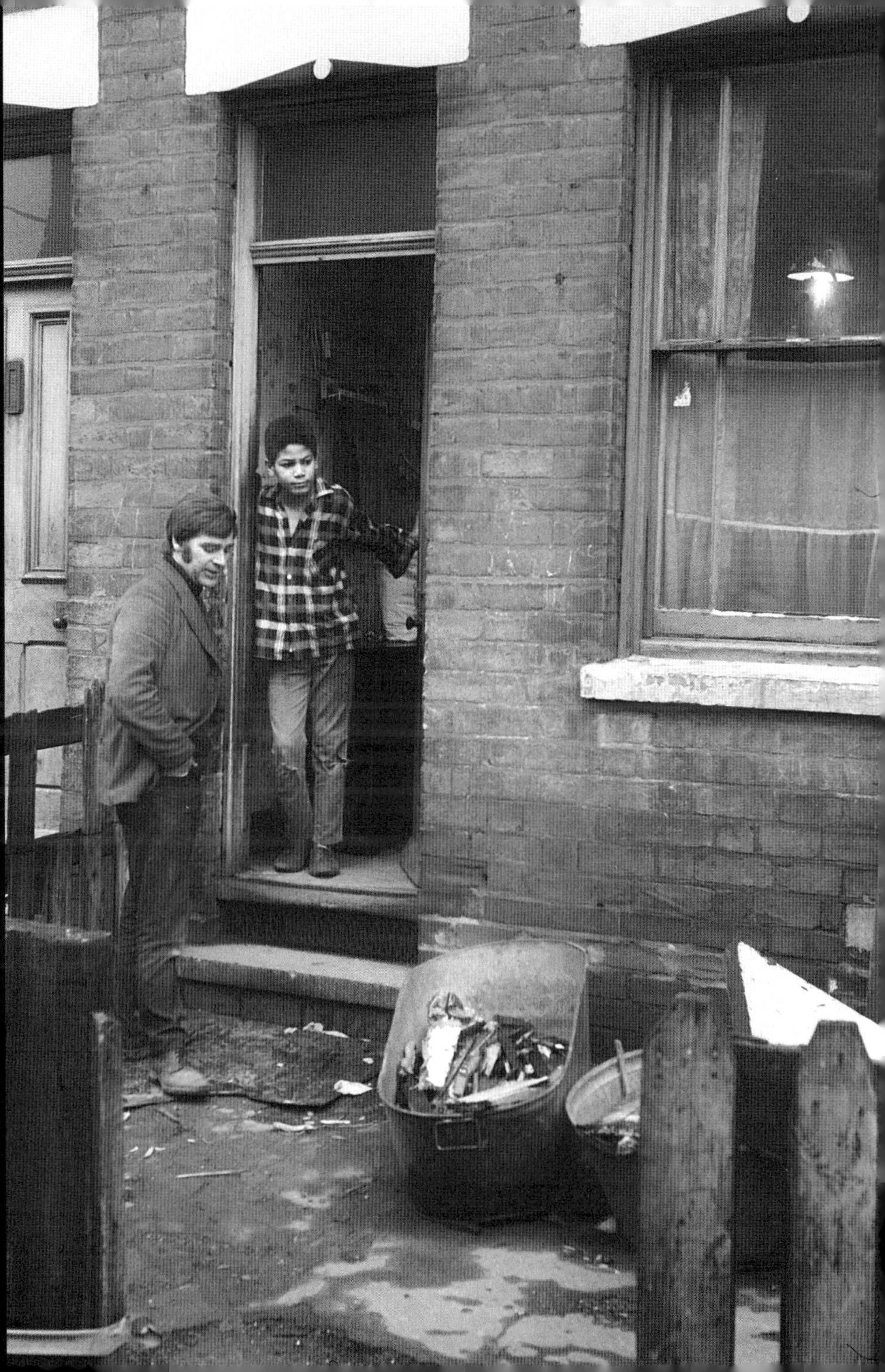

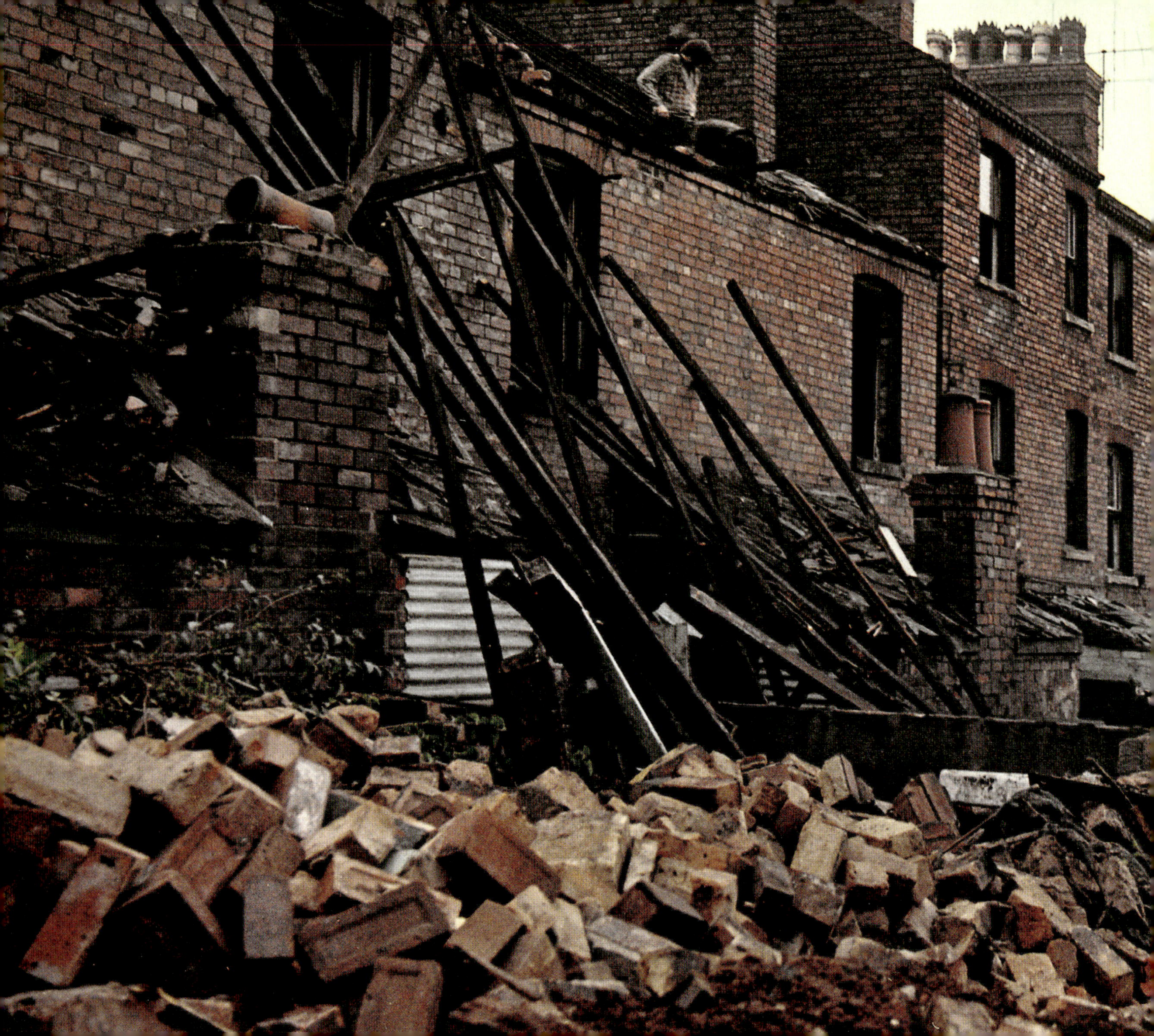

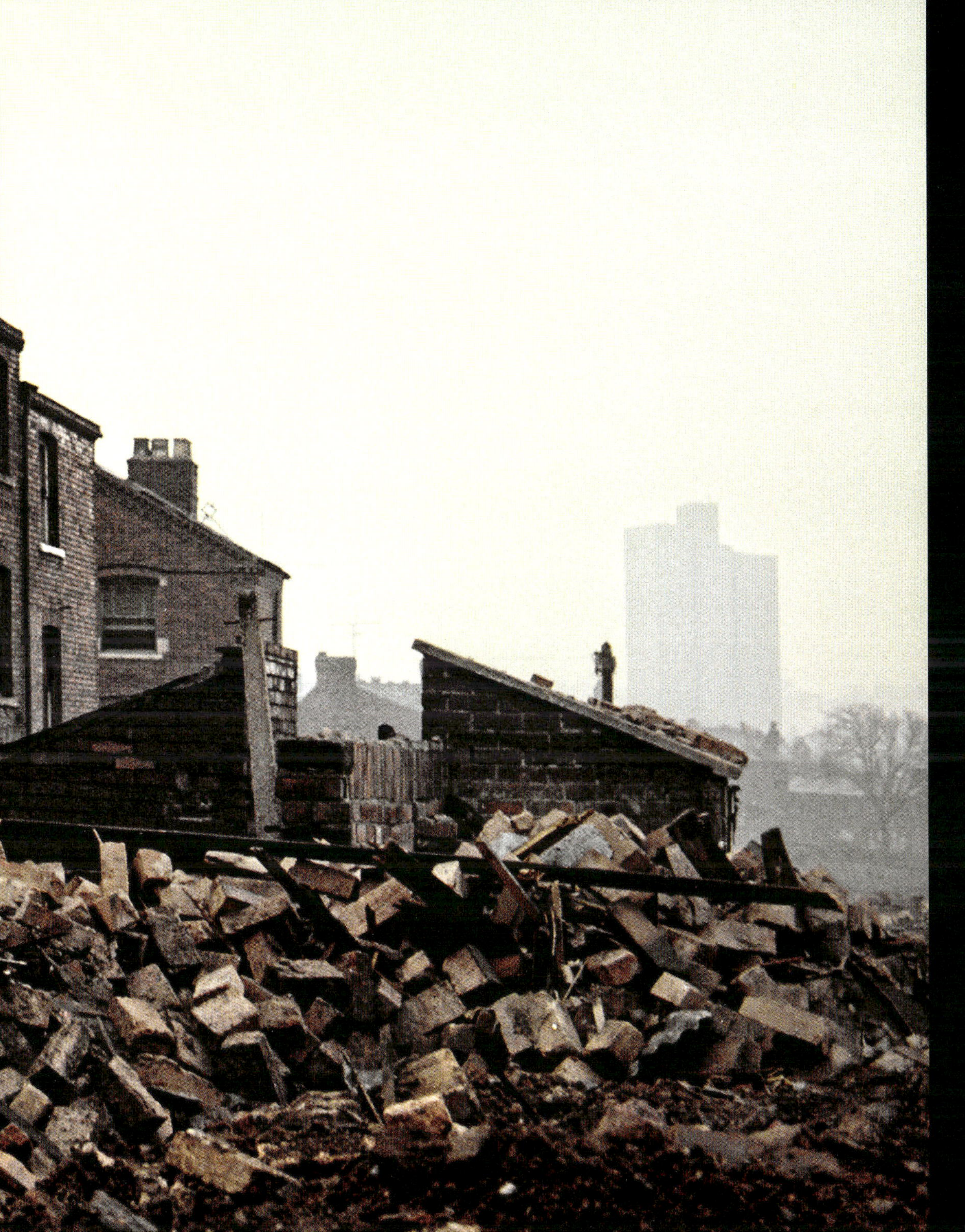

"St Ann's wasn't prosperous, but it was full of life. The new St Ann's would emerge, rebuilt and vastly different to the way it was."
"What people don't appreciate today is the sense of community that there was. The demolition hadn't really started, I had no concept of what was about to happen. I went back ten years later and everything had changed. Everything had gone. The only thing left was the layout of the road."

Mavis Baker

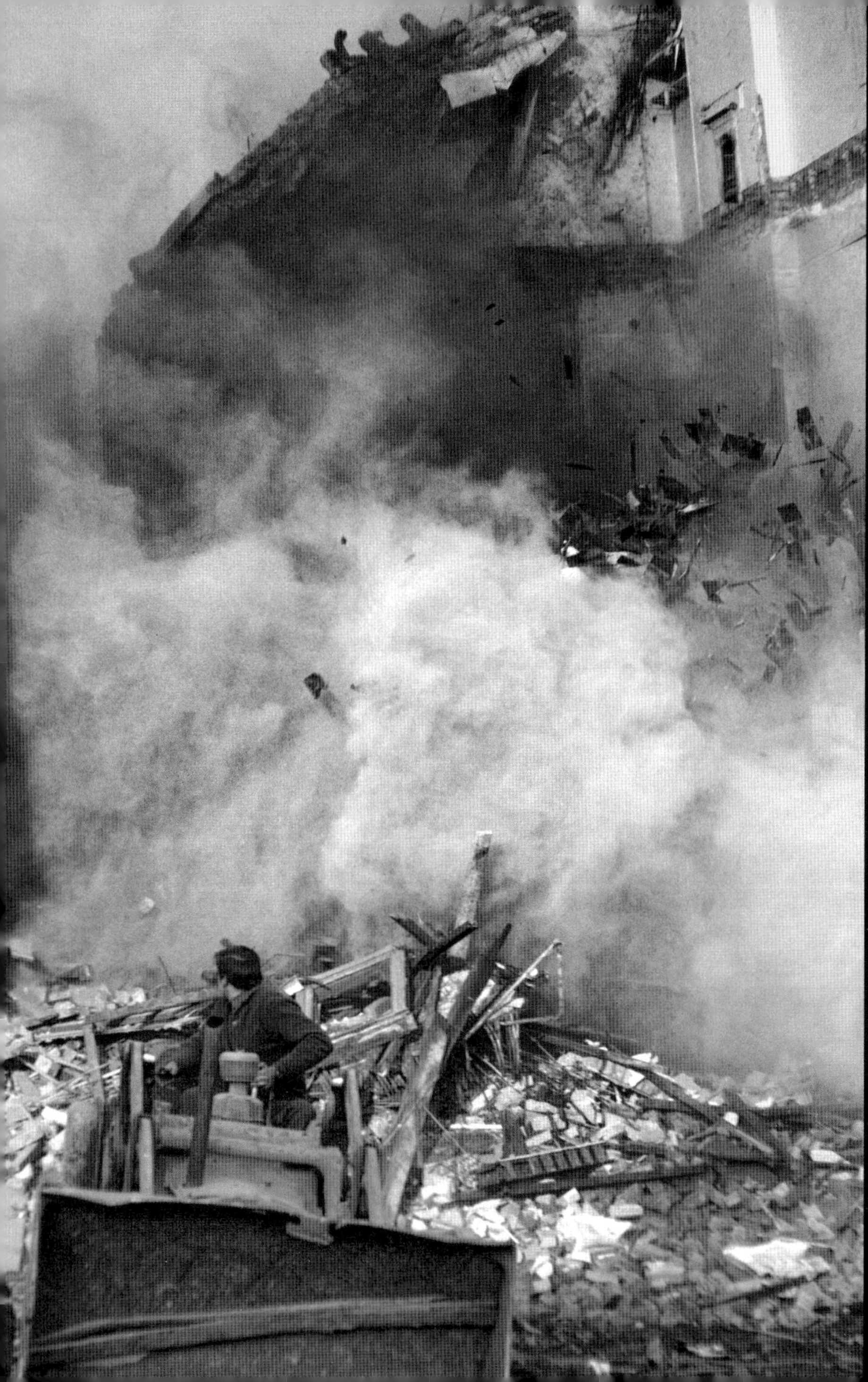

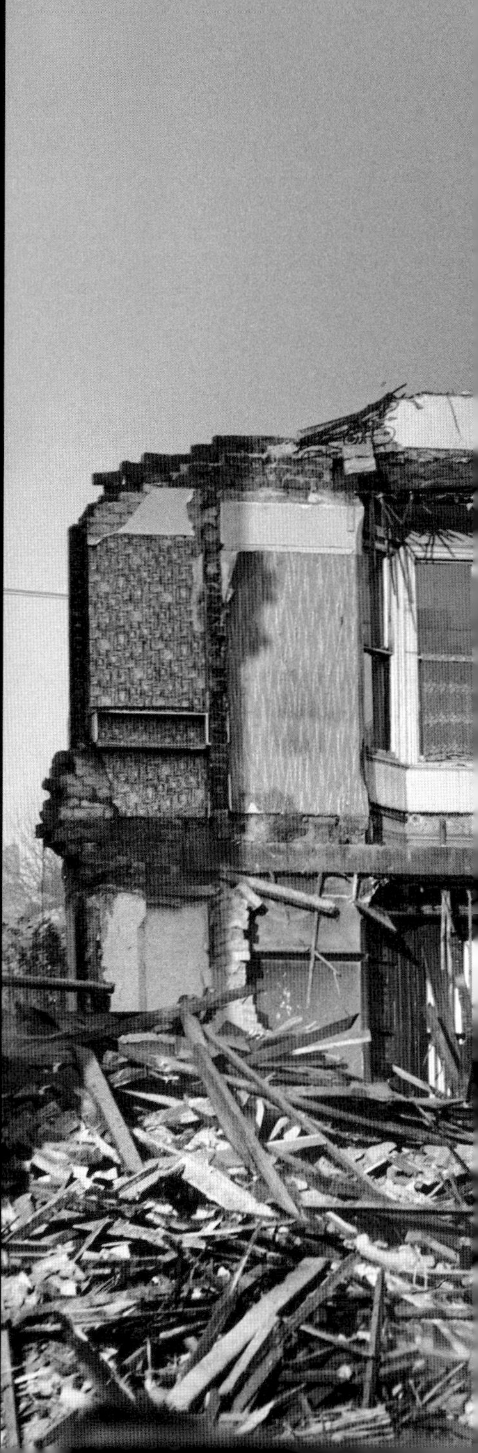

Bulldozers move in to demolish the houses

After the dust has settled the interiors of peoples former homes are exposed.

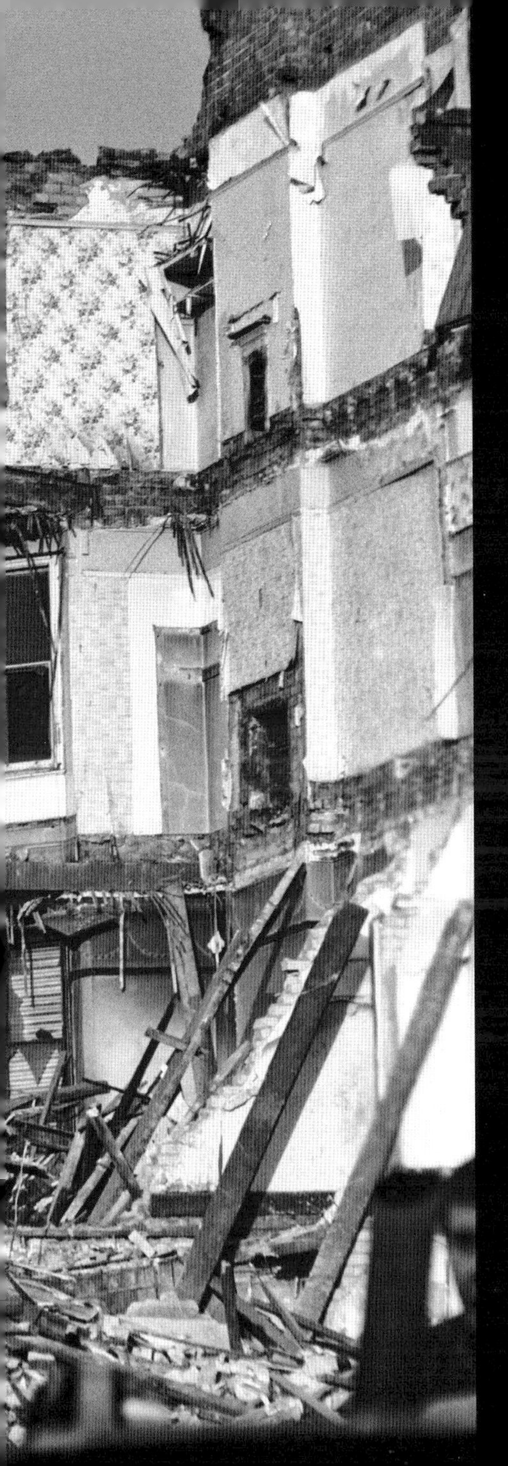

"Many, now,
would say the
soul flew out
with the brick
dust left by
the demolition
men."

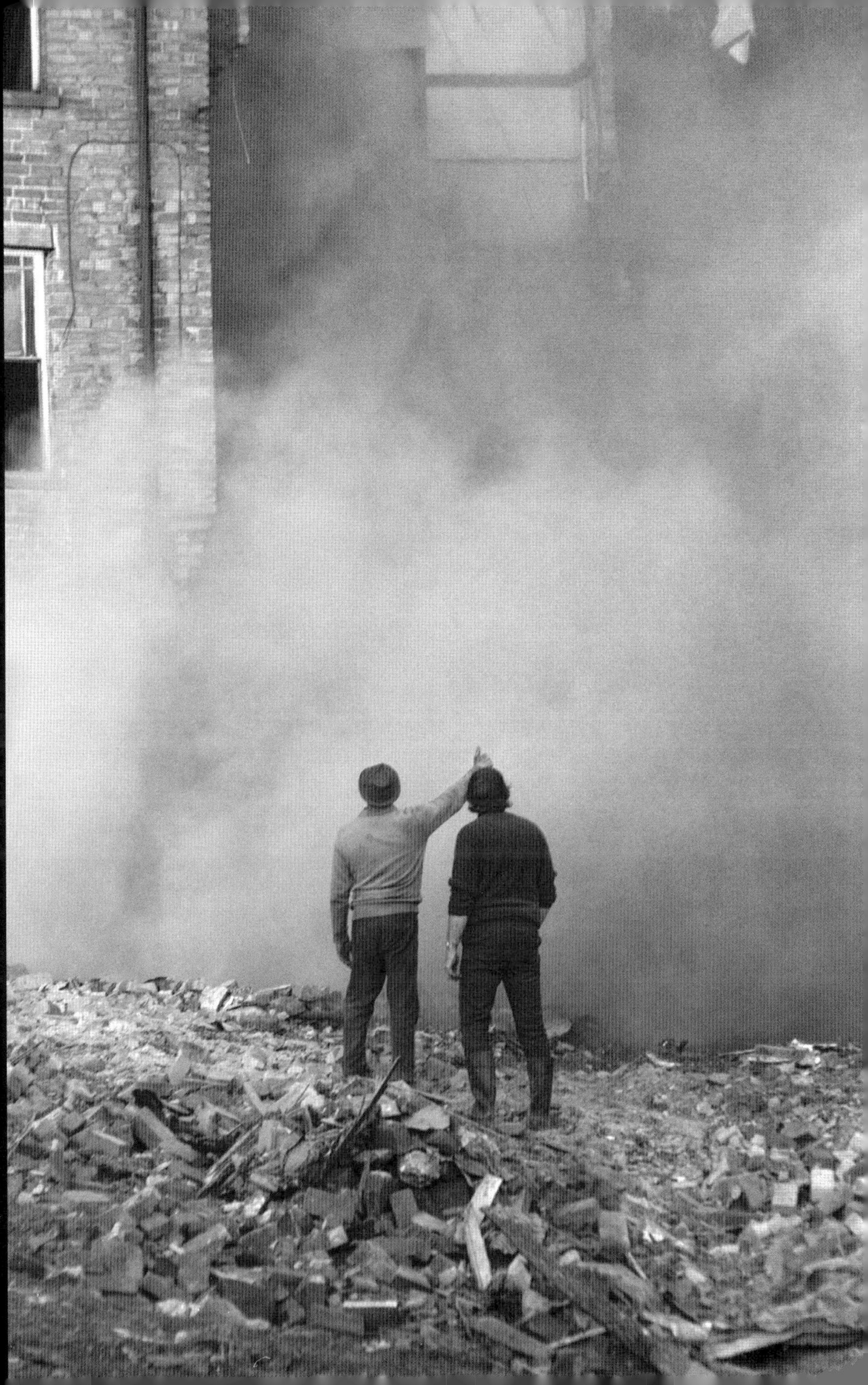

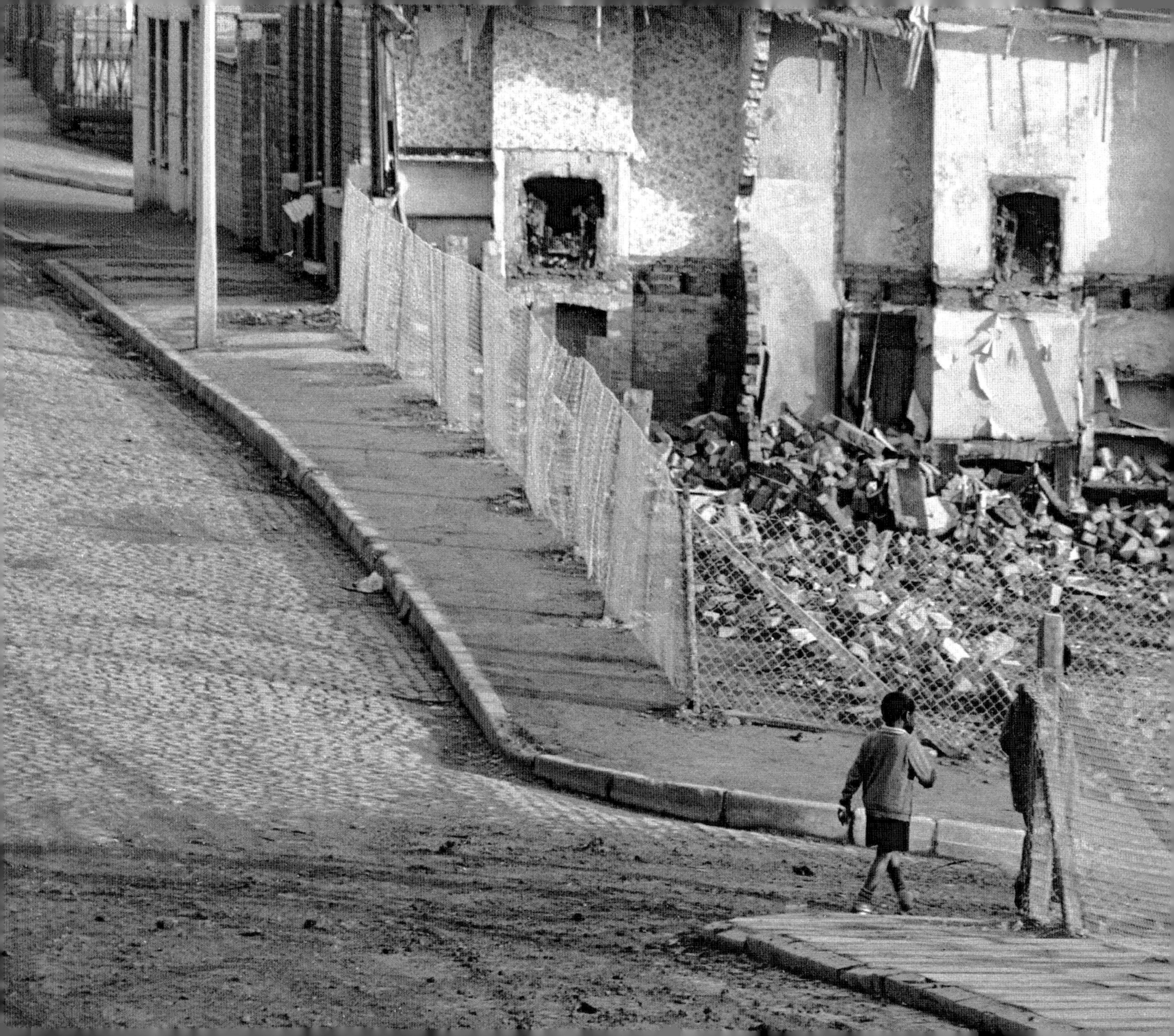

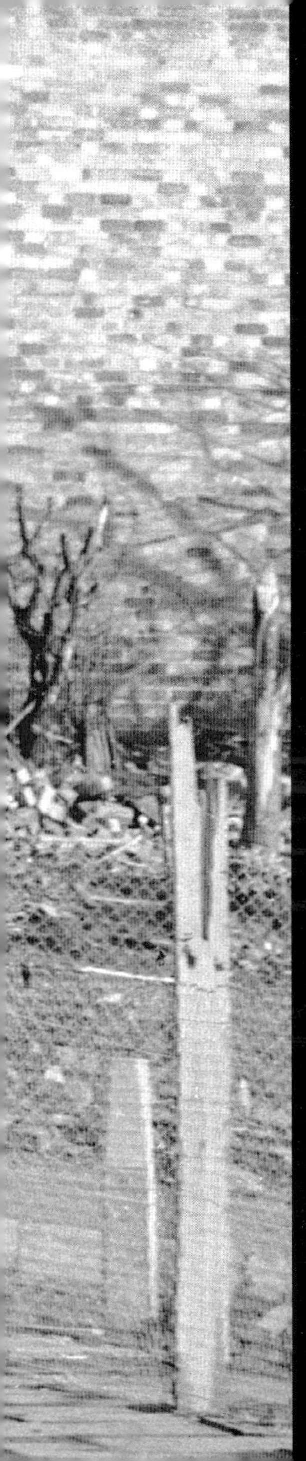

Left: Children walking along streets of part-demolished houses on their way to school

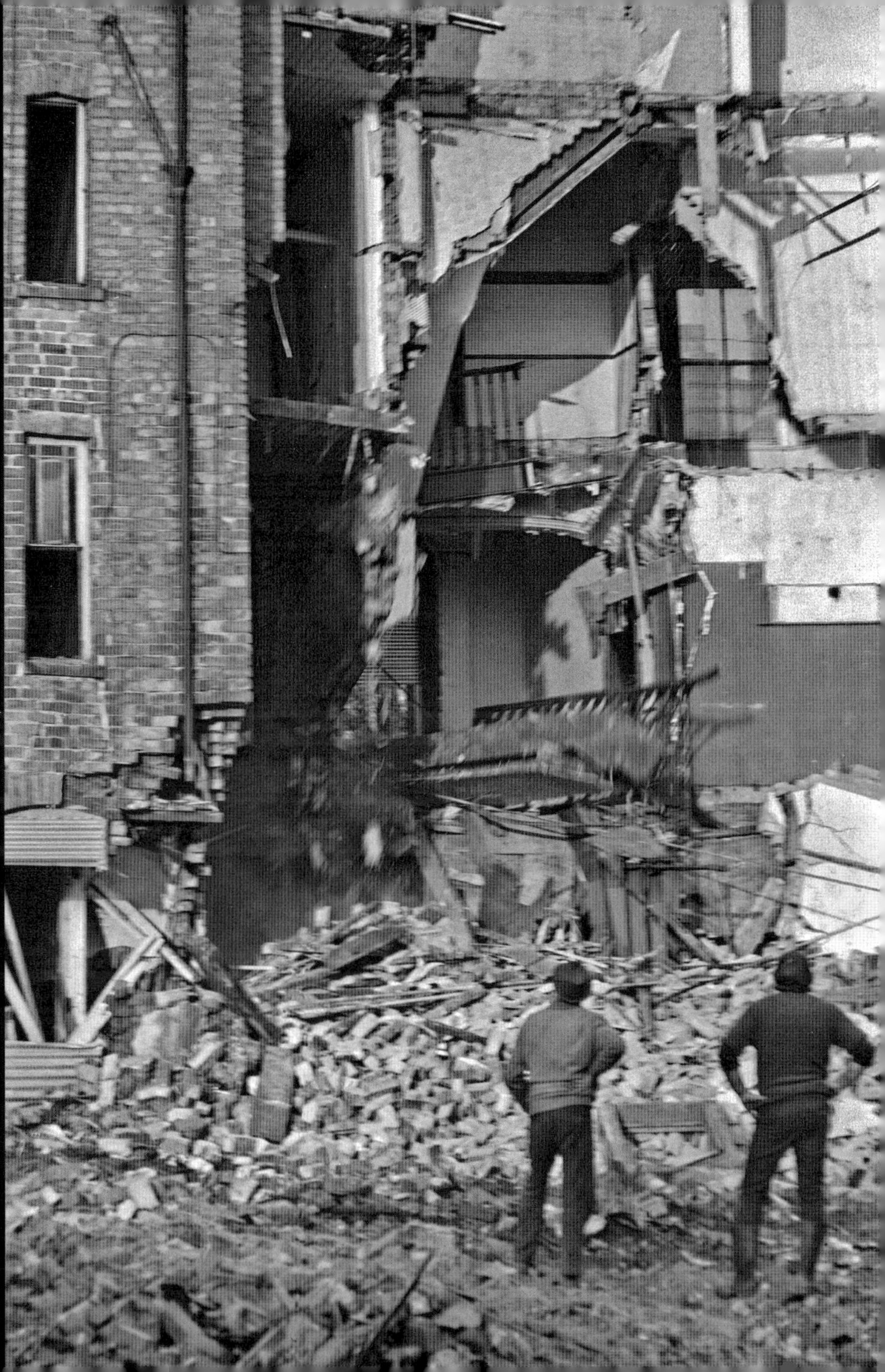

Right: Demolition contractors look on as a house is demolished

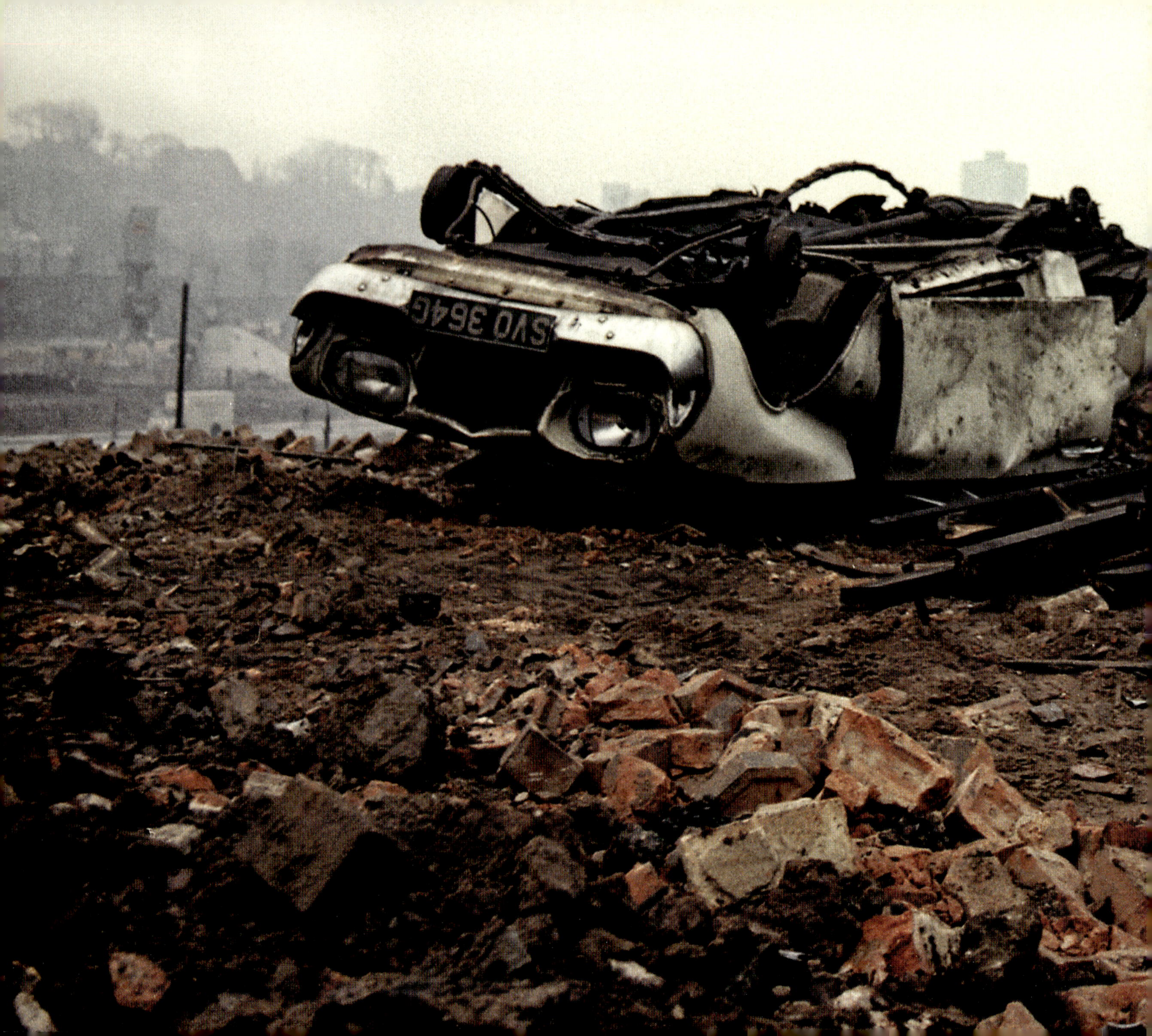
SVO 364G

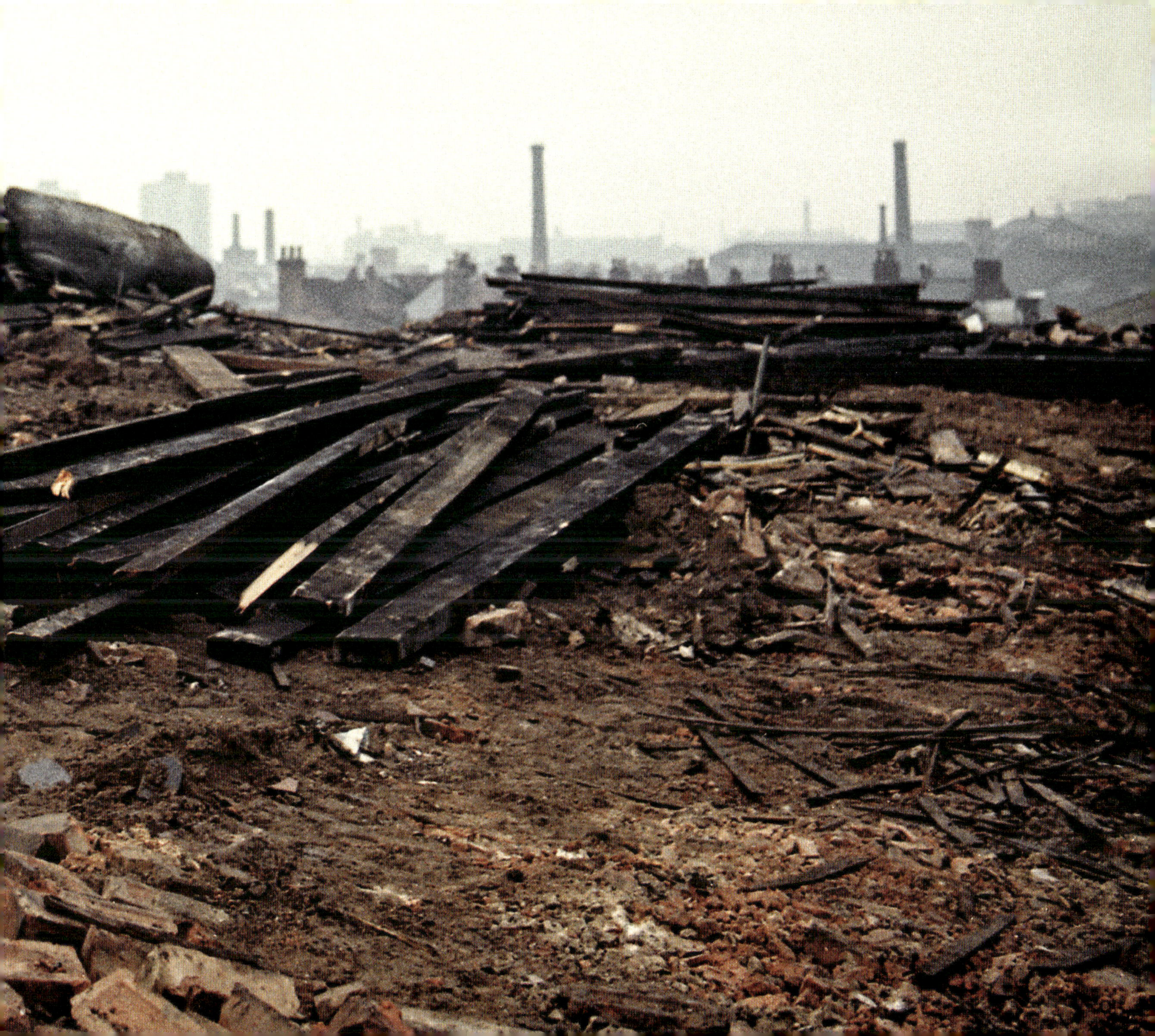

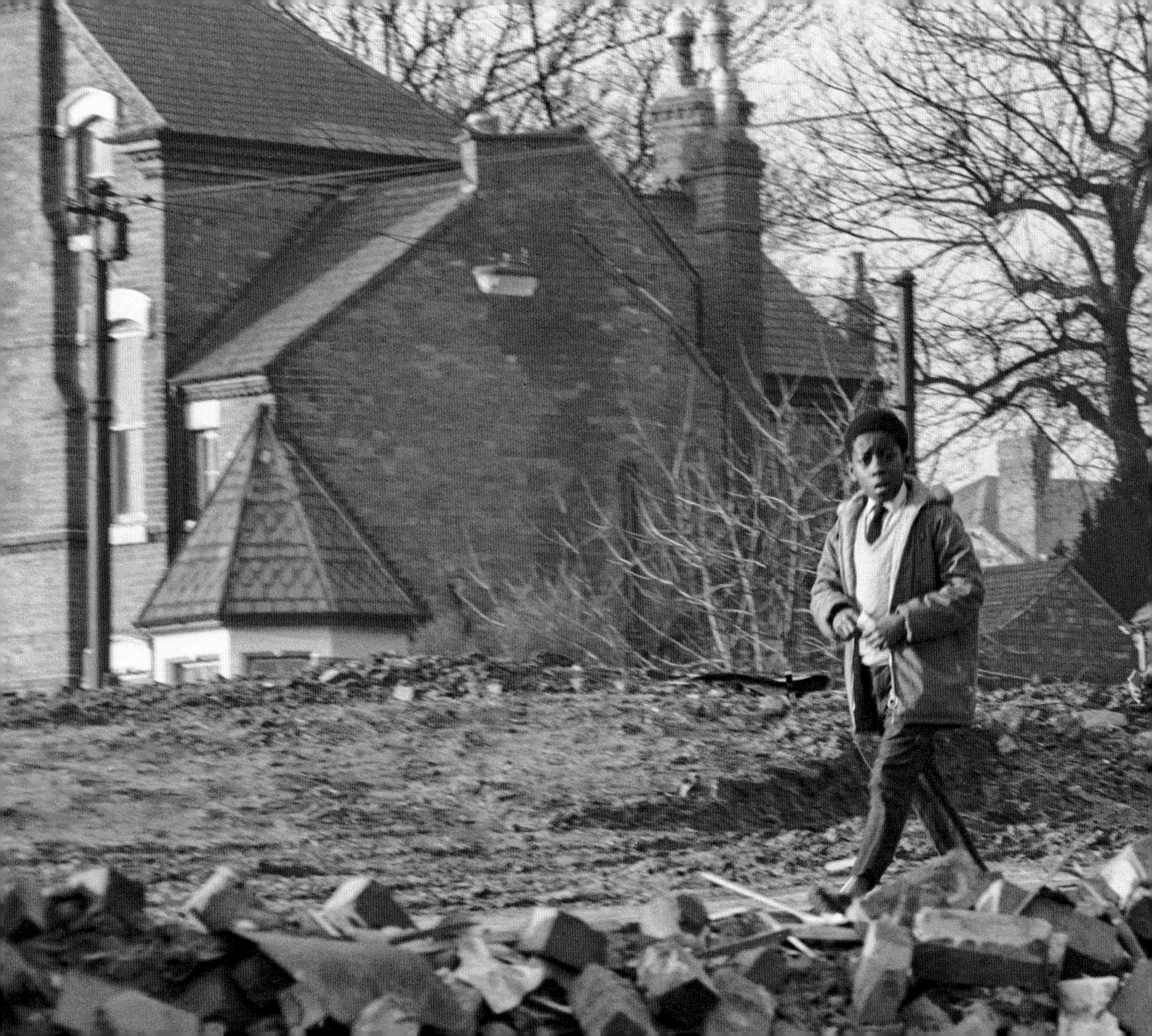

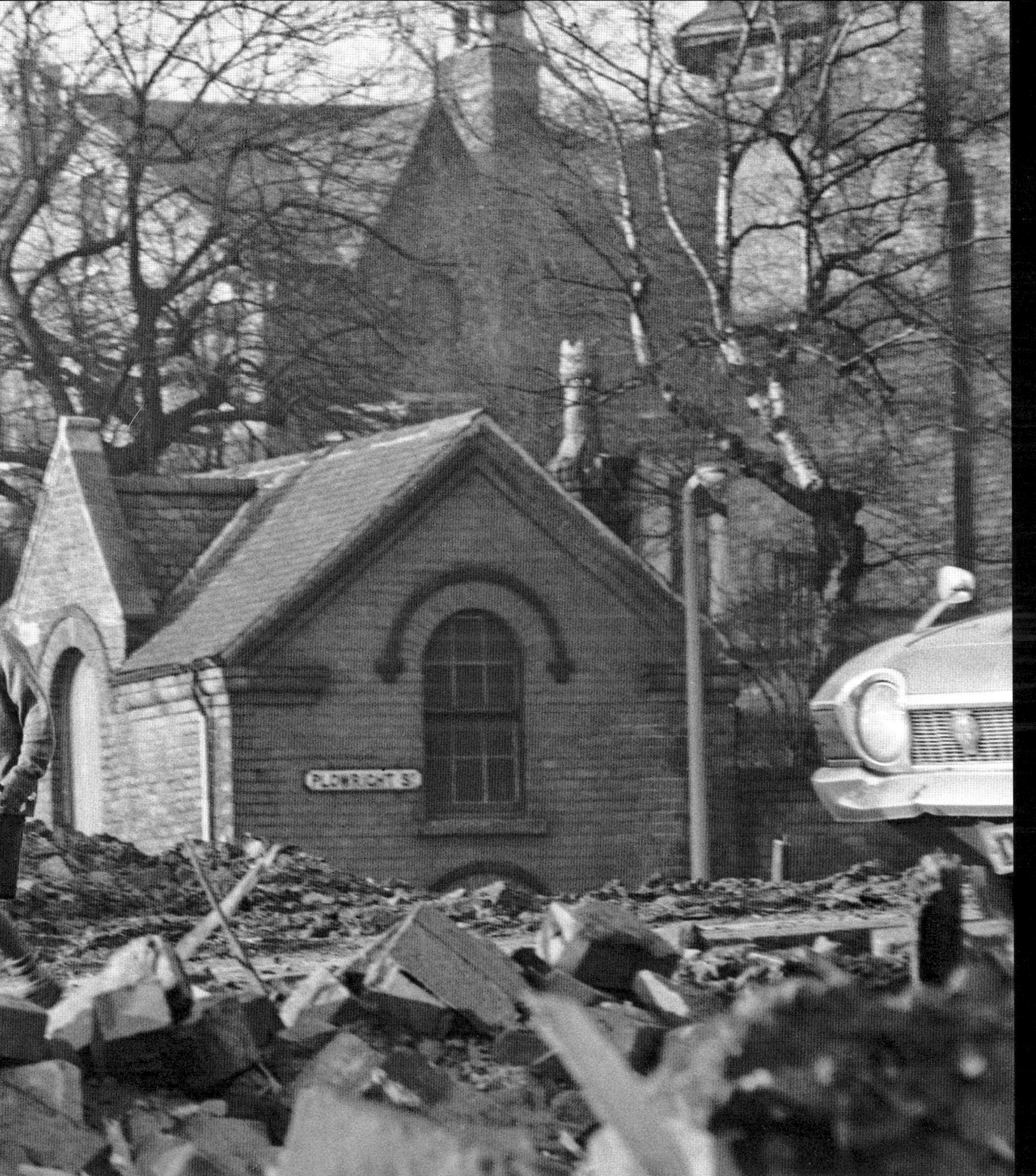

Manning Street at the junction with Woodborough Road

Schoolchildren making their way through the rubble on their journeys to and from school.

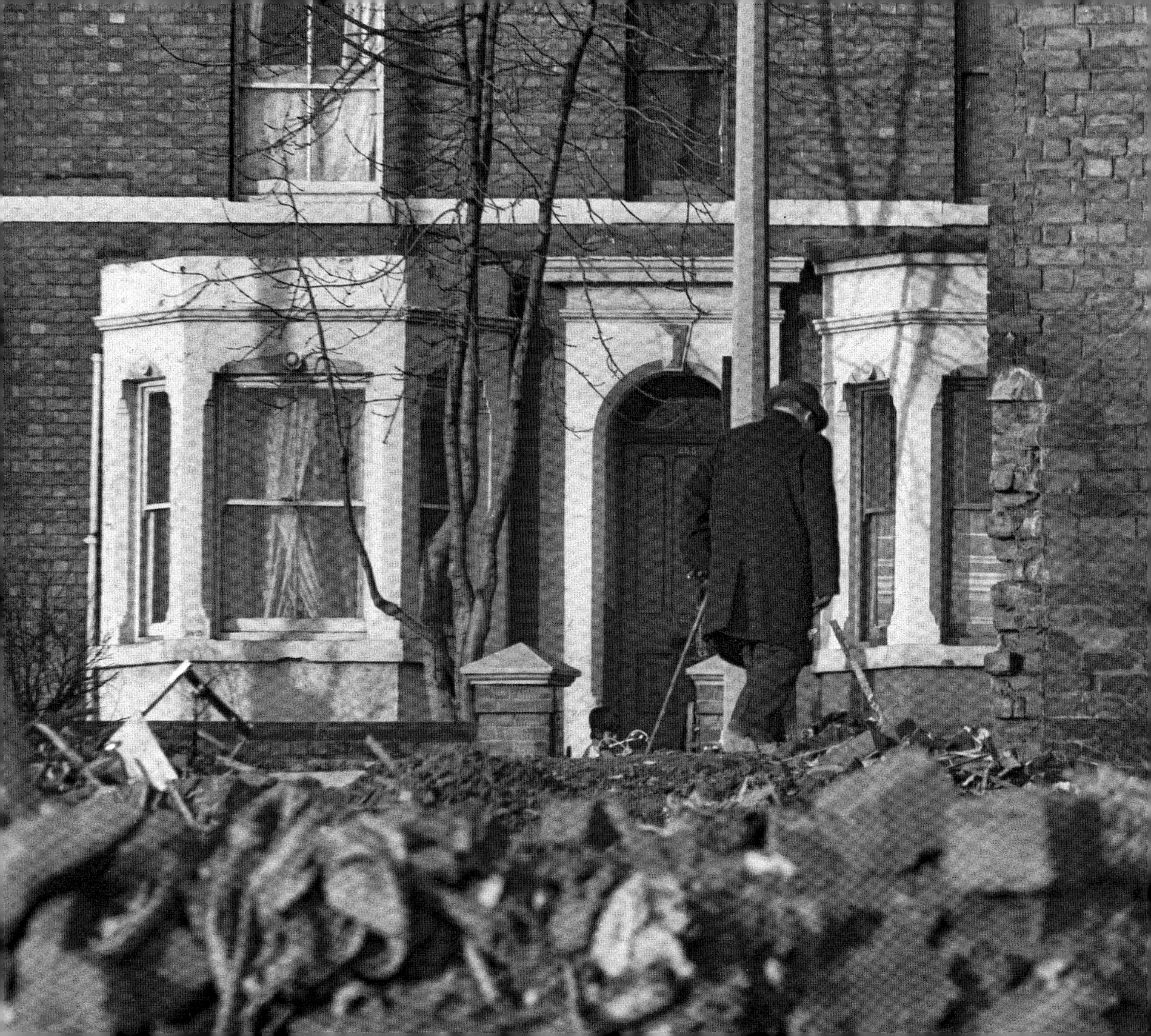

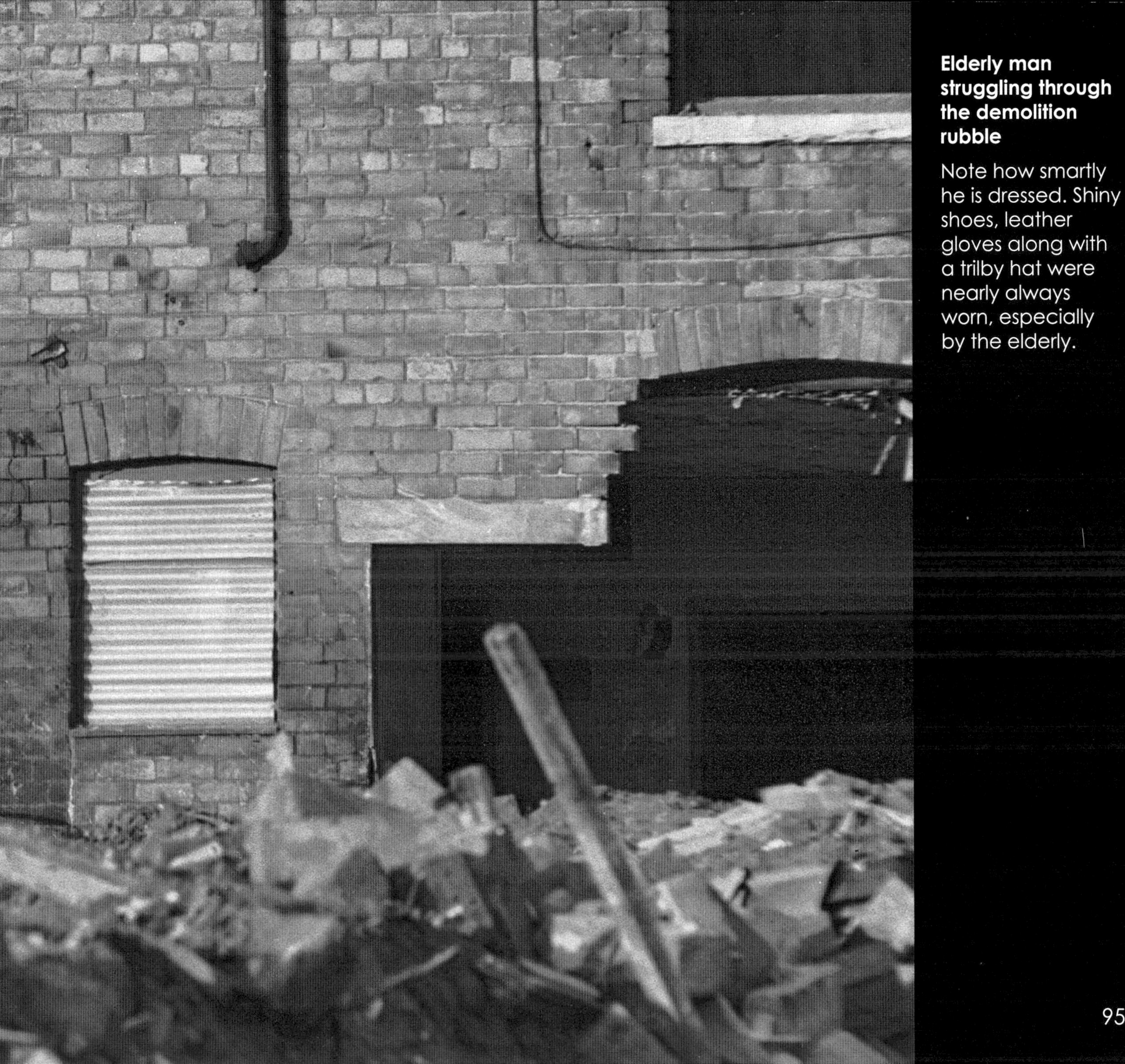

Elderly man struggling through the demolition rubble

Note how smartly he is dressed. Shiny shoes, leather gloves along with a trilby hat were nearly always worn, especially by the elderly.

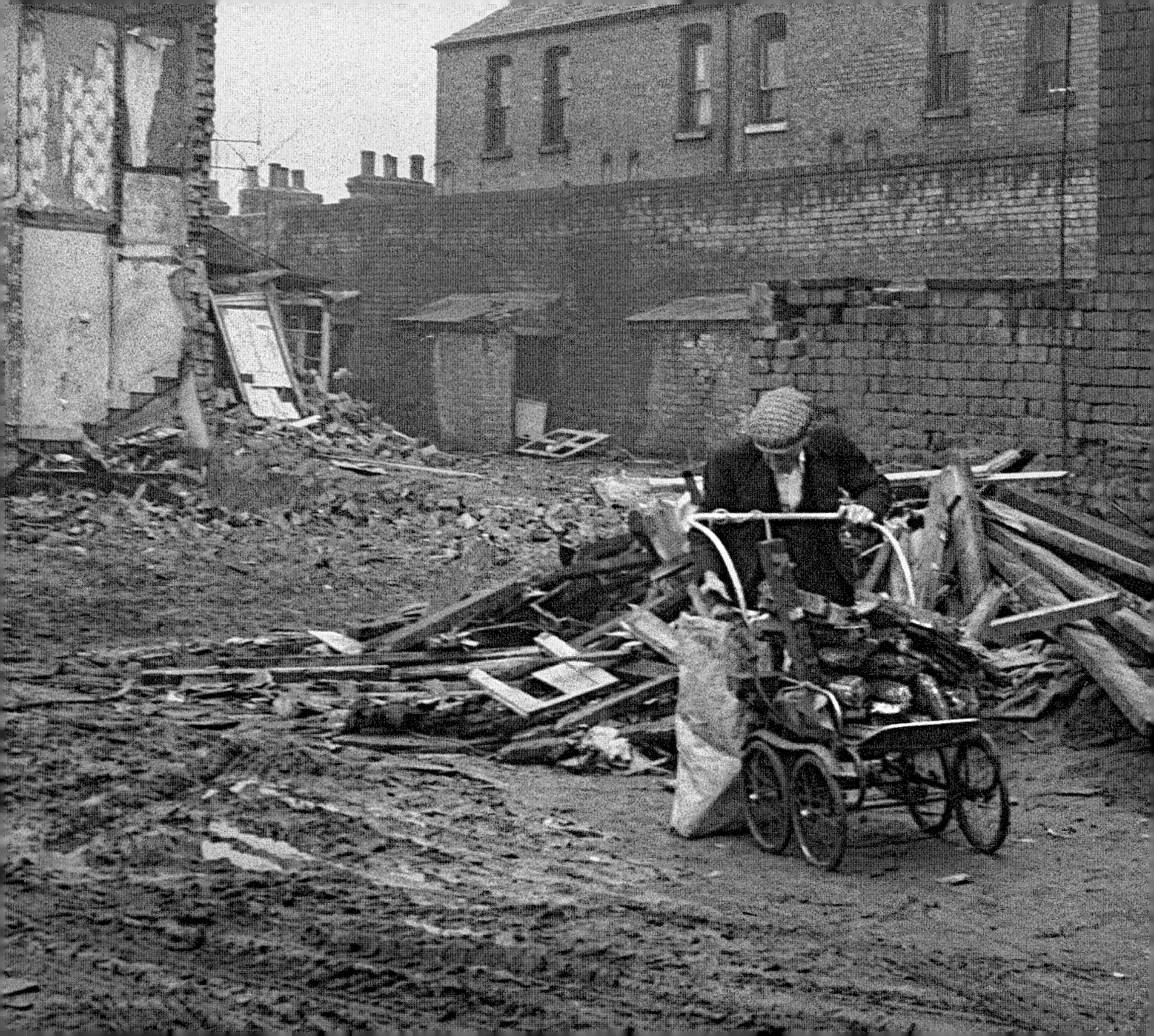

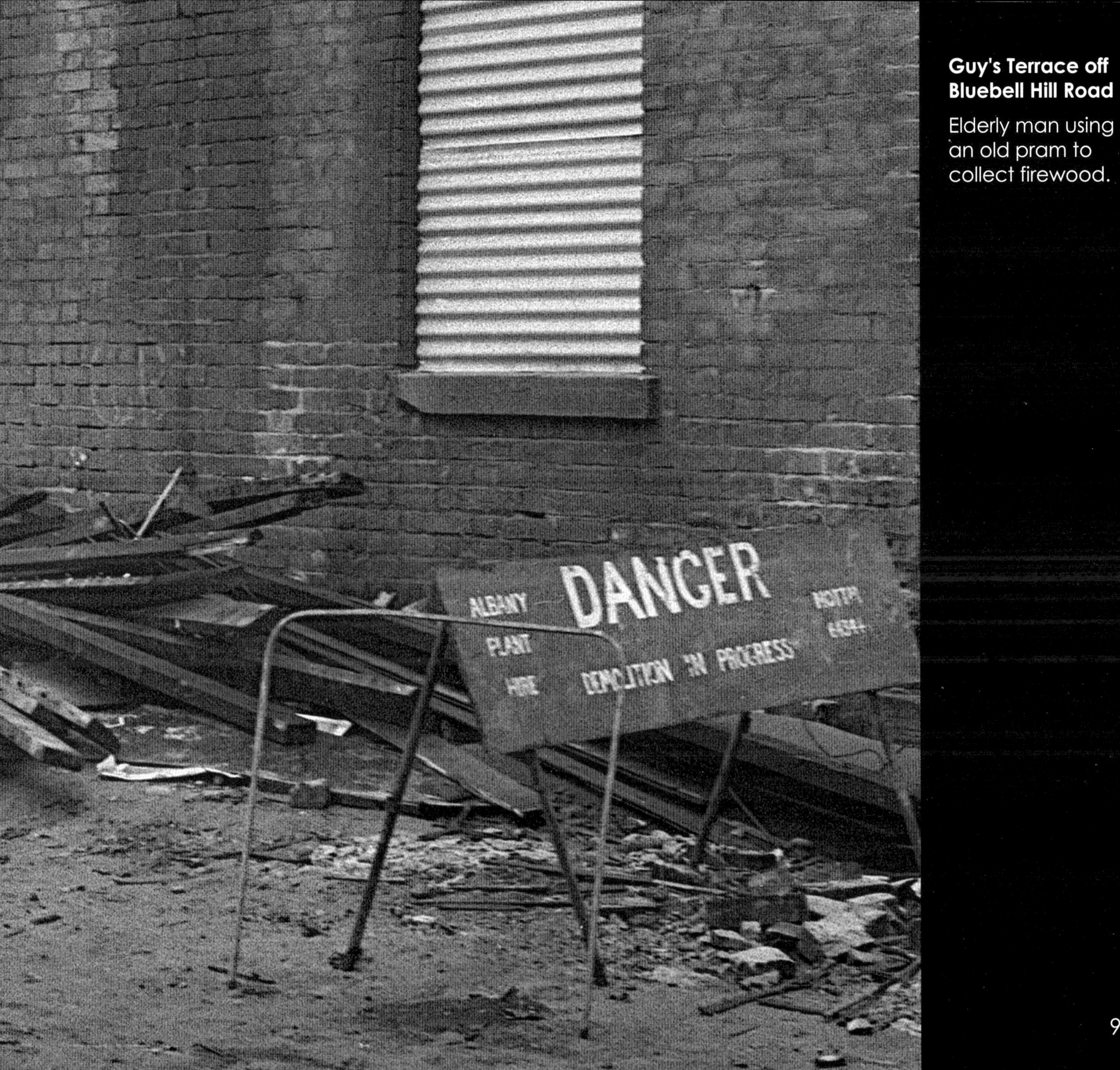

Guy's Terrace off Bluebell Hill Road

Elderly man using an old pram to collect firewood.

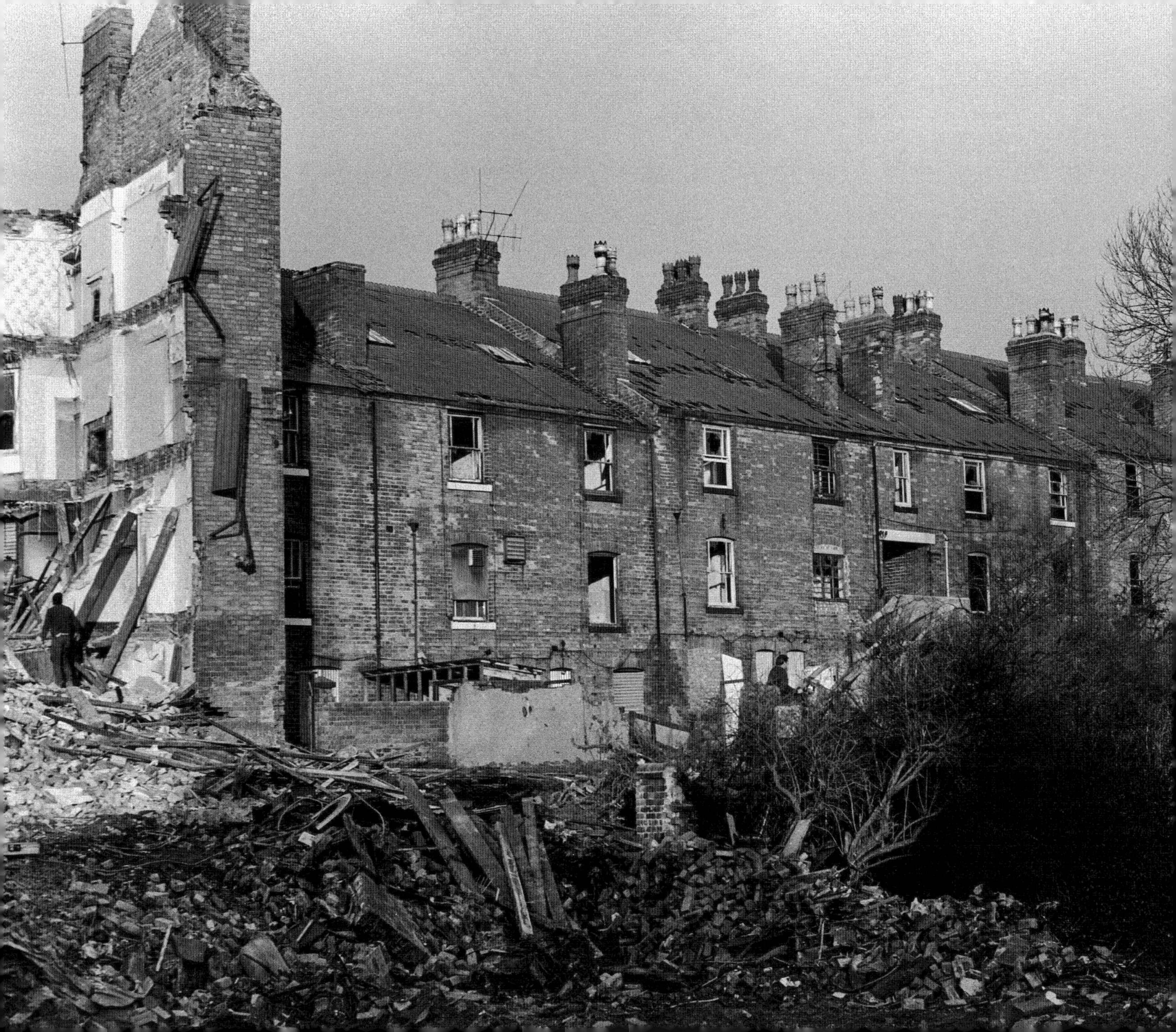

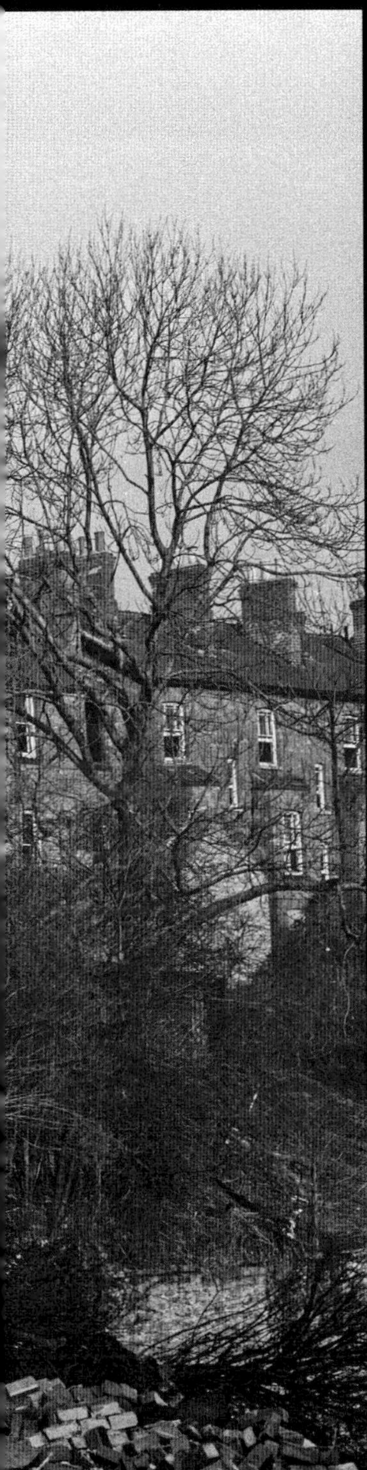

Rows of empty houses awaiting demolition and a street of part-demolished houses

"It's a good idea to remember the past. It was a great place to live, it was very friendly and had good neighbours. It was a community, everybody was there for everybody. If you wanted anything you could ask a neighbour."

Beryl Morris

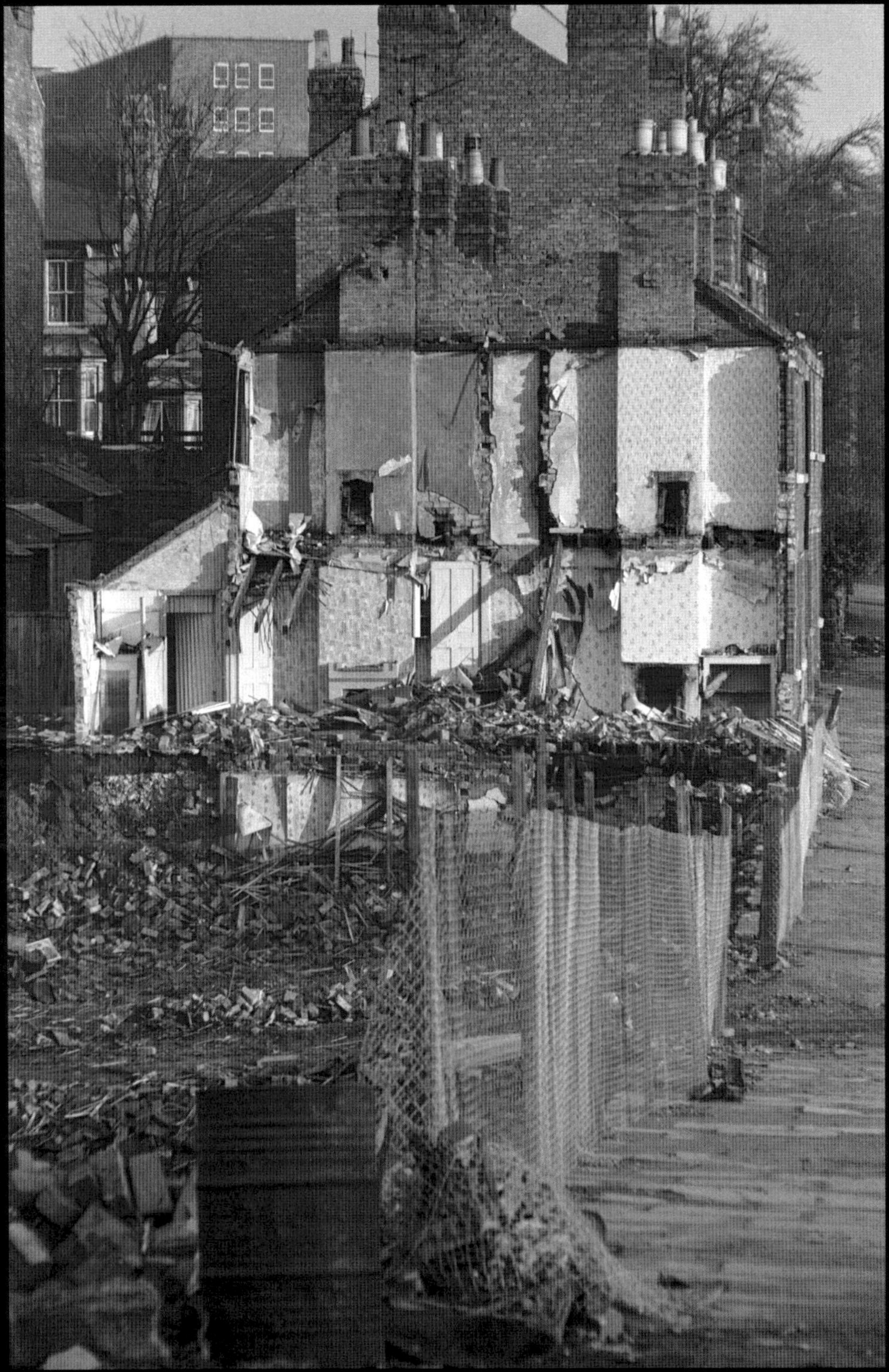

Protest and Travellers

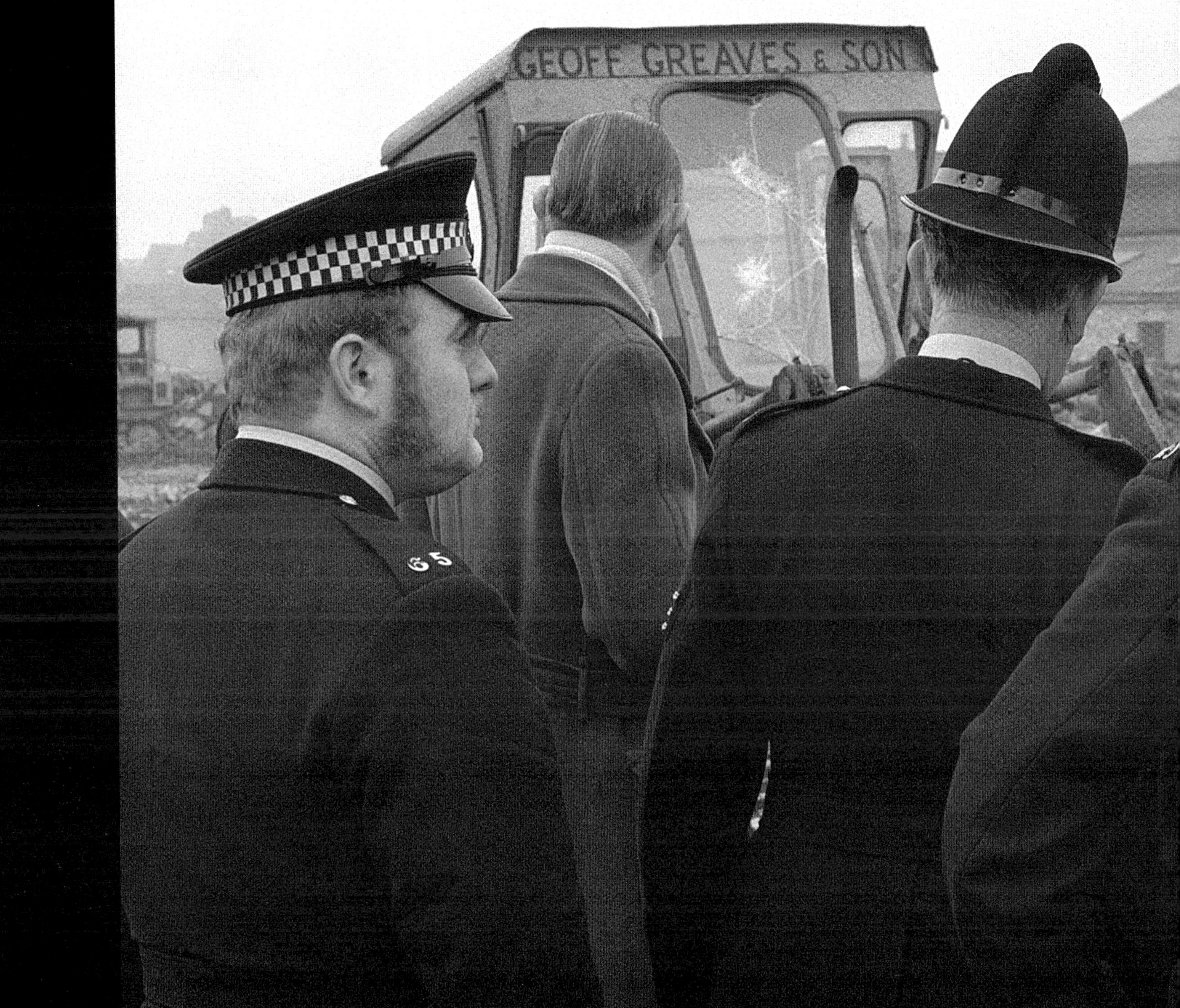

GEOFF GREAVES & SON

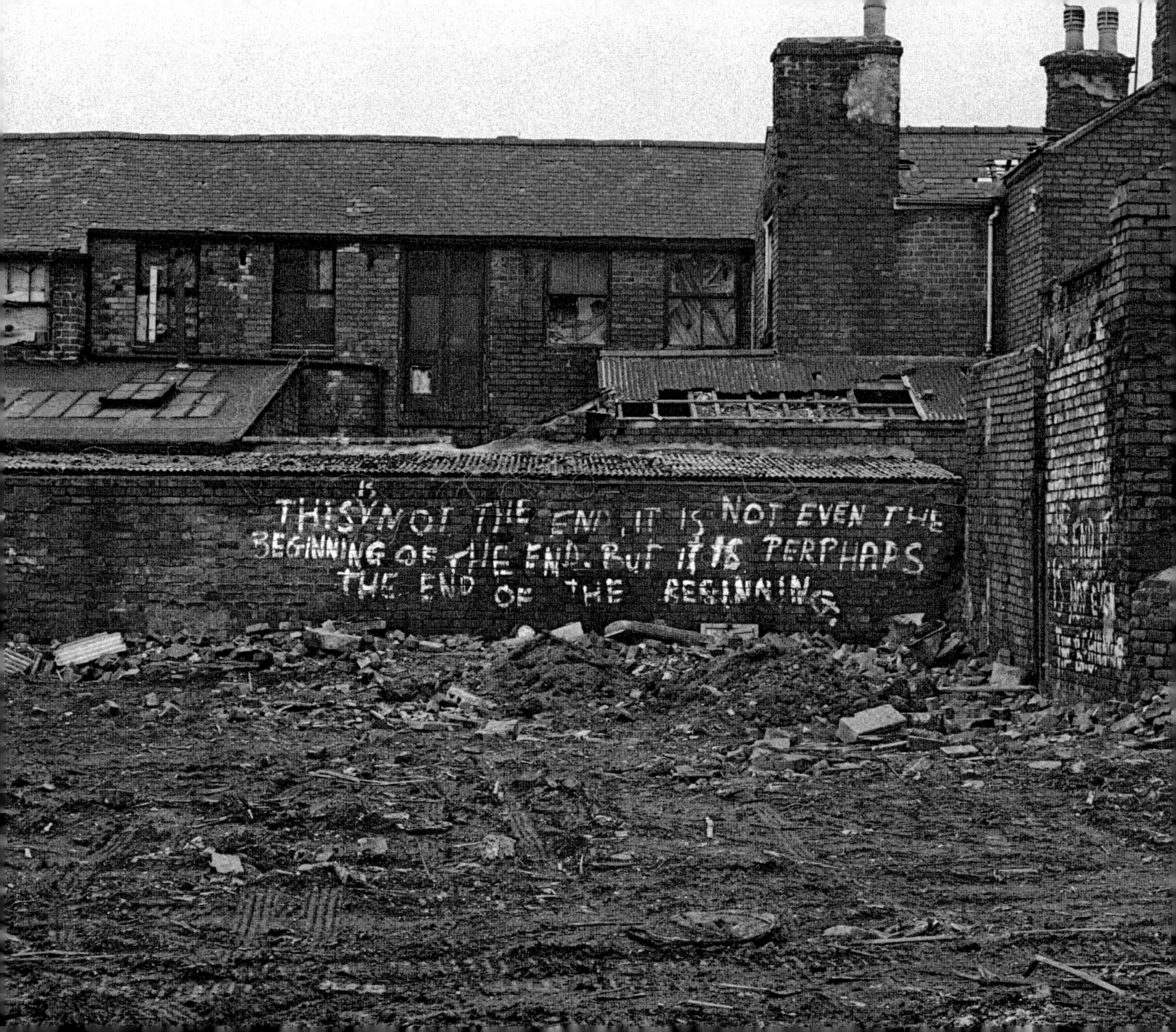
THIS IS NOT THE END, IT IS NOT EVEN THE
BEGINNING OF THE END. BUT IT IS PERPHAPS
THE END OF THE BEGINNING.

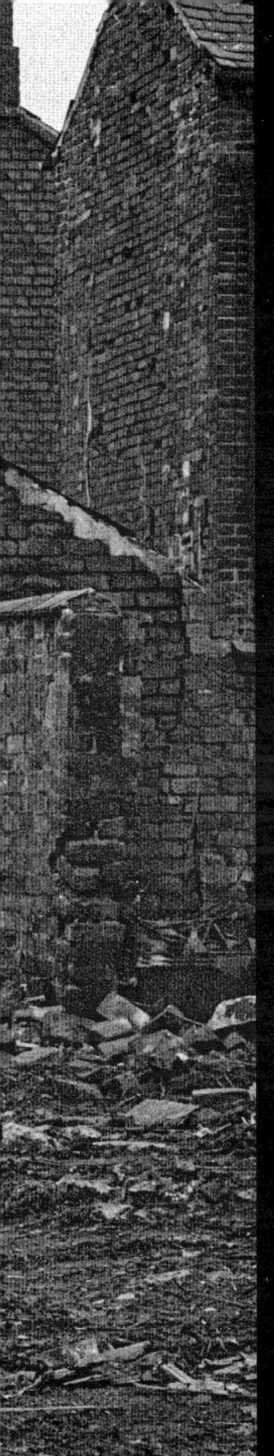

Left: Famous Churchillian saying chalked on a wall

"This is not the end, it is not even the beginning of the end. But it is perhaps the end of the beginning."

This was a reference to a turning point in the Second World War. To many in St Ann's the demolition and rehousing was a turning point in their lives after living in what was classed as 'slums'.

Right: Protest took many forms

People sometimes vented their anger on the demolition companies and their machinery. This bulldozer with its smashed windscreen is an example of such anger. Residents resented the council's wholesale approach of knocking down houses that would have lasted for generations to come.

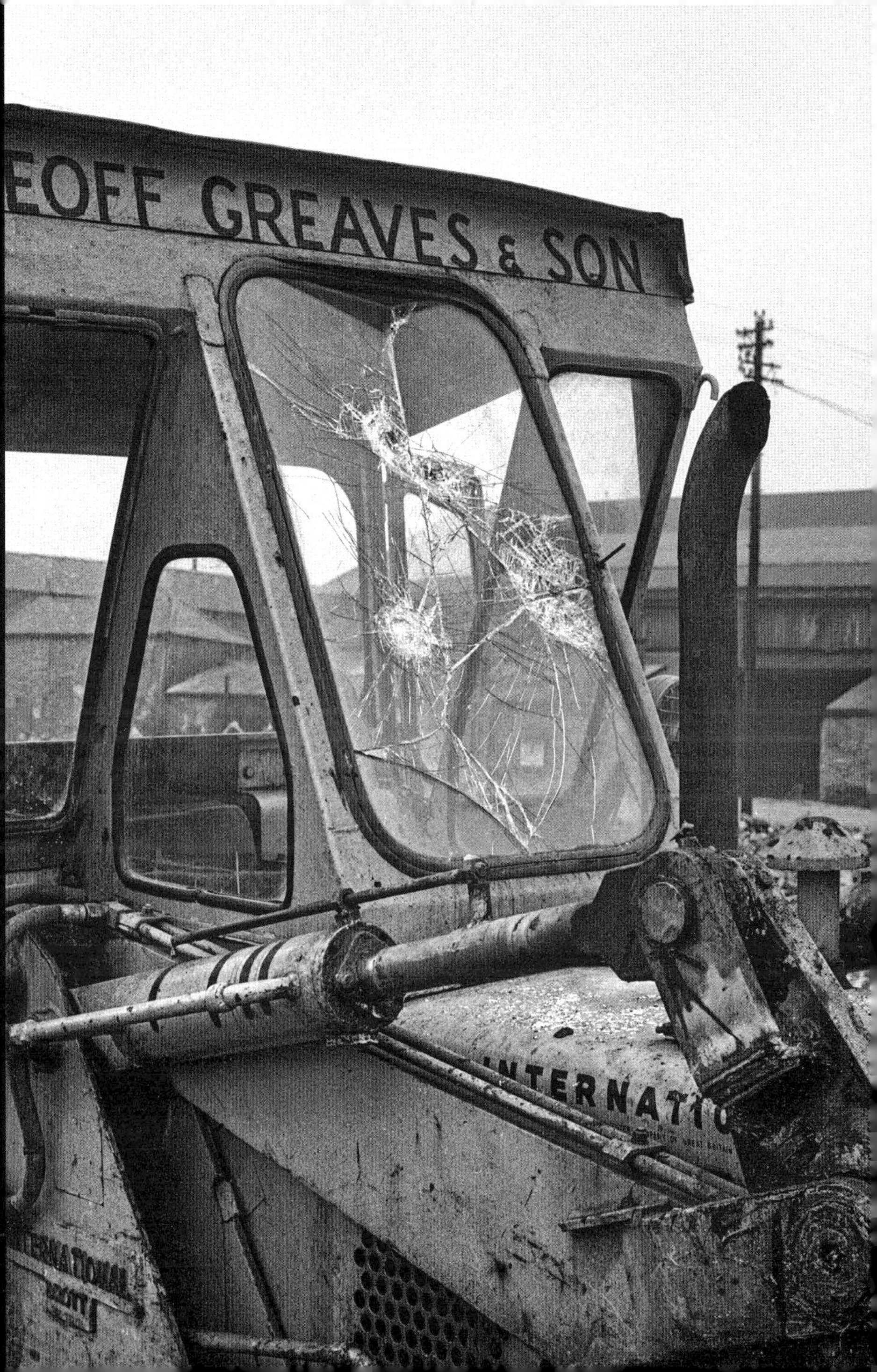

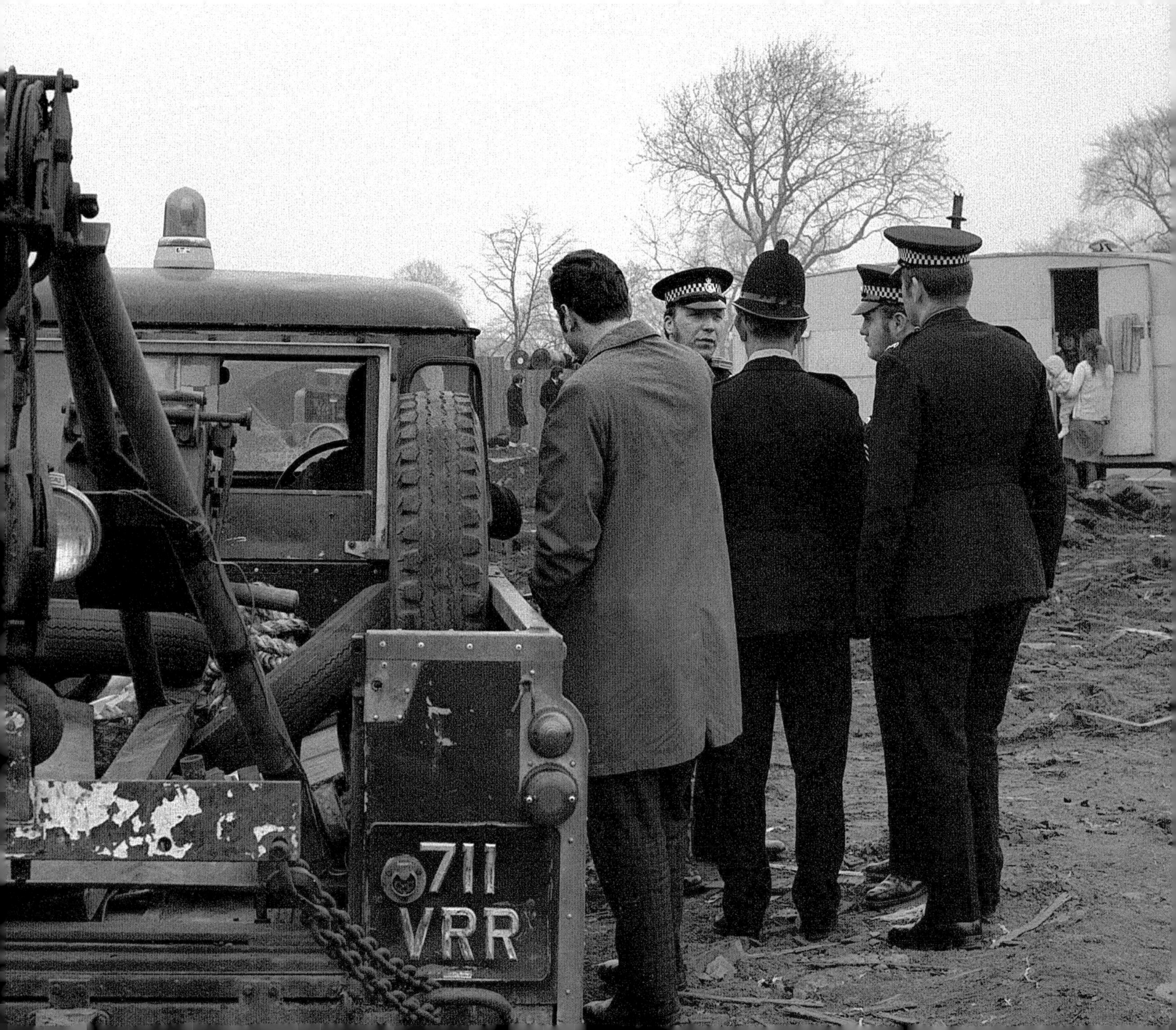
711
VRR

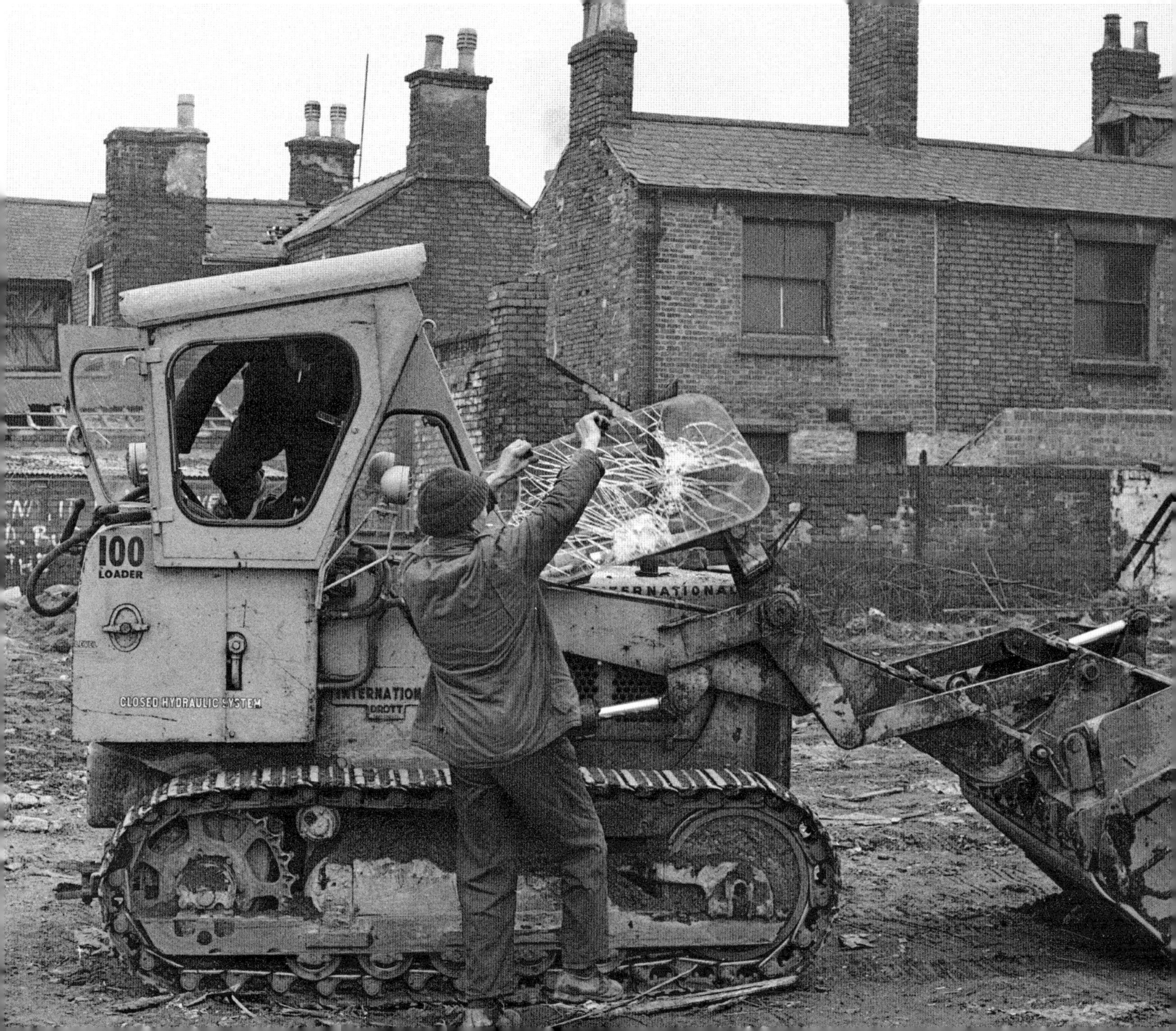

100
LOADER
CLOSED HYDRAULIC SYSTEM
INTERNATIONAL
DROTT
INTERNATIONAL

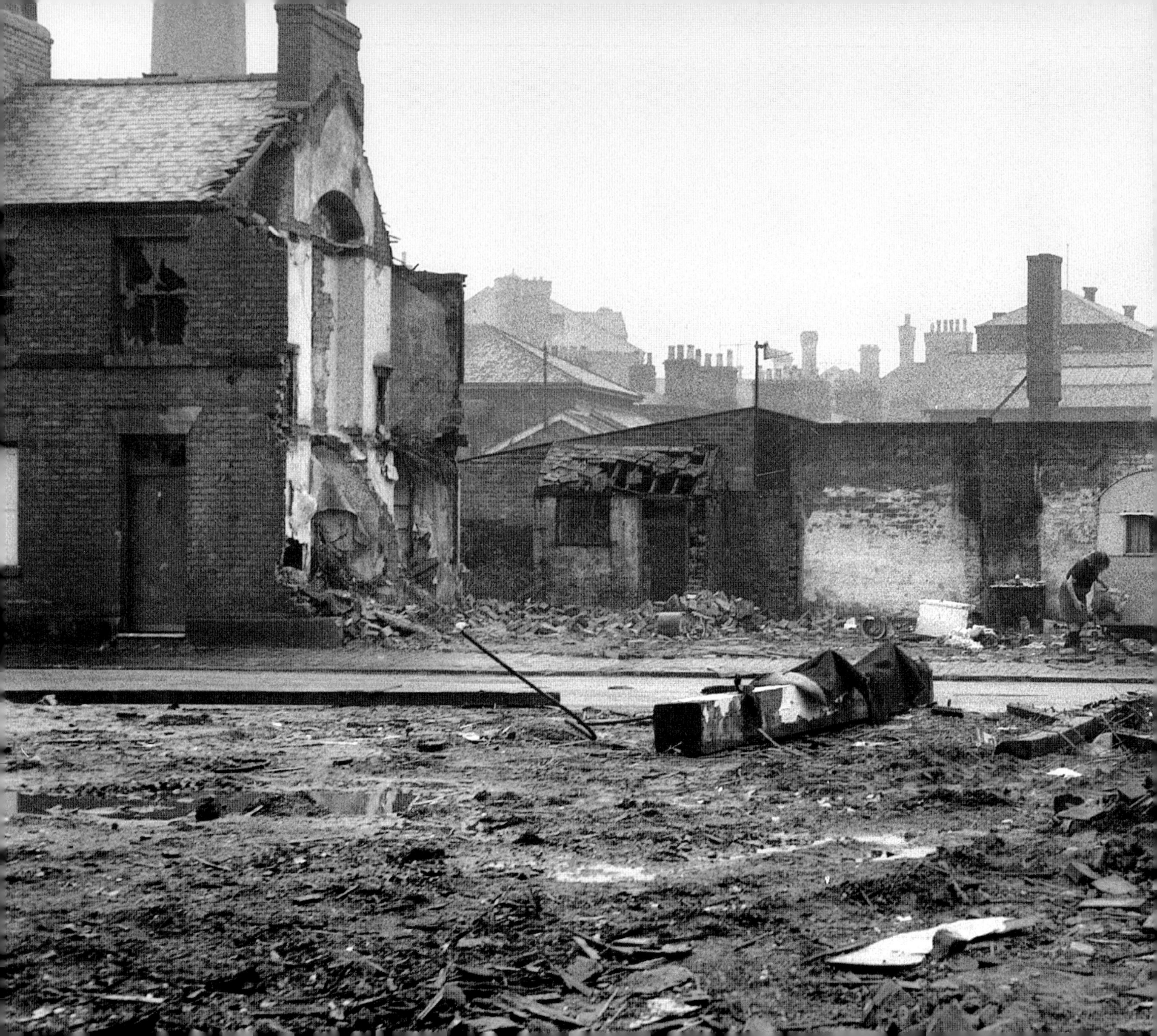

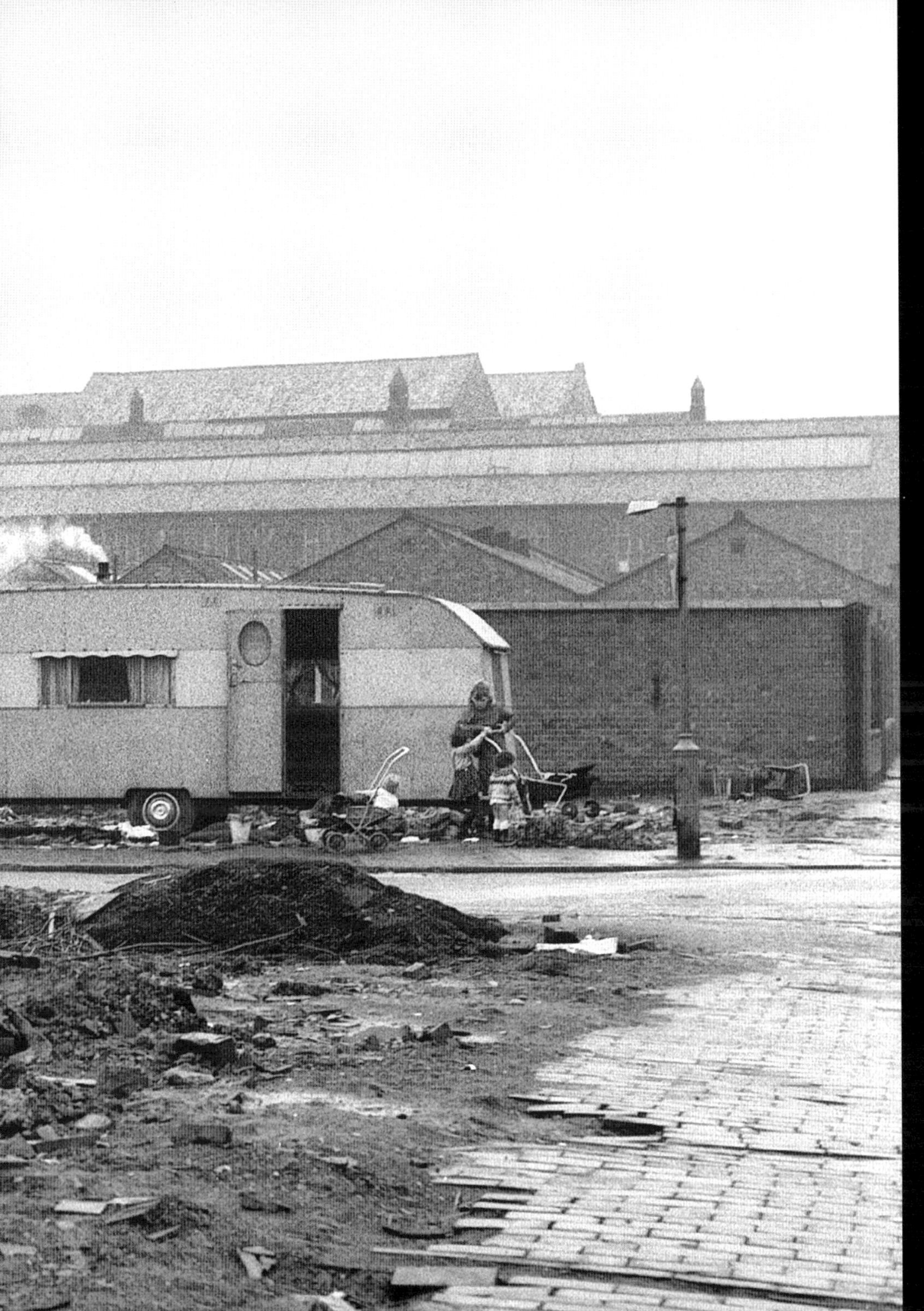

When the bulldozers moved out, the Travellers moved in

Travellers took advantage of the empty land and any scrap they could salvage. Their caravans had wood-burning stoves so they made good use of the plentiful supply of firewood from the demolished buildings.

They were constantly moved on by the police, only to settle on other areas of wasteland.

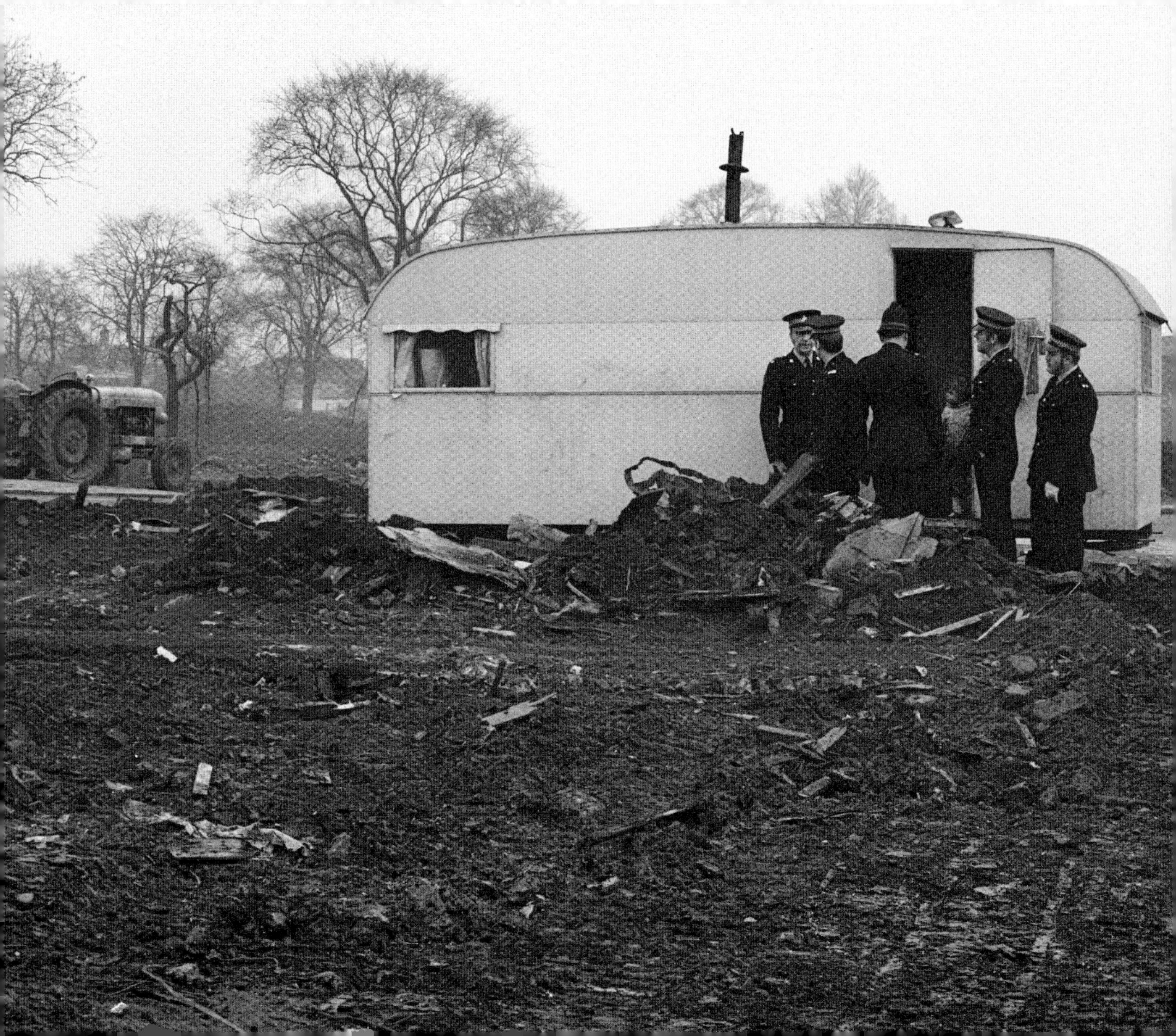

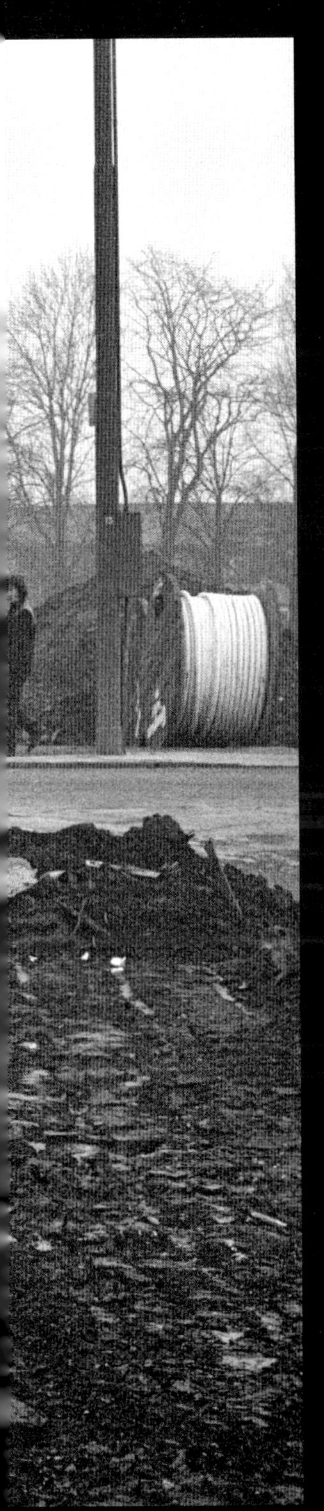

Police were frequently called to investigate cases of criminal damage

Travellers were often blamed, either rightly or wrongly, and made to move on.

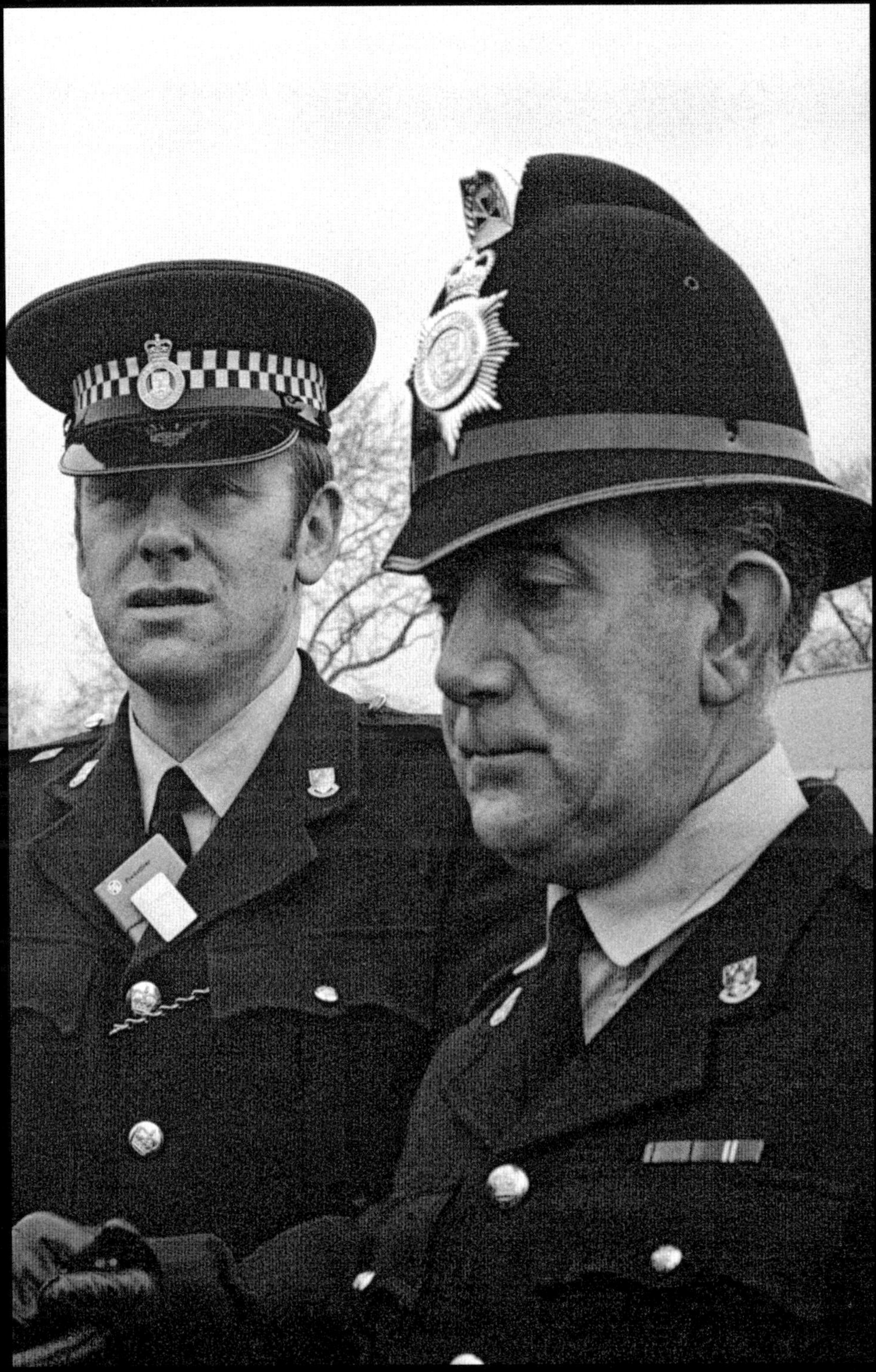

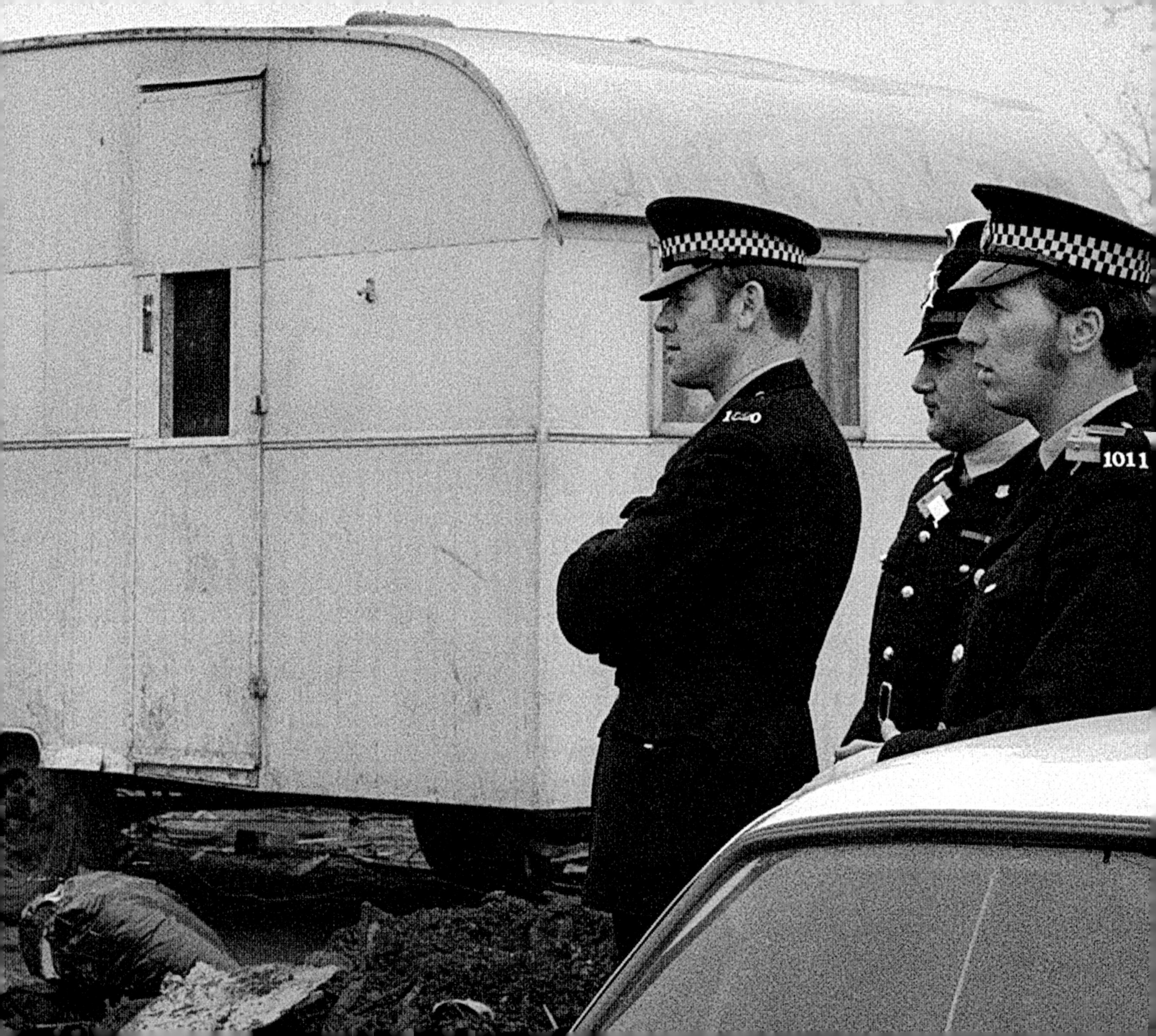

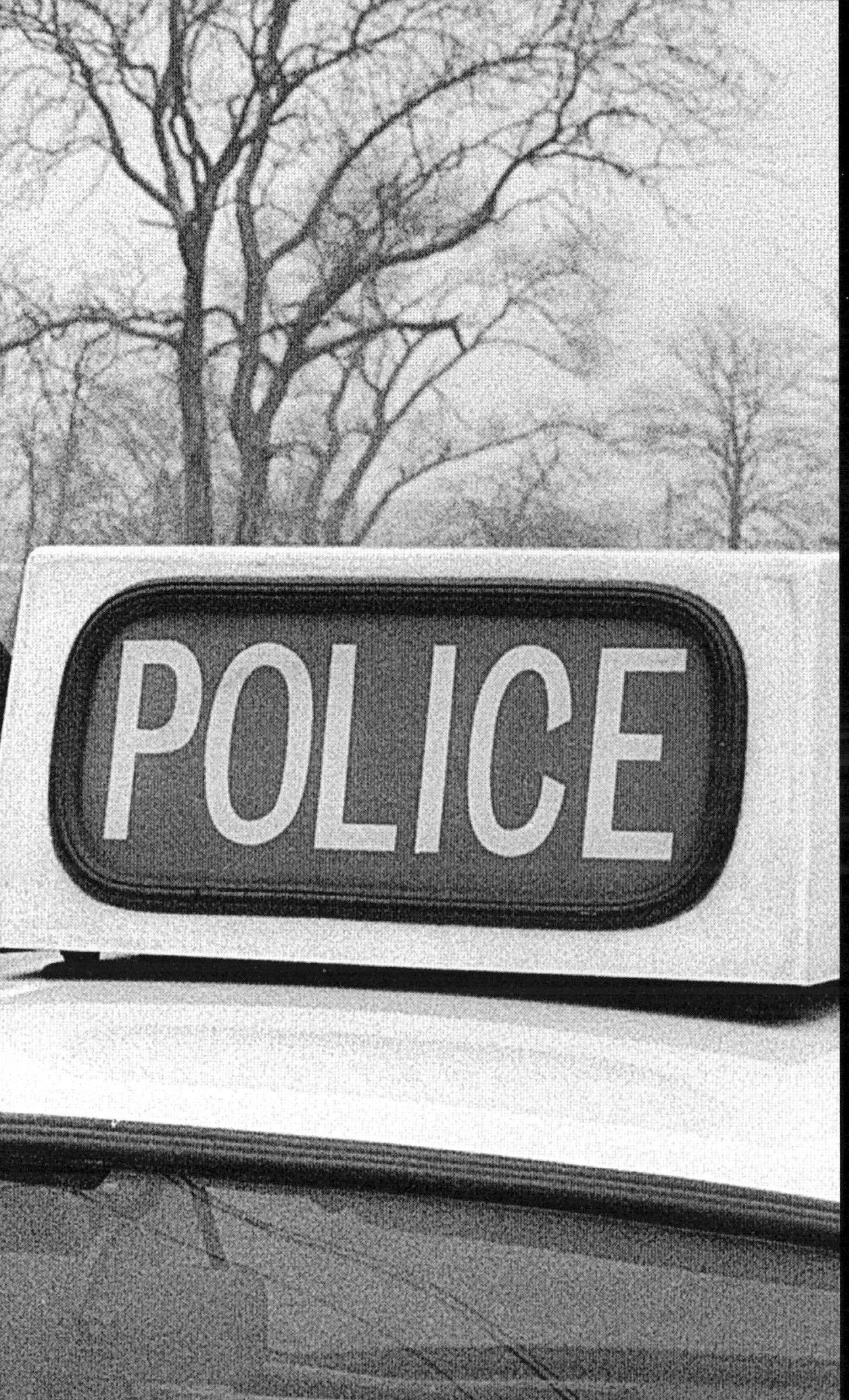

The police visit another Traveller family

There was no shortage of police manpower back in the 1970s.

"Can you remember the proper policemen? We on St Ann's respected our policemen. I crossed the road at the sight of the police, always in twos, even if I did nothing wrong: always this respect. Can you remember them in shop doorways at night with blacked out badges? Not easy to see. I remember walking to the baths with Huntingdon Street School and passing the police box at the bottom of St Ann's and waving to Sergeant Douglas, whose son was in our class."

Richard Greenhaigh

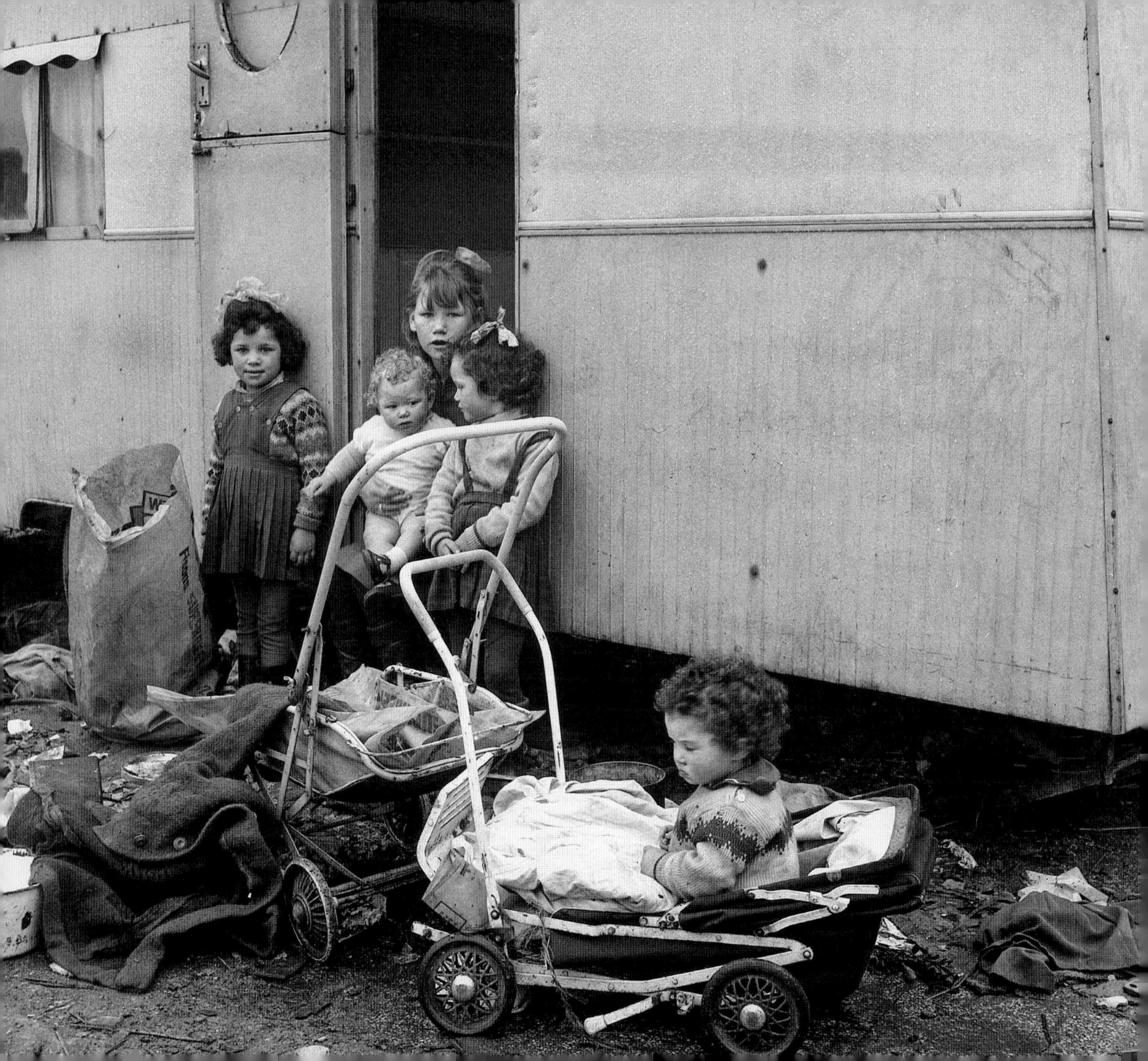

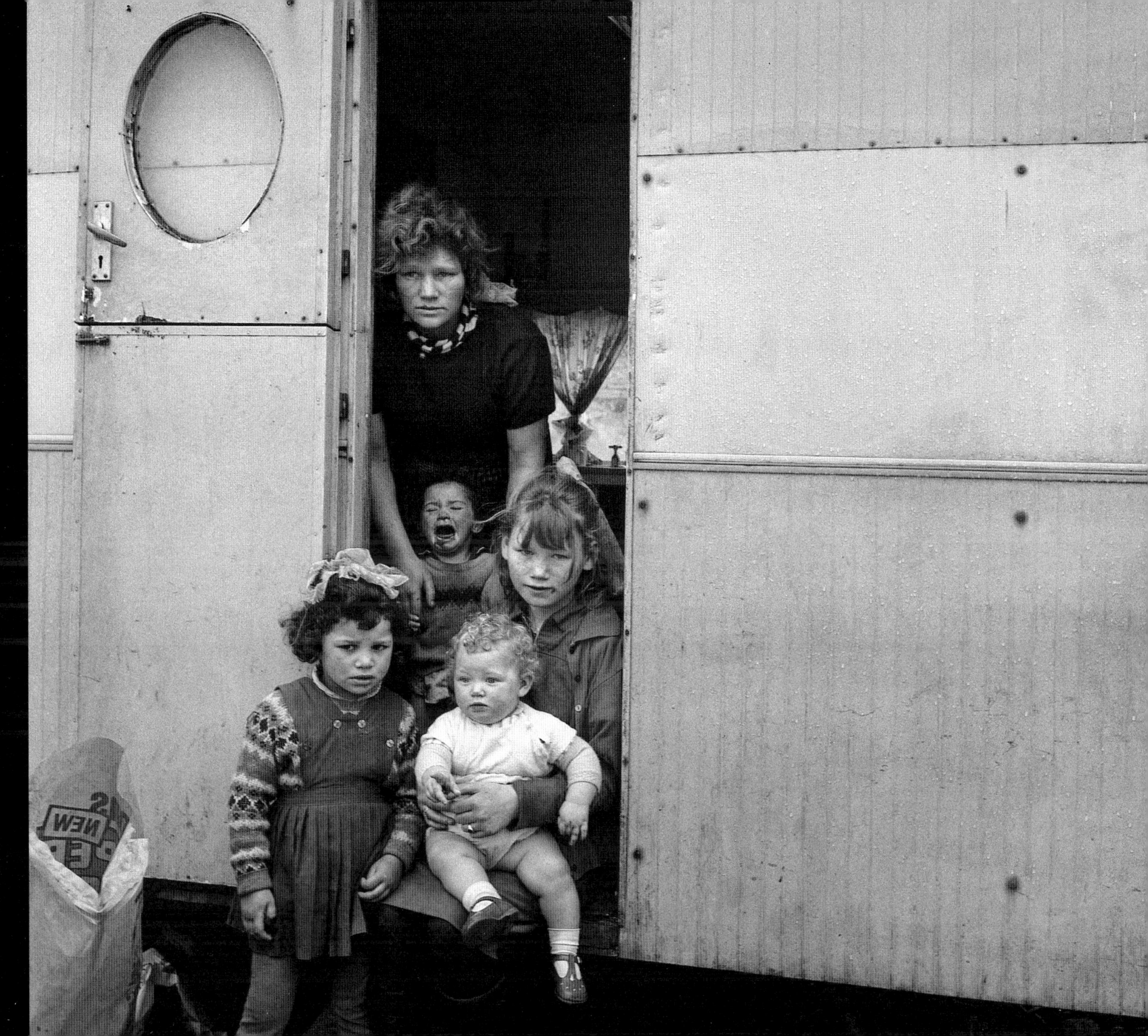

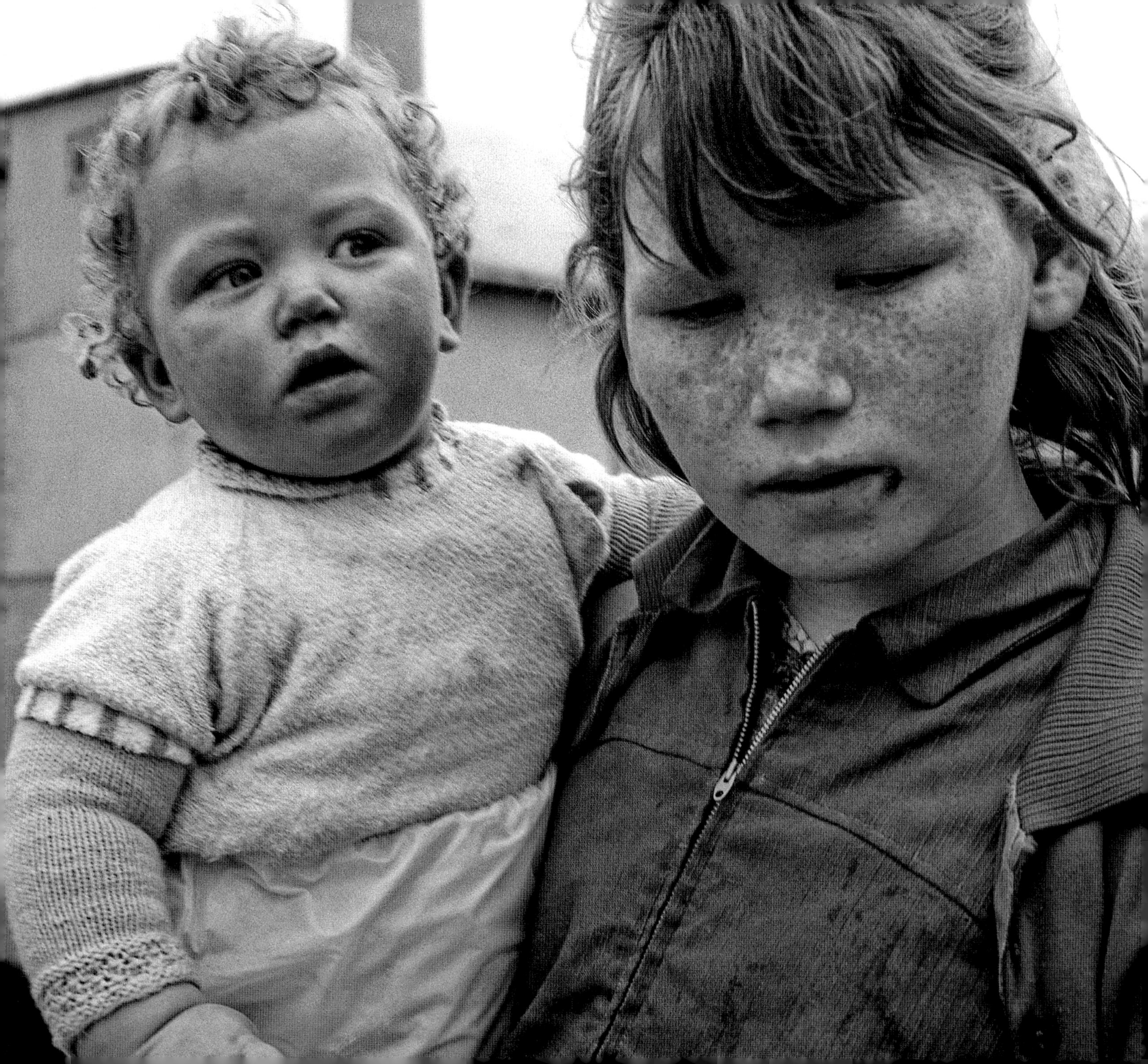

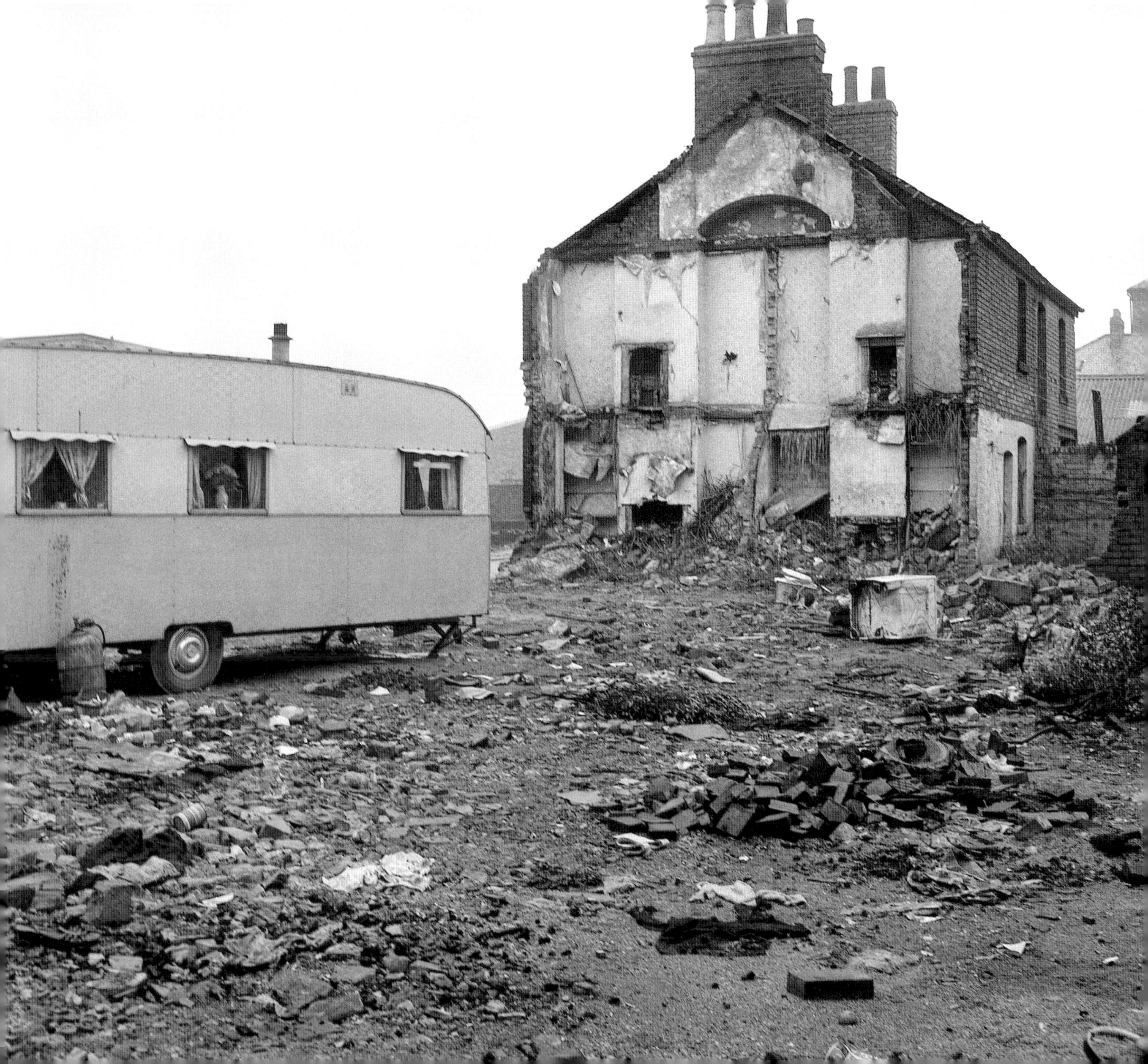

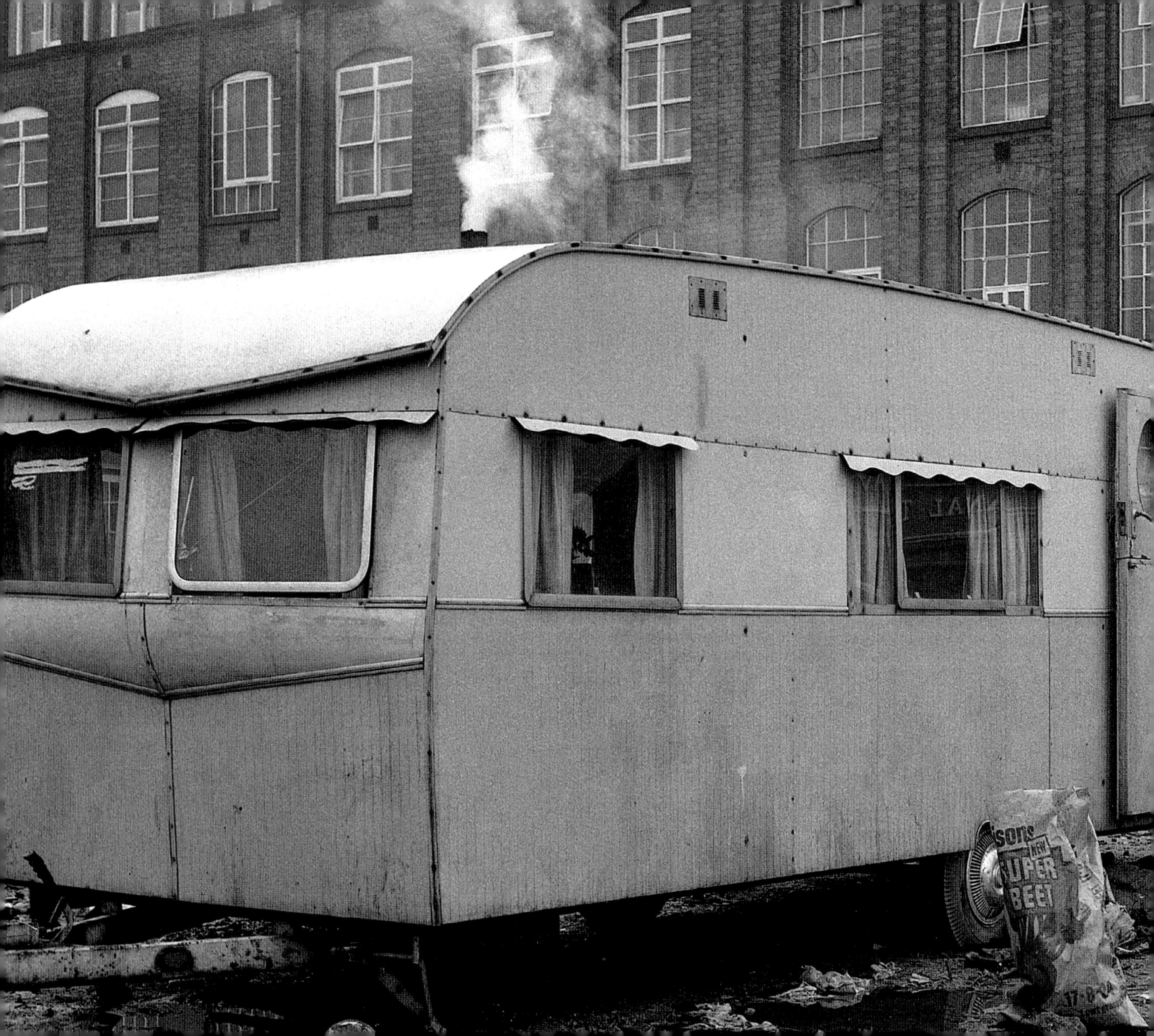
isons
NEW
SUPER
BEET

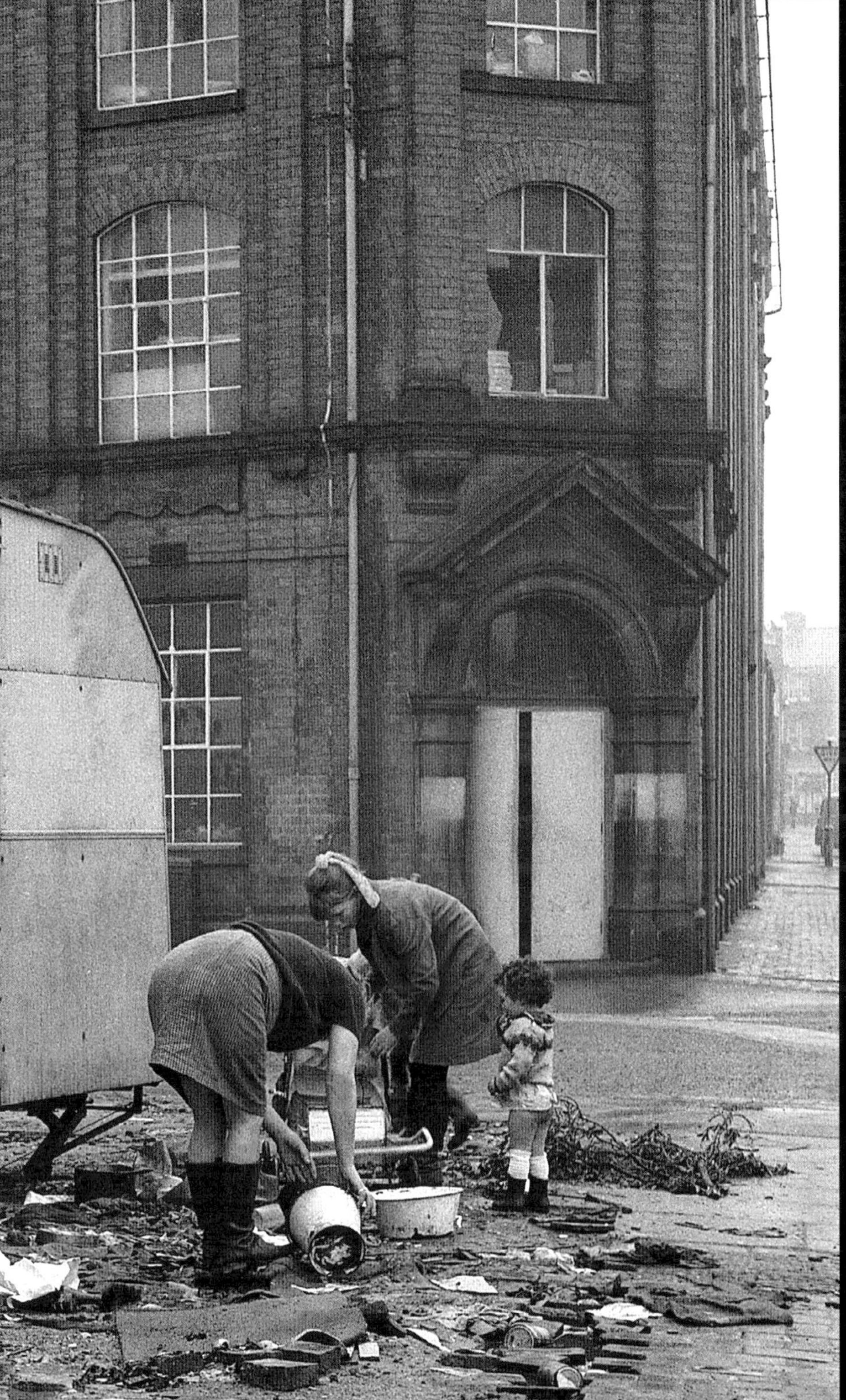

A Traveller family pictured outside their mobile home

This family set up on the site of cleared housing adjacent to a large factory which appears to be still in use, judging by the intact windows. Like the local youngsters, the children played amongst the rubble.

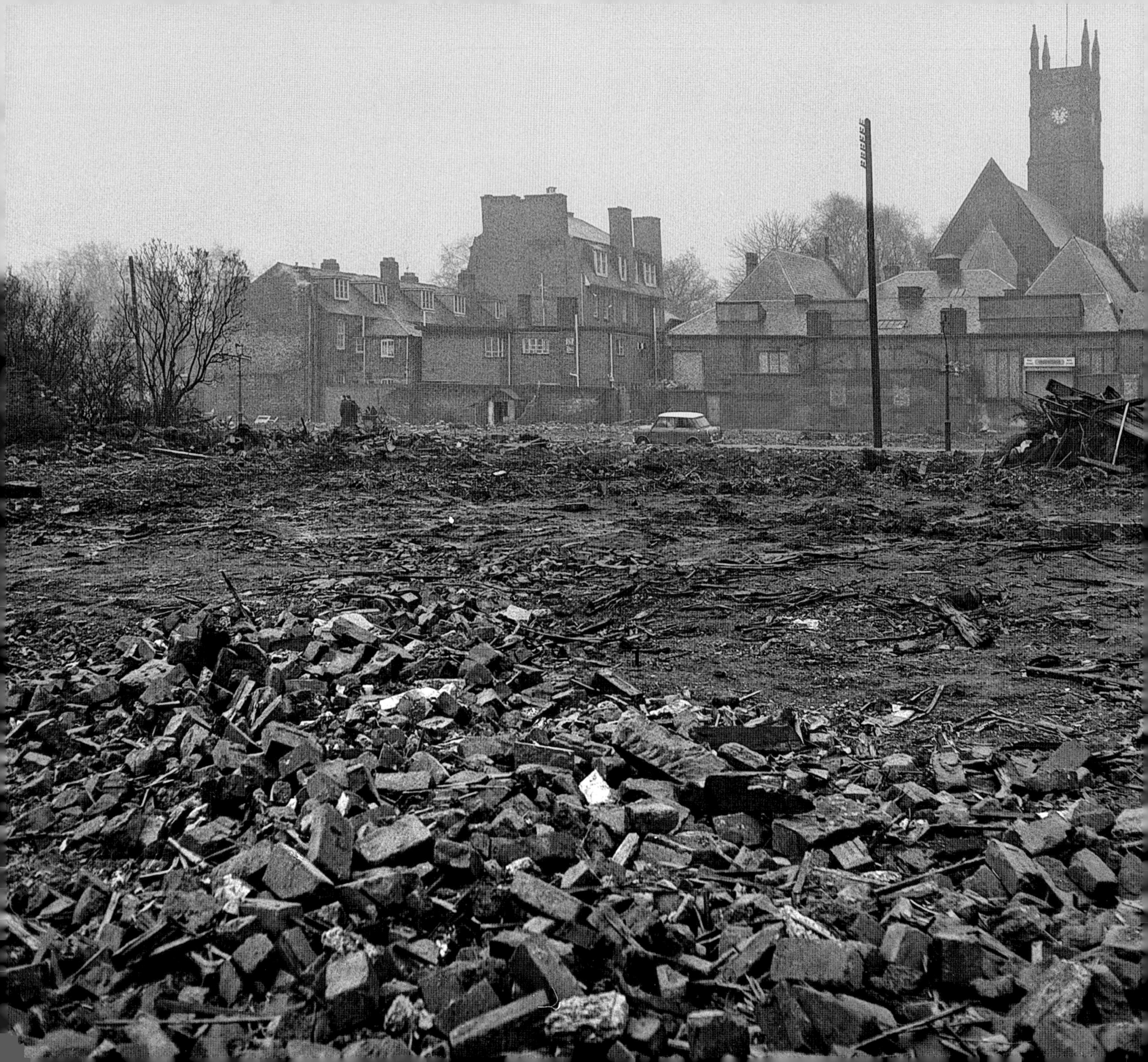

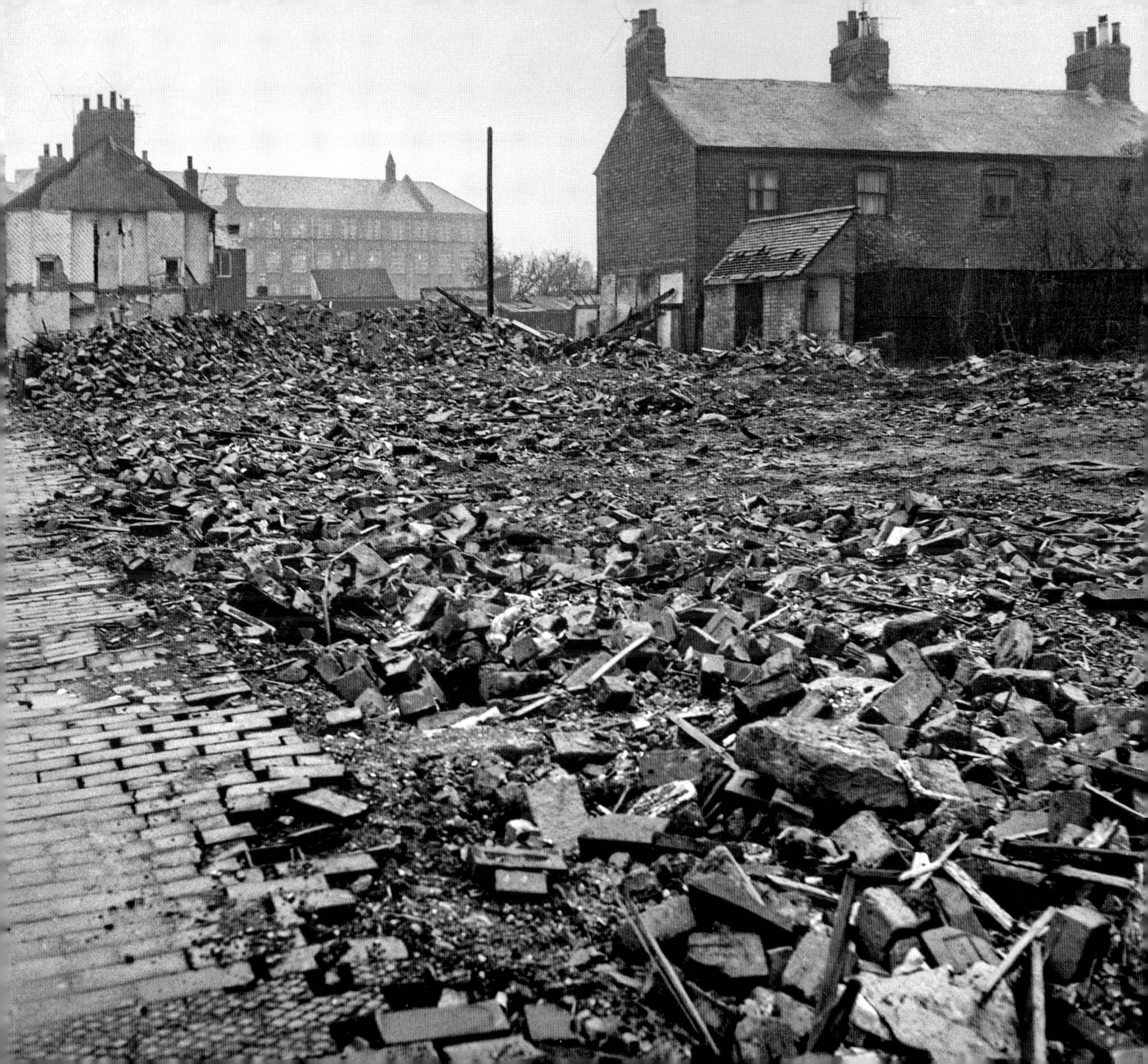

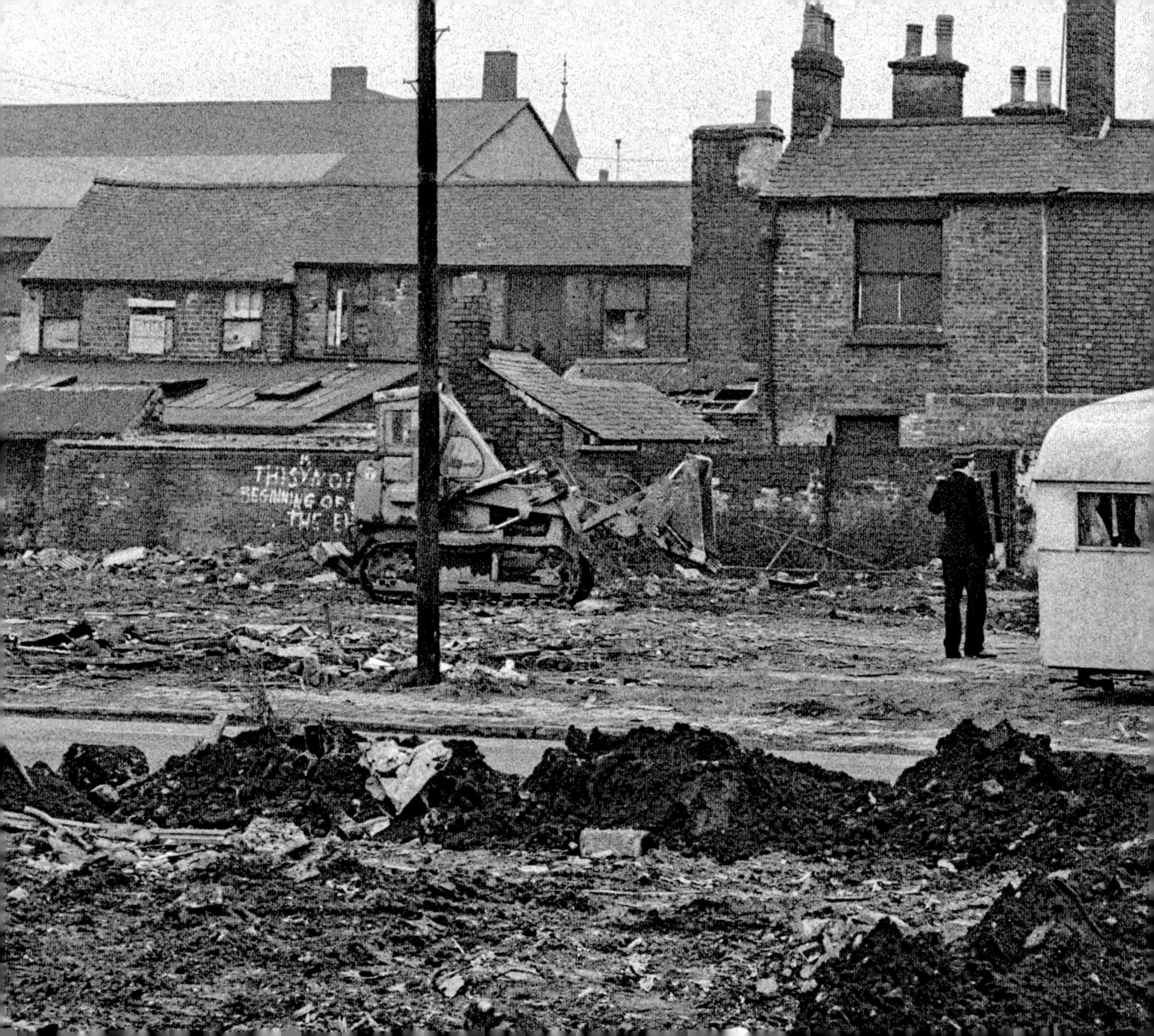

THIS IS NOT
BEGINNING OF
THE E

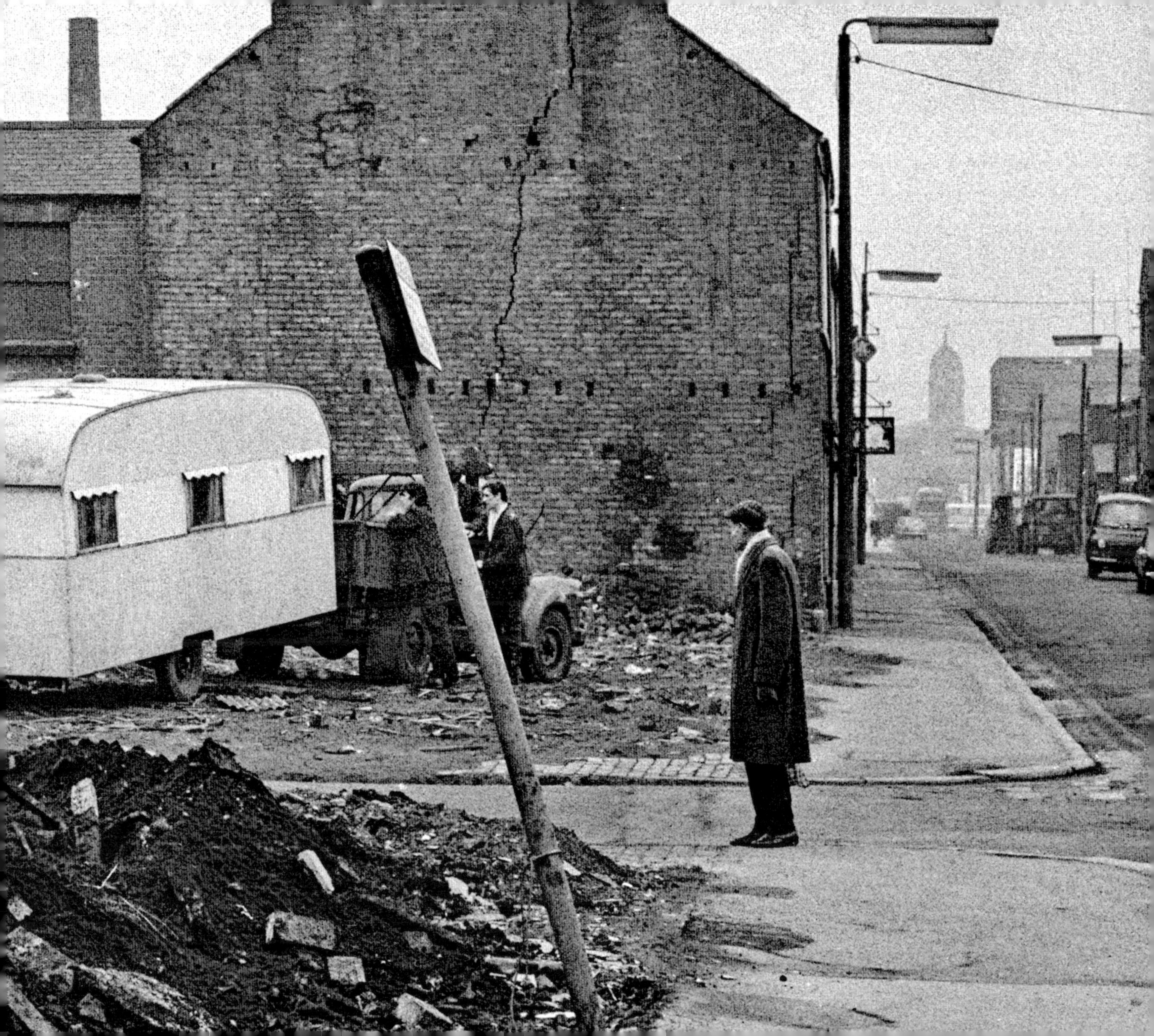

Acknowledgements

I would like to thank Tony Miller and Mavis Paskulich, joint founders of the St Ann's Well Road Pre-Demolition (1970) website, for their selfless assistance in the production of this book. I would also like to thank everyone who has willingly volunteered information and supplied anecdotes used in the book. I have tried to acknowledge each contribution where possible, apologies to anyone who I may have missed out. I have endeavoured to make the information within this book as accurate as possible, although please bear in mind the photographs were taken fifty years ago, and I apologise for any errors.

The majority of the anecdotes were sourced from the St Ann's Well Road Pre-Demolition (1970) website, which includes some interviews carried out by Trent & Peak Archaeology Department (St. Ann's Research Document 080/2014). Others were supplied direct to me via the St Ann's website.

The stories in this book, though genuine, are not about or told by the people in the photographs they accompany.

Further information and contact details:

St Ann's Well Road Pre Demolition (1970): www.stanswellroad.weebly.com

Peter Andrew Richardson: email peterrichardsonphoto@me.com